SEVENTY-FIVE YEARS OF THE TURKISH REPUBLIC

SEVENTY-FIVE YEARS OF THE TURKISH REPUBLIC

Editor

Sylvia Kedourie

LONDON AND NEW YORK

First published in 2000 in Great Britain by
Routledge
2 Park Square, Milton Park, Abingdon, Oxon, OX14 4RN
270 Madison Ave, New York NY 10016

Transferred to Digital Printing 2007

Website: www.routledge.com

British Library Cataloguing in Publication Data

Seventy-five years of the Turkish Republic
1. Turkey – Politics and government – 1909– 2. Turkey – History – 20th century 3. Turkey – Foreign relations
I. Kedourie, Sylvia
956.1'02

ISBN 0-7146-5042-0 (cloth)
ISBN 0-7146-8099-0 (paper)

Library of Congress Cataloging-in-Publication Data

A catalog record for this book is available
from the Library of Congress

This group of studies first appeared as a special issue of *Middle Eastern Studies*, Vol.35, No.4, October 1999 (ISSN 0026-3206), published by Routledge.

Publisher's Note

The publisher has gone to great lengths to ensure the quality of this reprint but points out that some imperfections in the original may be apparent

Contents

Atatürk and the Kurds

ANDREW MANGO

Is Mustafa Kemal Atatürk, the founding father of the Turkish Republic, to blame for his country's troubled relationship with its Kurdish-speaking citizens? In his foreword to Jonathan Rugman's fair-minded account of the problem, John Simpson, foreign affairs editor of the BBC, wrote:

> In terms of ethnicity and culture, Turkey is varied, complex and intermixed. Yet the myth which Atatürk bequeathed to his fellow-countrymen insists that there is a single ethnic group, the Turks. Nowadays the effects of this myth can be brutal; it can never, in the long run, be successful. While Turkey gives no legal recognition to its large Kurdish minority, the problem that dissident Kurds pose for the Turkish state cannot be solved.[1]

The seriousness of the problem is undeniable. According to figures given at the end of June 1998 by the head of the anti-terrorist department of the Turkish police, the radical Kurdish nationalist organization PKK (Partiya Karkeren Kurdistan – Kurdistan Workers Party), had by that time launched nearly 19,000 attacks since the beginning of its armed campaign in 1984. These caused the deaths of 5,121 members of the security forces and of 4,049 civilians, while 17,248 persons described as terrorists were killed.[2] In spite of repeated assurances by the security forces that the back of the insurrection has been broken and that the PKK now numbers only 5,000 armed militants, the death toll continues to mount. As Şükrü Elekdağ, the former Turkish Ambassador in Washington, has recently pointed out, 'the problem of the south-east' (that is, the Kurdish problem) is acquiring a growing international dimension and constitutes the main and most urgent threat facing Turkey.[3] In the circumstances, an elucidation of the genesis of the problem is a matter of current political, as well as of historical, importance. And since the actions and statements of Atatürk remain a source of inspiration of Turkish government policy, and tend to be used to legitimize it, it is as well to be clear about Atatürk's attitude towards the Kurds.

Mustafa Kemal Paşa, as he then was, did not acquire first-hand experience of Kurdish-speaking areas until April 1916, when he was promoted Brigadier-General at the age of 35, and sent to Diyarbekir (now Diyarbakır) at the head of the 16th corps, a part of the 2nd Ottoman army, which was transferred from Thrace after the withdrawal of the Allies from Gallipoli. Enver Paşa, the Ottoman deputy commander-in-chief (theoretically, deputising for the elderly Sultan Mehmet V), had prepared an ambitious plan, requiring the 2nd Army in the south-east and the 3rd Army in the north-east to close in on the Russian troops, which had occupied Erzurum and were fanning out to the west and south. The plan failed, but Mustafa Kemal acquitted himself well, regaining the towns of Muş and Bitlis in the Kurdish area in August 1916. A little later, a Russian counter-offensive forced him out of Muş, and the front then remained more or less stable until the Russian Revolution the following year. In November 1916, Mustafa Kemal became deputy commander of the 2nd Army, when the commander Ahmet İzzet Paşa, a general of Albanian origin, went on leave to Istanbul. In March 1917, Ahmet İzzet Paşa was made commander of all the armies on the eastern front and Mustafa became substantive commander of the 2nd Army. He remained in the area until July 1917, when he was appointed commander of the 7th Army, part of the Lightning (Yıldırım) Group, brought together in Syria under the German general (Marshal in the Ottoman army) Erich von Falkenhayn for the purpose of recapturing Baghdad from the British.[4]

Mustafa Kemal kept a diary between 7 November and 24 December 1916 during his service with the 2nd Army.[5] He records the books he read (a French novel and two books on philosophy), his thoughts on army discipline and on the emancipation of women, and a few impressions of the ravaged countryside: Bitlis made him think of the ruins of Pompeii and of Nineveh. There is a brief mention of a volunteer detachment, organized by a local Nakşibendi sheykh, of hungry Kurdish refugees, of a meeting with the tribal leader Hacı Musa who commanded the Mutki Kurdish militia. Mustafa Kemal's tone is remarkably detached: he observes his surroundings with the curiosity of an outsider. He does not express any views on the Kurds.

His chief of staff, Lt. Col. İzzettin (later General İzzettin Çalışlar) is more forthcoming in his diary.[6] 'In the villages, there are many men capable of bearing arms', he noted on 2 May 1916. 'The enemy is pressing hard against their land. Yet most of them are not rushing to defend it. They will have nothing to do with military service. They do not know Turkish. They do not understand what government means. In brief, these are places which have not yet been conquered. Yet one could make good use of these people. They obey their tribal leaders and sheykhs, who are very influential in these parts.'[7] On 11 November 1916, İzzettin commented: 'One must gradually set up a military organization among the Kurds. One must begin by forming units from among those who are comparatively more used to the government and are more friendly. At the same time, the government must organize to do more and increase its influence.'[8] Like Mustafa Kemal, İzzettin notes the poverty and backwardness of local people. He hopes for a transfer from 'these sorrowful surroundings' and says that anyone posted from the west to the east faces a hard time.[9]

Mustafa Kemal had one close military supporter who had a good knowledge of the Kurds. This was Col. Fahrettin (later General Fahrettin Altay, the renowned cavalry commander in the Turkish War of Independence). Born in Scutari in Albania, Fahrettin was posted to the 4th Army in eastern Anatolia in 1904, after graduating from the staff college in Istanbul.[10] Fahrettin describes the posting as exile, saying that the regime of Sultan Abdülhamit suspected him of holding liberal views.[11] However, he stayed on after the Young Turkish coup of 1908, and took part in a punitive expedition against Kurdish tribes in the Dersim (now Tunceli) mountains, west of Erzurum. The expedition was one of several mounted by the Young Turkish regime against dissident tribes – Druzes, Arab tribes in the Yemen, Albanians – which found the new constitutional order even less to their liking than Abdülhamit's absolutism, and which were, in consequence, smitten harder than at the time of that manipulative sovereign.

Fahrettin accepted the submission of the Dersim Kurds, on condition that they paid taxes and desisted from banditry. But the arrangement he made with a tribal leader was disallowed. He comments in his memoirs: 'It was that breakdown which made it necessary to mount another punitive expedition in these parts 28 years later.'[12] The reference is to the suppression of the Dersim rebellion by the armed forces of the Turkish Republic in 1937. In 1909, Fahrettin was put in charge of the reorganization of the Hamidiye Kurdish tribal regiments, which were renamed Tribal Cavalry Regiments (Aşiret Süvari Alayları). He claims that he would have preferred a Turkish name, such as 'Oğuz regiments', on the grounds that some of those who considered themselves Kurds were of Turkish origin, but that he was overruled by the Ottoman War Minister, Mahmut Şevket Paşa.[13] In 1913, Fahrettin led some of these tribal forces against the Bulgarians in eastern Thrace at the close of the second Balkan War. There were instances of looting by the Kurds, as 'our soldiers, who did not know Turkish, mistook local (Turkish) people for Bulgarians, on account of their dress'.[14] Fahrettin says that he made the looters return stolen goods and saved them from execution by firing squad. His views match those of Major İzzettin: the Kurds were rough diamonds, their land was a place of hardship for a Turkish officer, but they could be managed if one knew how to approach them. Civilization would come with education – in the Turkish language – and would reinforce loyalty to the Ottoman state.

The same approach had been tried by Abdülhamit, who, apart from establishing the Hamidiye regiments (modelled on Rusian Cossacks), had inspired the foundation of the Tribal School (Mekteb-i Aşair or Aşiret Mektebi) in Istanbul.[15] But the sons of Arab and of Kurdish chieftains came to blows in the school, and it was closed down in 1907, apparently when the authorities realized that the students were tending to a nationalist critique of the administration.[16] Abdülhamit was brought down by the close link between education, which he promoted, and disaffection, which he tried in vain to contain. Nevertheless, the Young Turks, and Atatürk after them, kept the faith in the merits of education in civilization, while redefining its content.

The original source of inspiration of Mustafa Kemal Atatürk, as of other Young Turks, was Namık Kemal, the 'poet of liberty'. Namık Kemal had written in 1878: 'While we must try to annihilate all languages in our country, except Turkish, shall we give Albanians, Lazes and Kurds a spiritual weapon by adopting their own characters? ... Language ... may be the firmest barrier – perhaps firmer than religion – against national unity.' Elsewhere, Namık Kemal said: 'If we set up regular schools... and carry out the programmes which are now not fulfilled, the Laz and Albanian languages will be utterly forgotten in twenty years.'[17]

Mustafa Kemal did not have to deal with Kurdish tribes until 1916, but he was aware of the experience of his fellow-officers and was imbued with the ideology of Ottoman liberals among whom Turkish nationalism took shape. He had also encountered other tribesmen in his military career. His active military service had started in Syria in 1905–6, where he took part in operations against rebellious Druzes and was threatened by Circassians.[18] Then he saw service in the suppression of the Albanian revolt in 1910; and he organized Cyrenaican Arab tribesmen against the Italians in 1911. Immediately after his appointment as commander of the 7th army in Aleppo in 1917, he criticized an agreement made by Kress von Kressenstein (Kress Paşa), German commander in Gaza, with a local Arab tribal leader, Sheykh Hajim. In a letter to the Lightning Group commander, von Falkenhayn, Mustafa Kemal argued that while relations with tribal leaders were necessary, it was dangerous to single out one leader for an agreement and give the impression of downgrading the others. To allow officials to enter into relations with individual sheykhs would only serve to create confusion. He would, therefore, deal impartially with all tribal leaders and show no preference to Sheykh Hajim.[19]

Mustafa Kemal's ability to orchestrate relations with tribal leaders – in this case, Kurdish tribal leaders – was put to the test when he arrived in Anatolia on 19 May 1919 and set about organizing Turkish national resistance against the Allies. The signature of the armistice of Mudros on 30

October 1918 and the subsequent arrival of Allied troops in Istanbul and at various points in Anatolia had inspired the hope among some Kurdish leaders that they could advance their personal ambitions with British help. Mehmet Şerif Paşa, an Ottoman official of Kurdish origin, who had spent the Great War as an exile in Paris, informed the British in May 1919 that he was willing to become Amir of an independent Kurdistan.[20] In Istanbul, a Kurdish notable, Seyyit Abdülkadir, became president of a Society for the Rise of Kurdistan (Kürdistan Teali Cemiyeti), which was supported by the Bedir Khans (Bedirhanoğulları), a Kurdish princely dynasty from the area round Diyarbekir (Bohtan in Kurdish, Jazirat ibn-'Umar in Arabic, El-Cezire in Ottoman Turkish).[21] Another Bedir Khan, Süreyya, was the moving spirit of the Committee for Kurdish Independence in Cairo, which appealed for British help in January 1919.[22] In Sulaimaniyya (Süleymaniye), Sheykh Mahmud Barzinji, began co-operating with British troops as soon as they arrived at the end of 1918. Kurdish tribal leaders of lesser importance sought contact with the British elsewhere in south-eastern Anatolia.[23]

On 23 May 1919, four days after his arrival in Samsun as Inspector of the 9th Army, Mustafa Kemal requested a situation report from Ahmet Cevdet, deputy commander of the 13th corps in Diyarbekir. In his reply, dated 27 May, Cevdet detailed the activity of the tribes and of the British in his area, and said that the Kurdish club in Diyarbekir, working for Kurdish independence, was co-operating increasingly with the club of the Ottoman party Concord and Freedom (İtilâf ve Hürriyet, known as Entente Libérale in the West), whose policy was in conformity with that of the Istanbul government. The army corps was following closely the anti-government propaganda of the Kurdish club. This telegram and subsequent communications to and from Mustafa Kemal on Kurdish affairs were published in 1996 by the Military History Department of the Turkish General Staff (ATASE – Askerî Tarih ve Stratejik Etüt Başkanlığı), as part of a series of extracts from Atatürk's private archive.[24] The book comprises 67 documents, from May 1919 to April 1920, with photocopies of the original handwritten Ottoman Turkish texts, followed by transcription into Latin characters. Twenty of them are signed by Mustafa Kemal, first as Inspector of the 9th Army, then of the 3rd Army (when the 9th Army was renumbered, following a reorganization), and later as 'former Inspector', then as Chairman of the General Congress (in Sivas), and finally 'on behalf of the Representative Committee (*Heyet-i Temsiliye*, i.e. permanent executive)' of the Society for the Defence of (National) Rights in Anatolia and Rumelia. These 20 telegrams give a clear idea of Mustafa Kemal's tactics *vis-à-vis* the Kurds in the critical months which preceded the formation of the government of the Turkish Grand National Assembly in Ankara in April 1920.

The first telegram from Mustafa Kemal in the collection was sent from Havza (inland from Samsun) on 28 May 1919 to four Kurdish tribal leaders, including Hacı Musa of Mutki. In it he announces his appointment by 'our master, the Sultan and Glorious Caliph' and expresses the hope of visiting their area in the near future. In the meantime, he is certain that his addressees would do all in their power to show to the world that the independence of the country could be ensured if internal order was maintained and if everyone was totally obedient to the state (pp.10–11). On the same day, Mustafa Kemal sent a telegram to Kâmil, a deputy in the Ottoman parliament, who was a member of the Kurdish club in Diyarbekir. Again he speaks of his intention to visit his 'old friends' in Diyarbekir at the earliest opportunity. Referring to reports that animosity had arisen between the Kurdish club and Turks in Diyarbekir, Mustafa Kemal warns that this could produce sad consequences for both 'brothers-in-race' (*ırk kardeş*). He goes on to ask Kâmil to urge on the Kurdish club that national unity was essential and that to allow the external enemy to make use of 'problems which should be settled within the family, such as those concerning the principles of administration and the defence of the rights of the races' would constitute the greatest treachery (p.14). The word 'race' (*ırk*) tended at the time to be used to denote an ethnic community (*ethnie*).

The following day (29 May 1919) Mustafa Kemal asked the General Staff in Istanbul to notify him where exactly the British were promoting the cause of an independent Kurdistan. He notes that he had in the meantime given the necessary advice to 'many famous Kurdish emirs, whose gratitude and affection I had won fully during the war' (p.19). The Chief of the Ottoman General Staff, Cevat Paşa (Çobanlı), replied on 3 June that it could be deduced that the British wanted to set up a Kurdish government between 'Iraq, Armenia and Turkey'. As a result of pressure by General Allenby, the General Staff had to agree to disband the 13th Army corps in Diyarbekir. It would be redesigned as a gendarmerie unit. Presumably to safeguard this fiction, Cevat Paşa asked Mustafa Kemal to be careful in his communications with the 13th Corps and to make sure that his name was not bandied around in its area (p.21).

Mustafa Kemal's message to the Kurds is particularly clear in the telegram he sent on 11 June 1919 to a Diyarbekir notable, Kasım Cemilpaşazade. The plan to create an independent Kurdistan, he declared, had been hatched by the British for the benefit of the Armenians. However, 'Kurds and Turks are true brothers [*öz kardeş*, i.e. children of the same father and mother] and may not be separated'. 'Our existence requires that Kurds, Turks and all Muslim elements [*anasır* – ethnic components of the state] should work together to defend our independence and prevent the partition of the fatherland.' Mustafa Kemal went on: 'I am in favour of granting all manner of rights and privileges (*hukuk ve imtiyazat* – the Latin transcription substitutes three dots for *imtiyazat*) in order to ensure the attachment [to the state – *merbutiyet*] and the prosperity and progress of our Kurdish brothers, on condition that the Ottoman state is not split up' (p.33). In a covering letter, Mustafa Kemal asks the 13th corps commander to facilitate the visit to Sivas of men trusted by three named Kurdish notables (p.35). In his reply of 25 June 1919, the commander, Ahmet Cevdet, objects that the notables kept brigands in their suites, and that they were, in any case, quarrelling among themselves: people would respond to Mustafa Kemal's invitation only if it served their interests. However, delegates had been elected to the congress which was to meet in Erzurum, and the Kurdish club had been closed down. It was impossible to win over many of its members. 'They do not want Ottoman rule, and prefer British rule, believing that [their area] would [then] develop and become prosperous like Egypt.' Ahmet Cevdet explained that the Cemilpaşa family and their friends, who made up the Kurdish club, wanted a change in government in order to escape prosecution for their part in the expulsion and killings (of Armenians) (pp.38–9).

Mustafa Kemal had in the meantime moved from Havza to Amasya for a meeting with his nationalist comrades, Hüseyin Rauf (Orbay), Ali Fuat (Cebesoy) and Refet (Bele). The strongest Ottoman military force in Anatolia at that time was the 15th Corps, commanded by General Kâzım Karabekir in Erzurum. On 16 June 1919, Mustafa Kemal sent him a telegram from Amasya to explain his views on the Kurds (pp.40–4). The Kurdish club in Diyarbekir, he wrote, had been closed down because it aimed at the formation of a Kurdistan under British protection. In any case, the club had been formed by a few 'vagabonds' (*serseri*) and did not represent the Kurds. However there was a problem: the people of the eastern provinces which were threatened by Armenian bands realized the need for unity. But in 'tranquil' parts of Anatolia, the position was different, as local people, who had been made the plaything of politicians, were now unwilling to join any organization. He had, therefore, made every effort to explain the need for National Defence Societies, as an instrument of national unity. Fortunately, the co-operation of military and civil officials in spreading his message had borne fruit and he had received telegrams 'from everywhere' showing that the people had seen the need to organize and that the work of organizing (resistance to the Allies) had begun.

Mustafa Kemal told Karabekir that he was determined to 'grasp the Kurds like true brothers' and thus unite the whole nation through the Societies for the Defence of National Rights. Two days later, Mustafa Kemal sent an optimistic telegram to Col. Cafer Tayyar, the nationalist commander of the 1st Corps in Edirne (Adrianople in Turkish Thrace), declaring 'British propaganda for the formation of an independent Kurdistan under British protection, and supporters of this project, have been eliminated. Kurds have joined forces with Turks' (p.54). On 23 June, Mustafa Kemal wrote in the same vein to the Chief of the General Staff in Istanbul, General Cevat (Çobanlı). 'Important telegrams' he had received from Diyarbekir and Mamuretülaziz (now Elâzığ) proved conclusively, he declared, that the idea of an independent Kurdistan under British protection had been 'destroyed'. 'We are always ready to provide an administration which would guarantee the prosperity and happiness of Kurdistan. We expect important people from that area to come to Sivas soon', Mustafa Kemal concluded (p.57).

This suggests that Mustafa Kemal did not expect any important Kurdish personalities to turn up at the congress of eastern provinces, which had been organized under the auspices of Kâzım Karabekir in Erzurum. Events proved him right. The provinces of Diyarbekir and Mamuretülaziz (or Harput) were not represented. It seems that supporters of the Society for the Rise of Kurdistan prevented any election of delegates from Mamuretülaziz to the congress in Erzurum, and prevented delegates who had been elected in Diyarbekir from going to Erzurum.[25] True, the largely Kurdish provinces of Bitlis and Van, and Kurdish districts of the province of Erzurum did send delegates, but they were small fry: retired Ottoman officials, clerics, etc.[26]

The congress of Erzurum opened on 23 July; elected Mustafa Kemal to be its chairman on the same day and on 7 August issued a proclamation, which was to form the basis of the National Pact – the charter of the Turkish nationalist movement in the War of Independence. The proclamation began by stating that the Black Sea and East Anatolian provinces (including the main Kurdish provinces of Diyarbekir, Mamuretülaziz, Van and Bitlis) were an inseparable part of the Ottoman community and that 'all Islamic elements [i.e. ethnic communities], living in this area, are true brothers, imbued with the sentiment of mutual sacrifice and respectful of their [i.e. each other's] racial [i.e. ethnic] and social circumstances'.[27] Article 6 of the proclamation extended this principle to all Ottoman territories within the lines of the armistice signed with the Allies on 30 October 1918, and repudiated any partition of these lands 'inhabited by our true brothers, of the same religion and race as ourselves, whom it is impossible to divide' (*yekdiğerinden gayr-ı kabil-i infikâk öz kardeş olan din ve ırkdaşlarımızla meskûn*). The formulation conceals an ambiguity: the Kurds were a 'race' (or ethnic community – *ırk*), but Turks, Kurds and all other Muslims in Anatolia and Eastern Thrace were of 'the same race' (*ırkdaş*).

The committee (or permanent executive) elected at the Erzurum congress included two representatives of predominantly Kurdish areas: Sadullah Efendi, the former Ottoman deputy for Bitlis, and the Kurdish tribal leader Hacı Musa of Mutki.[28] However, neither served on the committee: Sadullah Efendi excused himself on grounds of ill health, while Hacı Musa was unable to come because he was afraid of action by tribes opposed to him.[29] On 13 August 1919, Mustafa Kemal communicated the decisions of the Erzurum congress to two Kurdish leaders, Şeyh Abdülbaki Küfrevi of Bitlis and Cemil Çeto of Garzan. In his telegram to the latter, he regretted that conditions had not allowed him to realize his wish of visiting the area (*oralar*) (p.69). Çeto was later to stage a brief rising (May–June 1920) against the young Nationalist government in Ankara.[30]

Although Mustafa Kemal's party felt threatened by Dersim Kurds as they journeyed between Sivas and Erzurum,[31] and then back again, the Kurds did not impinge on the work of the Erzurum congress. The congress which followed in Sivas was not so lucky. On 26 August 1919, the 13th Corps commander Ahmet Cevdet had instructed military authorities in Malatya to arrest a number of Kurdish notables who had been charged with trying to establish a Kurdish state under British protection.[32] In fact, four of these notables, including Celadet and Kâmuran of the Bedirhan family, turned up in Malatya on 3 September, in the suite of Major E.M. Noel, who was indeed promoting the proposal put forward to the British government by Colonel (later Sir) Arnold Wilson, acting British commissioner for the Persian Gulf, that an independent Kurdistan should be formed under British auspices.[33] Two days before Noel's arrival, the provincial governor (*vali*) of Harput (Mamuretülaziz), Ali Galip, had instructed the district governor of Malatya, who was a member of the Bedirhan family, to collect a small force of Kurdish cavalry. On 7 September, Major Noel noted that Ali Galip intended to despatch the Kurds against the Turkish nationalists assembled in Sivas.[34]

The Sivas congress had opened in the meantime on 4 September. It was meant to represent Societies for the Defence of National Rights throughout the country – from eastern Thrace to eastern Anatolia. However, only 38 delegates turned up, including Mustafa Kemal and his party. There was no delegate from any of the Kurdish areas. But a former Ottoman governor (and supporter of the Committee of Union and Progress), Mazhar Müfit (Kansu), was present as delegate of Hakkâri, and a delegate of Diyarbekir, İhsan Hamit (Tiğrel), arrived after the congress had ended.[35] Mustafa Kemal co-opted İhsan Hamit into the Representative Committee, the permanent executive of the countrywide society which became the source of his authority until he was elected president of the Grand National Assembly on 24 April 1920. As the nine members of the committee elected earlier in Erzurum were transferred *en bloc*, Sadullah Efendi and Hacı Musa of Mutki also became members of the new 16-member nationwide Representative Committee formed at Sivas.[36] But they remained sleeping members.

The proclamation issued by the Sivas congress on 11 September 1919, refined the terms used in Erzurum. It declared in its first article that: 'All Islamic elements living in the abovementioned domains [the Ottoman lands within the armistice lines] are true brothers, imbued with feelings of mutual respect and sacrifice for each other, and wholly respectful of racial and social rights and local conditions' (*Memalik-i mezkûrede yaşayan bilcümle anasır-ı islâmiye yekdiğerine karşı hürmet-i mütekabile ve fedakârlık hissiyatiyle meşhun ve hukuk-u ırkiye ve içtimaiyeleriyle şerait-i muhitiyelerine tamamiyle riayetkâr öz kardeştirler*).[37] The wording would seem to imply that Kurdish ethnicity and Kurdish customs would be respected.

Some time during the Sivas congress, Mustafa Kemal was informed of Major Noel's presence in Malatya and of Ali Galip's intention of recruiting Kurdish tribesmen to raid Sivas. On 11 September, the day on which the congress issued its proclamation, Ahmet Cevdet, the corps commander in Diyarbekir, was informed by the 3rd Corps in Sivas that the plot had been hatched by the Interior and War ministers in Istanbul. Ahmet Cevdet had by then decided to reinforce his troops in Malatya and had ordered the arrest of the district governor and of Major Noel's Kurdish companions, although not of Major Noel himself.[38] Having heard of the order, Major Noel and his party left Malatya on 10 September. The following day Major Noel noted that Ali Galip had produced a decree (*irade*) from the Sultan ordering him to raise a force of Kurdish cavalry against Mustafa Kemal in Sivas. Pressed to assist in the project, Major Noel claims to have refused to commit himself publicly. A day later, 12 September, Major Noel noted that Ali Galip had decided to disperse the Kurdish tribal gathering, as the idea of marching on Sivas was too risky.[39]

As Ahmet Cevdet's measures, supported by Kâzım Karabekir in Erzurum, put a quick stop to Ali Galip's half-baked and half-hearted plan and secured the flight of Major Noel and his Kurdish companions, Mustafa Kemal sent a trusted and adventurous young officer, Lt. Recep Zühtü, on a special mission to Malatya in order to rally local support.[40] Some Kurdish leaders hastened to send messages of support to Sivas. On 15 September, in a telegram to Cemil Çeto in Siirt, Mustafa Kemal expressed the thanks of the congress for 'the loyalty of all our Kurdish brothers to this religion and state and their attachment to the sacred institution of the caliphate' (p.101). The following day, he congratulated the mayor of Malatya for having seen through the plot financed with 'British gold' (p.108).

Mustafa Kemal made maximum use of the Ali Galip plot to discredit the government of Damat Ferit, who had to resign on 30 September 1919 and was succeeded by Ali Rıza Paşa, a general sympathetic to the Turkish national movement.[41] On 6 November, as elections were being organized for the last Ottoman Chamber of Deputies, Mustafa Kemal sent a circular telegram to governors of five provinces in Eastern Anatolia, regretting claims made in the capital that the Kurds opposed the Turkish national movement, and asking that 'our Kurdish brothers, who are a noble [constituent] element of [the people of] Eastern Anatolia, should express their support for [Turkish] 'national forces' [*kuva-yı milliye*] and their opposition to the Society for the Rise of Kurdistan' (p.155). Messages of support duly followed. Replying on 3 December 1919 to one such message from the much-cited Hacı Musa of Mutki, Mustafa Kemal declared that 'the whole world knows that the noble Kurdish people [*Kürt kavm-i necibi*] feels a religious attachment to the sacred institution of the caliphate and constitutes an indivisible heroic mass with its Turkish brothers' (p.168). On 15 January 1920, Mustafa Kemal thanked a number of Kurdish tribal leaders for the telegrams which they had sent to the government and to representatives of foreign powers in Istanbul to express their solidarity with their Turkish brethren, considering that 'Kurdistan is an indivisible portion of the Ottoman community' (p.192). In another telegram sent on the same day, Mustafa Kemal spoke of Turks and Kurds as 'two true brothers joining hands in their determination to defend their sacred unity' (p.195).

On 20 February 1920, on the eve of the dissolution of the last Ottoman Chamber of Deputies in Istanbul and the subsequent opening of the Grand National Assembly in Ankara, Mustafa Kemal sent a private letter to the exiled Young Turk (CUP) triumvir Talât Paşa. It began with these words: 'The national unity created under the aegis of the Society for the Defence of [National] Rights in Anatolia and Rumelia aims at saving Turkey, as bounded by the national borders of the Turks and Kurds [*Türk ve Kürt millî hudutlariyle tahdid edilen Türkiye'yi*] ... in accordance with the principles established at the general congresses in Erzurum and then in Sivas.'[42]

Mustafa Kemal put his views in a more general framework in his first long speech to the GNA on 24 April 1920. The Erzurum congress, he said, had marked out the borders of the country by claiming the territory within the line along which the armistice had been declared on 30 October 1918, a line which encompassed the province of Mosul. This was not only a military, but a national frontier. 'However it should not be imagined', Mustafa Kemal went on, 'that the Islamic elements within this frontier all belong to the same nation. There are within it Turks, Circassians and other Muslims. This is, however, the national frontier of brotherly nations living together and genuinely sharing the same aims. But in addition, every one of the Muslim elements living within the borders of this fatherland has its own specific environment, customs and race, and privileges relating to them have been accepted and confirmed, mutually and in all sincerity. Naturally, these have not been detailed, because this is not the time for it. The matter will be settled and resolved between brothers when our existence is assured...'[43] Mustafa Kemal did not mention the Kurds specifically in this passage. But when he returned to the subject of frontiers on 1 May 1920, he said: 'The gentlemen making up your august assembly are not only Turks, or Circassians or Kurds. They are a sincere gathering of all Islamic elements.' He went on: 'There are Kurds as well as Turks north of Kirkuk. We have not distinguished between them.'[44]

However, the ambiguity about race (*ırk*) persisted. In his speech opening the third session of the GNA on 1 March 1922, Mustafa Kemal said, 'The people of Turkey is a social entity united in race, religion and culture, imbued with mutual respect and a sense of sacrifice and sharing the same destiny and interests.'[45] Nevertheless, the expression 'people of Turkey' (*Türkiye halkı*) rather than 'Turkish people' (*Türk halkı*) is significant, and Mustafa Kemal used it again when welcoming the French writer Claude Farrère in İzmit on 18 June 1922.[46]

Unlike the congresses of Erzurum and Sivas, the GNA which first came together on 23 April 1920 had genuine Kurdish members. The most colourful was Diyap Ağa of Dersim, one of several tribal leaders elected to the assembly. The first constitution (lit. Law of Fundamental Organization, *Teşkilât-ı Esasiye Kanunu*), which the GNA adopted on 20 January 1921 extended the powers and status of local government, which had been established on the French model in the Ottoman state. Article 11 of the constitution declared that provinces were autonomous in local affairs. Provincial councils, elected for two years, were given the right to administer pious foundations, educational and health services, public works, farming and economic affairs generally, in accordance with the laws of the GNA.[47] Moreover, the term used for these councils was changed significantly from *meclis* to *şura*. Chosen originally by Ottoman reformers as an indigenously Islamic term for a consultative assembly, *şura* acquired after the Bolshevik revolution the connotation of 'soviet' (in modern Persian *showra*, *showravi* are the standard translations of the noun and adjective 'Soviet', respectively). The government which the Ottoman army left behind when it was forced to evacuate Kars after the armistice was called 'Kars Millî İslâm Şurası', which, I believe, can be rendered as Kars National Muslim Soviet. There was another example of Soviet inspiration in the 1921 constitution: the term used to designate the Ankara government was '*icra vekilleri heyeti*', an exact translation of 'committee of executive commissars' (shortened in Russian as *Ispolkom*), the name of the Bolshevik government in Moscow. In French texts *vekil* was translated as *commissaire* (Halide Edib in *The Turkish Ordeal* uses the word 'Commissary').

Mustafa Kemal referred to the constitutional provisions on local government in the instructions he sent to Nihat Paşa (Anılmış), who had been appointed commander of the southern (El-Cezire) front in June 1920.[48] The instructions deserve to be quoted in full:

> 1. Our domestic policy requires the gradual establishment in the whole country and on a vast scale of local administrations in which popular masses will be directly and effectively involved. As for areas inhabited by Kurds, we consider it a necessity both of our domestic and of our foreign policy to set up a local government gradually.
>
> 2. The right of nations to determine their destinies by themselves is a principle accepted worldwide. We too have accepted this principle. It is expected that the Kurds will by that time have completed the organization of their own local government, and that their leaders and notables will have been won over by us in the name of this objective; when they express their votes, they should, therefore, declare that they prefer to live under the administration of the Grand National Assembly, where they are already masters of their own destiny. The command of the El-Cezire front is responsible for directing all the work in Kurdistan in line with this policy.
>
> 3. The general lines of accepted policy include such objectives as to raise by means of armed clashes to a permanent level the animosity of the Kurds in Kurdistan against the French and particularly the British on the border with Iraq, to prevent any accord between the Kurds and foreigners, to prepare gradually for the establishment of local government bodies and thus win for us the hearts of the Kurds and to strengthen the links which bind Kurdish leaders to us by appointing them to civil and military positions.
>
> 4. Domestic policy in Kurdistan shall be coordinated and administered by the command of the El-Cezire front. The front command will address its communications on the matter to the office of the president of the GNA. Leading civil officials will report on the subject to the front command, since the latter will regulate and cordinate action by provincial authorities.
>
> 5. The El-Cezire front command shall propose to the government such administrative, judicial and financial changes and reforms as it deems necessary.[49]

Nihat Paşa did not win the hearts and minds of Kurdish notables, at least not of all Kurdish notables, in his area. Some of them complained to the Assembly in Ankara, accusing him of high-handed and illegal activity. Having heard his defence, the judicial committee of the Assembly reported that no action should be taken. The report was accepted on 22 July 1922, in spite of loud protests by some deputies, notably Feyzi Efendi of Malatya. Nihat Paşa was, however, transferred to Ankara where he was appointed president of the military court of appeal.[50] Mustafa Kemal did not intervene, as he had done in an earlier case concerning 'bearded' Nurettin Paşa who, as commander of the central army, had repressed the rising of the Koçgiri Kurds on the northern edges of the Dersim mountains between April and June 1921.

Nurettin Paşa's severity and, particularly, his use of the irregulars led by the notorious Lame Osman (*Topal* Osman) of Giresun, were condemned in a motion by Emin Bey, deputy for Erzincan in whose constituency the rising had taken place. Speaking at a secret session of the assembly on 4 October 1921, Emin Bey declared that the punitive action taken against the people of Dersim would be unacceptable even for 'barbarians in Africa', and that such atrocities had not been committed even against the Armenians.[51] The Assembly decided to send a commission of inquiry, which was also to look into the consequences of Nurettin Paşa's behaviour during the deportation of Greeks from Samsun. The Assembly wanted to put Nurettin Paşa on trial, but in the secret session on 16 January 1922, Mustafa Kemal argued that although Nurettin had been relieved of his command, the accusations against him needed further investigation. This was accepted,[52] and the trial never took place. There was no love lost between Mustafa Kemal and Nurettin, but, as Mustafa Kemal said in a telegram to Kâzım Karabekir on 13 November 1921, he was worried by attacks in the assembly against military commanders he needed for the prosecution of the war.[53]

Robert Olson[54] says on the strength of British intelligence reports that, in addition to the Koçgiri commission, another commission drew up a bill concerning the administration of Kurdistan, which, it was decided, was to be debated at a secret session on 10 February 1922. The bill, whose text is given in British documents, was apparently rejected by 373 votes to 64, most Kurdish deputies voting against it. David McDowall speaks of a debate on Dersim at a secret session of the GNA on 9 October 1921, followed by a decision on 10 February to establish 'an autonomous administration for the Kurdish nation in harmony with their national customs'.[55] But according to the published minutes, there were no secret sessions of the GNA either on 9 October 1921 or on 10 February 1922. There was a debate on the Koçgiri rebelion (and Dersim) on 3 October, when a five-member committee of inquiry was elected. The debate was continued on 4 and 5 October. On the last day, the commissioner (or minister) for the Interior, Refet (Bele) Paşa, argued against requests he had received from the people of Dersim that their district should acquire separate administrative status, and said that it was much better off as part of the richer province of (Mamuret) Elaziz.[56] On 16–17 January 1921, when the GNA debated the possible committal for trial of Nurettin Paşa, a member of the committee of inquiry, Yusuf İzzet Paşa, said that the committee had completed its work, but was awaiting the return of two of its five members to draw up its report. In the meantime, he claimed that Nurettin Paşa had not exceeded his authority.[57] There is no reference in the debate either to a second committee or to any autonomy plan for Kurdistan.

The report of the committee of enquiry seems to have sunk without trace. Neither is there any reference to any autonomy plan in the long defence submitted by the El-Cezire front commander, Nihat Paşa, who says simply that 'the provinces of Kurdistan can be won over to the national government only by the hand of totally uncorrupt officials'.[58] Unless evidence to the contrary is found, I would suggest that the British reports quoted by Olson and McDowall concerning the existence of a precise Turkish plan for the autonomy of Kurdistan are inaccurate, like so many other British intelligence reports. The information was probably obtained from Kurdish sources, possibly Seyyit Abdülkadir, in Istanbul and was based either on documents having no legal validity, or simply on wishful thinking.

That Mustafa Kemal had not changed his mind – and continued to think of Kurdish autonomy in the framework of local government throughout the country – emerges clearly from his reference to the Kurds in the briefing he gave to journalists in İzmit on 16/17 January 1923, at a time when the Lausanne conference was in recess. Once again, the statement deserves to be quoted in full. Mustafa Kemal said:

> There can be no question of a Kurdish problem, as far as we, i.e. Turkey, are concerned. Because, as you know, the Kurdish elements within our national borders are settled in such a way that they are concentrated only in very limited areas. As their concentration decreases and as they penetrate among Turkish elements, a[n ethnic] frontier has come about in such a way that if we wished to draw a border in the name of Kurdishness [*Kürtlük*] it would be necessary to destroy Turkishness and Turkey. It would, for example, be necessary to have a frontier extending to Erzurum, Erzincan, Sivas and Harput. One should not forget also the Kurdish tribes in the Konya desert. Therefore, rather than envisage Kurdishness as such, local autonomies of a sort will in any case come about in accordance with our constitution [lit. Law of Fundamental Organization]. As a result, wherever the population of a district [*liva*] is Kurdish, it will govern itself autonomously. Aside from this, whenever one speaks of the people of Turkey [*Türkiye'nin halkı*], they [i.e.the Kurds] should also be included. If they are not included, it is always possible that they

> would make a grievance of it. Now, the Turkish Grand National Assembly is made up of empowered representatives both of Turks and of Kurds, and the two elements have joined their interests and destinies. They know that this is something held in common. To try and draw a separate frontier would not be right.[59]

The same line was taken by İsmet (İnönü), as head of the Turkish delegation at the Lausanne conference, as he defended his country's claim to the province of Mosul, arguing that the government of Turkey was the government of the Kurds as well.[60] But I think it would be wrong to attribute Mustafa Kemal's attitude to the governance of the Kurds of Turkey to the hope of regaining Mosul, for in the same briefing to journalists in İzmit, he expressed his personal opinion that it was impossible to take Mosul by war, in other words by fighting the British (*Musul'u harben almak gayr-ı mümkündür*), even although he said that the British wanted to set up a Kurdish government in Mosul, and that, if they did so, the idea might spread to the Kurds within Turkey's borders.[61]

In an immensely long address to the people of Izmir on 2 February 1923, Mustafa Kemal referred once again to Turkey's multiethnic character, saying, 'There is a primary element which has established the Turkish State. Then there are [other] elements which have joined their endeavours and their histories with those of this primary element. There are citizens from these elements too.'[62] The example which Mustafa Kemal gave this time was not Circassians or Kurds, but Jews, who certainly came more readily to the mind in İzmir, since their neighbourhood in the city had survived the great fire the previous year, and the Jewish community had allowed delegates to the first Economic Congress, held later that month, to lodge in its orphanage.[63]

The Turkish Socialist politician and publicist Doğu Perinçek who has drawn our attention both to Mustafa Kemal's instructions to Nihat Paşa and to his İzmit statement on the Kurds, wonders what happened after 1923 to prevent the incorporation of Mustafa Kemal's ideas in the 1924 constitution.[64] Why, in other words, was not a solution sought within the framework of the constitutional provisions on local government and on the basis of the recognition of the Kurds and of other ethnic elements in Turkey?

Elections were held soon after Mustafa Kemal's statements in İzmit and İzmir. Mustafa Kemal opened the first session of the second Grand National Assembly on 13 August 1923 with a speech in which he stressed the establishment of order as the first duty of the government. But he also said that the new Turkish state was a people's state.[65] The Assembly elected a committee to draw up a new constitution (*Kanun-u Esasî Encümeni*). Its chairman was the journalist Yunus Nadi, a Turkish nationalist with radical ideas – ideas which were left-wing in the sense that Fascism was, at the start, a left-wing movement. Another influential member was Ahmet Ağaoğlu, an intellectual born in Azerbaijan and formerly active in the CUP. He tended to a liberal nationalist position. Sabiha (Sertel), who describes herself at the time as a utopian Socialist and who had newly returned from the United States, observed the discussions of the committee when she went to Ankara to join her husband Zekeriya, who had been appointed Director General of the Press.[66] Mustafa Kemal, she says, often took part in the work of the constitutional committee, which met in the stationmaster's house in Ankara. According to Sabiha Sertel, there was an intense argument on the article 4 (of the 1921 constitution) which stated 'The Grand National Assembly is made up of members elected by the people of the provinces'.[67] It appears from her account that the word 'province' was taken to mean 'chief town of a province', and that objectors argued that the people of smaller towns and villages should also be represented. She argues that behind the objections lay the fear that the provincial elites – military commanders, notables, landowners – were largely in Mustafa Kemal's pocket and that the members of the assembly they would elect would strengthen his position as a dictator. However that may be, the text was changed to 'the Grand National Assembly of Turkey is made up of deputies elected by the nation in accordance with the relevant law'.[68]

Sabiha Sertel also claims that she complained to one of Mustafa Kemal's close companions, Mazhar Müfit (Kansu), who was at the time deputy for Denizli,[69] saying that there was nothing in the constitution about land reform and workers' rights, to which Mazhar Müfit replied: 'Mustafa Kemal wants to carry out many reforms. On land reform, he has talked here to landowners [*ağa*], particularly Kurdish landowners and to Kurdish deputies such as Feyzi Bey.[70] This problem of reform is very difficult. It is impossible to explain land reform to the *ağas*. Tackling the reform means losing all the *ağas* and notables. So for the moment we have closed the book on land reform.'[71]

Sabiha Sertel's testimony should be seen in the light of her subsequent commitment to the communist cause. But it is a fact that there were landowners from the south-east in the second GNA: two deputies from Malatya are identified as *ağa*,[72] and none as a tribal leader, a designation which had been applied to several deputies in the first Grand National Assembly.[73] The main point at issue in the deliberations of the constitutional committee and then of the GNA, when the draft constitution was debated, was the power of the president, Mustafa Kemal, and matters which had a bearing on it. Local government, within whose structure Kurdish ethnicity was to have been accommodated, attracted no attention. According to

Professor Suna Kili, 'there was very little discussion on the section of the Constitution which was devoted to the administration of the provinces'.[74] In the GNA debate one deputy, Halis Turgut of Sivas (who was hanged in 1926 for his alleged complicity in the plot to assassinate Mustafa Kemal in İzmir)[75] complained that provincial councils (modelled on the French *conseils généraux des départements*) had no real powers, and that provinces should be able to run their own affairs.[76] It made no difference. The term 'autonomy' (*muhtariyet*) was dropped from the provisions of local government; so was the term *şura* for council. The six articles on local government in the 1921 constitution were reduced to two brief articles in 1924: article 90 'Provinces, cities, towns and villages are legal entities', and article 91, 'Provincial affairs are administered in accordance with the principles of extending (delegated) powers and distiguishing between functions [*tevsi-i mezuniyet ve tefrik-i vezaif esası*]'.[77] The constitution was adopted by a near-unanimous vote of the Assembly on 20 April 1924.[78]

At the time there was no official opposition in the Assembly, most of whose members had been hand-picked by Mustafa Kemal. But this had not prevented successful moves to limit the president's powers in such matters as the dissolution of parliament and sending back laws for reconsideration. One of the deputies who spoke against giving the power of veto to the president was the lawyer Feridun Fikri (Düşünsel), deputy for the predominantly Kurdish province of Dersim,[79] who later became a member of the opposition Progressive Republican Party.[80] But neither he nor anyone else referred to the idea, discussed by Mustafa Kemal a year earlier, of granting predominantly Kurdish provinces the right to self-government within the framework of devolved local government. The plan had completely dropped out of the public debate. Why should this have been so?

The Mosul question was still unresolved, and, therefore, the need to secure the support of the Kurdish population of northern Iraq still remained, at least in theory. But as has been noted, the İzmit briefing in January 1923 suggests that Mustafa Kemal had written off Mosul. One could say cynically that the question of Kurdish self-government within Turkey was pushed aside as soon as the Lausanne treaty was signed on 24 July 1923, and the Turkish government's sovereign rights over its territory were recognized. But this does not explain the failure of the legal opposition and of the opposition press to pay any attention to the multiethnic character of the country's population, which Mustafa Kemal had recognized during the War of Independence.

I would suggest that the answer to the always difficult question why the dog did not bark – in this instance why Kurdish self-government dropped out of Ankara and Istanbul politics in 1924 – lies in the fact that priorities had changed. For Mustafa Kemal the priority was to create a modern, secular Turkey. He needed absolute power to do it. Any kind of provincial self-government would have been an obstacle to his designs, particularly self-government in what he, along with the entire Turkish elite, considered to be a backward region. For the liberal opposition, the priority was to curb Mustafa Kemal's power. For the radical left, as witness Sabiha Sertel, Kurdishness or Kurdish nationalism (*Kürtçülük*) served the interests of landlords, feudal tribal leaders and other 'reactionaries'. It is beyond the scope of this study to examine at what stage Lenin's and then Stalin's adoption of what one could call phoney federalism, but what was called officially the nurturing of cultures national in form but socialist in content, was taken on board by Turkish Communists and *Marxisants*. But it was not a factor in the crucial year of 1924.

After 1923 Mustafa Kemal's principal intervention in the Kurdish question occurred in February/March 1925 at the time of the rebellion of the Kurdish Şeyh Sait. The government of Fethi (Okyar) declared martial law and put in train military measures against the rebels. The opposition Progressive Republican Party supported these government measures. But Mustafa Kemal decided that a firmer hand was needed. He summoned his trusted lieutenant İsmet (İnönü) from Istanbul and saw to it that his People's Party disowned Fethi and brought İsmet to power to take drastic action to put down the rebellion. When İsmet's draconian Maintenance of Order Law was endorsed by the Assembly on 4 March 1925, by 122 votes to 22, 37 of the deputies representing Kurdish provinces voted with the government and only seven with the opposition.[81]

In his proclamation on 7 March 1925, Mustafa Kemal attributed the rebellion to certain notables, who had been found guilty by the courts (*kanunen mücrim olan bazı müteneffizan*) and who used the mask of religion to conceal their purposes. He went on to declare that law and order would be safeguarded as the foundation of social and economic life.[82] Opening the new session of the Assembly on 1 November 1925, he described the rebellion simply as a 'reactionary incident' (*irtica hadisesi*).

The opposition Progressive Republican Party was closed down in the aftermath of the Şeyh Sait rebellion. Yet the party's leader General Kâzım Karabekir had already in 1922/23 expressed the view that religious fanaticism had been used as an instrument to incite the Kurds to rebellion. Saying that what was important about the Kurds was not their number but the extent of the territory they occupied, Karabekir had proposed a characteristically idiosyncratic solution. Kurdish sheykhs, he said, should be replaced by intellectuals trained in the faculties of theology and law in Istanbul and taught Kurdish, and two Turkish corridors should be established, horizontally and vertically, around lake Van, thus ensuring that the government should dominate Kurdistan, militarily, politically and religiously.[83] Mustafa Kemal, Fethi (Okyar) and Kâzım Karabekir disagreed on methods for tackling Kurdish risings. But they all took it for granted that the writ of the central government should run throughout the country.

As the government was preparing to ban the opposition Progressive Republican Party, a friend of Rauf (Orbay), who had been one of Mustafa Kemal's original companions in Anatolia but had become by then a political opponent, was questioned by the police about his links with the Kurds. The friend's name was Ömer Fevzi Mardin. He was a retired officer who had been assigned by Enver Paşa to assist Rauf in his clandestine mission in Iran at the beginning of the Great War. Ömer Fevzi Mardin told his questioners that his mother was the daughter of Bedirhan Paşa. This, he said, was his only link with the Kurds. But as an officer he had always served the cause of the unity under one flag of all the races (*ırk*) – we would say ethnic communities – living in the country.[84] Mustafa Kemal had spoken in similar terms during the War of Independence. But times had changed.

On 8 December 1925, the Ministry of Education issued a circular banning the use of such divisive terms as Kurd, Circassian and Laz, Kurdistan and Lazistan.[85] Mustafa Kemal explained the new thinking in the manual of civics which he dictated in 1930 to his adopted daughter Âfet İnan. The relevant paragraph reads:

> Within the political and social unity of today's Turkish nation, there are citizens and co-nationals who have been incited to think of themselves as Kurds, Circassians, Laz or Bosnians. But these erroneous appellations – the product of past periods of tyranny – have brought nothing but sorrow to individual members of the nation, with the exception of a few brainless reactionaries, who became the enemy's instruments. This is because these individual members of the nation share with the generality of Turkish society the same past, history, concept of morals and laws.[86]

There is no specific mention here of common ethnic origin. But in the same year, Mustafa Kemal approved the publication of an *Outline of Turkish History* (*Türk Tarihinin Ana Hatları*) – a title reminiscent of Atatürk's favourite history book, *The Outline of History* by H.G. Wells. The Turkish *Outline* formulated the Turkish historical thesis which claimed that many if not most civilizations had been created by people of Turkish origin. The claim included some at least of the Medes,[87] whom the Kurds consider as their ancestors, as well as the Achaemenians and Parthians.

Then, on 14 June 1934, the Law of Resettlement (İskân Kanunu)[88] made assimilation (*temsil*) of all the country's citizens to Turkish culture – note the word 'culture' – official government policy. The insistence on 'culture' can, of course, be traced to Ziya Gökalp, one of the main ideologists of

Turkish nationalism. The model was, as ever, France, where Bretons, Occitanians, Savoyards, Flemings, etc. had all been assimilated to French culture. The government of the Turkish republic was determined not to repeat the mistake deplored the previous century by Namık Kemal when programmes – for education in Turkish – were not carried out. This time, there would be no negligence (*ihmal*).

Atatürk did not disapprove of this policy. Otherwise he would have stopped it. But his interests lay elsewhere – in the great project of modernization. Law and order was the province of İsmet İnönü's government, and Atatürk let him get on with it. As laws and institutions were changed and difficulties emerged, Atatürk made repeated tours of the provinces. But Diyarbekir and the south-east, which he promised to visit in 1919, were left out of his travels until the last year of his life. Finally, on 12 November 1937, Atatürk left Ankara by train for Diyarbekir in the company of his new prime minister Celâl Bayar. On the way, he visited the building site of a new textile mill in Malatya on 14 November. The following day he attended a concert at the People's House in Diyarbekir. 'After an interval of twenty years,' he said, 'here I am again in Diyarbekir, listening to beautiful modern music in one of the world's most beautiful and modern buildings, in the presence of civilized people, in this people's house.'[89] The following day, he inaugurated the work of extending the railway link through Diyarbekir to Iran and Iraq. He then stopped briefly at Elâziz (Mamuretülaziz): the authorities had made sure that the leaders of the last Dersim rising were executed before the visit.[90] Atatürk's adopted daughter, the military pilot Sabiha Gökçen, had earlier taken part in bombing raids against the rebels.

On 18 November, Atatürk was already in Adana. His stay in the south-east had lasted five days.[91] But it left a lasting mark, for during it he decreed that Diyarbekir should be renamed Diyarbakır and Elâziz should become Elazığ in accordance with the Sun Theory of Language which found Turkish roots for all and any words of foreign origin. On his return, Atatürk declared that he had been happy to see all the people of the eleven provinces he had visited give willingly to the state treasury, without any hesitation and in a spirit of self-sacrifice, all that was surplus to their daily needs, for the sake of a rich, strong and grandiose Turkish republic.[92]

Asım Us, a People's Party deputy and journalist, noted in his diary that, during his trip to the east, Atatürk had ordered the construction of military roads in Dersim (which was renamed Tunceli). But he cancelled the allocation of four million liras for the building of schools and of one million liras for the repair of damage done by bandits, on the grounds that it would be better to resettle mountain people in the fertile plains of the eastern provinces.[93]

To sum up, during the years of the War of Independence, Mustafa Kemal recognized specifically the multiethnic character of the Muslim population of Turkey, while insisting on its fraternal unity. He also promised that local government would accommodate ethnic specificity. After 1923, any idea of the self-rule of individual Muslim ethnic communities dropped out of the Turkish political agenda. Mustafa Kemal devoted his energy to the consolidation of his power and to his cultural revolution. He had little time for the Kurds. Did he change his views and, as John Simpson of the BBC suggests, did he propagate the myth that the Turks were the only ethnic group in Turkey? I would say that he did so only in the sense that since everyone of note in history was of Turkish origin, so too were the Kurds.

The ideology which has shaped the policy of the governments of the Turkish republic towards its Kurdish citizens antedates Atatürk. His main contribution was to manage the Kurdish problem successfully during the War of Independence. Thereafter, the requirements of creating a modern nation state took precedence. It is true that Atatürk's cultural revolution was an additional obstacle to the preservation of distinct ethnic cultures, let alone to the introduction of local self-rule. But there was no vocal demand in Turkish society for either. In the circumstances, Atatürk could delegate the management of the Kurds to his government.

Today the Turkish historical thesis has been dropped together with the Sun Theory of Language. The diverse ethnic roots of the people of Turkey are openly discussed, and the word 'mosaic' has become a cliché in describing the country's ethnic picture. We are thus back to the language which Mustafa Kemal (Atatürk) used and the ideas which he put forward during the War of Independence. Hence the importance of recording and analysing what the pragmatic founding father of the Turkish Republic said during that crucial period of Turkish history.

NOTES

1. *Atatürk's Children: Turkey and the Kurds* (London, 1996), p.11. The book was reviewed in *Middle Eastern Studies*, Vol.30, No.1 (January 1997), pp.155–6.
2. *Milliyet*, 30 June 1998, p.8.
3. 'Güneydoğu Sorunu' [The Problem of the South-East] in *Milliyet*, 10 August 1998, p.19.
4. Details in Celâl Erikan, *Komutan Atatürk* [Atatürk as a Commander] (Ankara, 1972), pp.184–217.
5. Extracts in Uluğ İğdemir, *Atatürk'ün Yaşamı* [Atatürk's Life], Türk Tarih Kurumu (Ankara, 1980), pp.79–87.
6. İzzettin Çalışlar, *Atatürk'le İkibuçuk Yıl* [Two and a half years with Atatürk] (Istanbul, 1993).
7. Çalışlar, op. cit., p.102.
8. Çalışlar, op. cit., p.134.
9. Çalışlar, op. cit., p.130.
10. ATASE [Military History Dept. of Turkish General Staff], *Türk İstiklâl Harbine Katılan Tümen ve Daha Üst Kademelerdeki Komutanların Biyografileri* [Biographies of Divisional

and More Senior Commanders in the Turkish War of Independence], 2nd ed. (Ankara, 1989), pp.113–15.
11. Fahrettin Altay, *On Yıl Savaş (1912–1922) ve Sonrası* [Ten Years of War (1912–1922) and After] (Istanbul, 1970), p.29ff.
12. Altay, op. cit., p.53.
13. Altay, op. cit., p.57.
14. Altay, op. cit., p.70.
15. Selim Deringil, *The Well-Protected Domains* (London, 1998), pp.101–4.
16. *Ana Britannica*, 1st ed. (Istanbul, 1986–87), Vol.II, p.471.
17. Quoted by Masami Arai, *Turkish Nationalism in the Young Turk Era* (Leiden, 1992), p.3.
18. Afetinan, *Atatürk Hakkında Hâtıralar ve Belgeler* [Reminiscences and Documents Concerning Atatürk] (Istanbul, 1984), pp.43–51.
19. Text of letter in Salih Bozok, *Hep Atatürk'ün Yanında* [Ever at Atatürk's Side] (Istanbul, 1985), pp.182–3.
20. David McDowall, *A Modern History of the Kurds* (London, 1996), p.121.
21. Ibid., p.123; *Encyclopaedia of Islam*, 2nd ed. (Leiden, 1958), Vol.I, p.871; *Ana Britannica*, Vol.XIV, p.185.
22. McDowall, op. cit., p.122.
23. McDowall, op. cit., pp.121–3.
24. ATASE, *Atatürk Özel Arşivinden Seçmeler* [Extracts from Atatürk's Private Archive], Vol.IV, Genelkurmay Basımevi [General Staff Press] (Ankara, 1996). Ahmet Cevdet's first report on pp.1–8.
25. Mahmut Goloğlu, *Sivas Kongresi* [The Sivas Congress] (Ankara, 1969), p.120.
26. Full list of delegates in Mahmut Goloğlu, *Erzurum Kongresi* [The Erzurum Congress] (Ankara, 1968), pp.78–80.
27. Text in Goloğlu, *Erzurum Kongresi*, pp.201–2.
28. Kemal Atatürk, *Nutuk: Vesikalar* [Speech: Documents], Atatürk Kültür, Dil ve Tarih Yüksek Kurumu, Atatürk Araştırma Merkezi, Ankara 1991, Document No.41, p.643.
29. Mazhar Müfit Kansu, *Erzurum'dan Ölümüne Kadar Atatürk'le Beraber* [At Atatürk's Side from the Erzurum Congress to His Death] (Ankara, 1988), Vol.II, pp.112–13.
30. Erikan, *Komutan Atatürk*, p.585.
31. Şevket Süreyya Aydemir, *Tek Adam* [The Only Man] (Istanbul, 1984), Vol.II, p.89; Mazhar Müfit Kansu, pp.198–203.
32. Date in *Diary of Major Noel* (Basra, 1919), p.19. Charge mentioned in Ahmet Cevdet's telegram of 12 September to Grand Vizier, copy 3rd Corps in Sivas (ATASE, p.78).
33. *Diary of Major Noel*, p.1.
34. *Diary of Major Noel*, p.21.
35. Goloğlu, *Sivas Kongresi*, pp.74, 124.
36. Mahmut Goloğlu, *Sivas Kongresi*, p.110.
37. Text in Goloğlu, *Sivas Kongresi*, pp.232–4.
38. ATASE, p.79.
39. *The Diary of Major Noel*, p.24.
40. Recep Zühtü's telegrams to 3rd corps in Sivas in ATASE, pp.91–7.
41. Sina Akşin, *İstanbul Hükûmetleri ve Millî Mücadele* [The Istanbul Governments and the National Struggle] (Istanbul, 1992), Vol.I, p.589.
42. İlhan Tekeli and Selim İlkin, 'Kurtuluş Savaşında Talat Paşa ile Mustafa Kemal'in Mektuplaşmaları' [Correspondence between Talat Paşa and Mustafa Kemal during the Liberation Struggle], *Belleten* (Ankara, 1980), Vol.XLIV, No.174, p.321.
43. *Atatürk'ün Söylev ve Demeçleri* (*ASD*) [Atatürk's Speeches and Declarations], Atatürk Kültür, Dil ve Tarih Yüksek Kurumu, Atatürk Araştırma Merkezi (Ankara, 1989), Vol.I, p.30.
44. *ASD*, Vol.I, pp.74–5.
45. *ASD*, Vol.I, p.236.
46. *ASD*, Vol.II, pp.37, 39.
47. Original wording of the text in Rona Aybay, *Karşılaştırmalı 1961 Anayasası* [Comparative (Text) of 1961 Constitution] (Fakülteler Matbaası, Istanbul, 1963), p.199.
48. ATASE, p.69.

49. *TBMM Gizli Celse Zabıtları* [Minutes of Secret Sessions of the Grand National Assembly] (Ankara, 1985), Vol.III, p.551.
50. ATASE, p.69.
51. *TBMM Gizli Celse Zabıtları*, Vol.II, p.270.
52. *TBMM Gizli Celse Zabıtları*, Vol.II, p.630.
53. Kâzım Karabekir, *İstiklâl Harbimiz* [Our War of Independence] (Istanbul, 1969), pp.978–9.
54. Robert Olson, *The Emergence pf Kurdish Nationalism and the Sheikh Said Rebellion, 1880–1925* (Austin, TX, 1989), pp.38–9.
55. McDowall, pp.187–8.
56. *TBMM Gizli Celse Zabıtları*, pp.248–80. The context shows that the word *müstakil* (independent) refers to *müstakil sancak* or *liva* (separate district or province) rather than full state independence.
57. *TBMM Gizli Celse Zabıtları*, Vol.II, p.623.
58. *TBMM Gizli Celse Zabıtları*, Vol.III, p.559.
59. Doğu Perinçek (ed.), *Mustafa Kemal: Eskişehir-İzmit Konuşmaları (1923)* [Mustafa Kemal: Speeches in Eskişehir and İzmit (1923)] (Istanbul, 1993), p.104.
60. Stephen Evans, *The Slow Rapprochement: Britain and Turkey in the Age of Kemal Atatürk, 1919–38* (Walkington, England, 1982), pp.85–6.
61. *Eskişehir-İzmit Konuşmaları*, pp.94–6.
62. Sadi Borak (ed.), *Atatürk'ün Resmi Yayınlara Girmemiş Söylev, Demeç, Yazışma ve Söyleşileri* [Atatürk's Speeches, Declarations, Correspondence and Interviews Which Have Not Been Included in Official Publications] (Istanbul, 1997), p.225.
63. Mahmut Goloğlu, *Türkiye Cumhuriyeti 1923* [The Republic of Turkey: 1923], p.94.
64. *Eskişehir-İzmit Konuşmaları*, p.13.
65. *ASD*, I, 337, 338.
66. Sabiha Sertel, *Roman Gibi* [Like a Novel] (Istanbul, 1969), pp.68–78.
67. Sabiha Sertel calls this article 4 of the draft. In fact it was article 4 of the 1921 constitution (see Aybay, op. cit., p.99).
68. Aybay, op. cit., p.99.
69. Goloğlu, *Türkiye Cumhuriyeti*, p.320.
70. She probably means Fevzi (Pirinççi), deputy for Diyarbekir (Goloğlu, *Türkiye Cumhuriyeti*, p.320).
71. Sabiha Sertel, p.76.
72. Goloğlu, *Türkiye Cumhuriyeti*, p.324.
73. Goloğlu, *Üçüncü Meşrutiyet* [The Third Constitution(al Period)], gives the tribal affiliations of three deputies from Dersim (p.328), one from Erzincan (p.329) and one from Van (p.343).
74. Suna Kili, *Assembly Debates on the Constitutions of 1924 and 1961*, Robert College Research Center (Istanbul, 1971), p.60.
75. Feridun Kandemir, *İzmir Suîkastinin İçyüzü* [The Inside Story of the İzmir Assassination Attempt], Ekicigil Matbaası (Istanbul, 1955), Vol.I, p.107.
76. Goloğlu, *Devrimler ve Tepkileri* [Reforms and Reactions To Them] (Ankara, 1972), p.38.
77. Aybay, p.200.
78. Goloğlu, *Devrimler ve Tepkileri*, p.49.
79. Goloğlu, *Devrimler ve Tepkileri*, pp.37–8.
80. Mete Tunçay, *T.C.'de Tek-Parti Yönetimi'nin Kurulması* [The Establishment of the Single-Party Regime in the Turkish Republic] (Istanbul, 1981), p.108.
81. İsmail Göldaş, *Takrir-i Sükûn Görüşmeleri* [The Debates on the Maintenance of Order Law] (Istanbul, 1997), pp.470, 491.
82. *ASD*, IV, pp.562–3.
83. Karabekir, *İstiklâl Harbimiz*, p.1034.
84. Rauf Orbay (ed. by İsmet Bozdağ), *Cehennem Değirmeni: Siyasî Hatıralarım* [The Mill of Hell: My Political Memoirs] (Istanbul, 1993), Vol.II, p.190.
85. Sami Özerdim, *Atatürk Devrimi Kronolojisi* [Chronology of Atatürk's Reforms] (Ankara, 1996), p.93.
86. Nuran Tezcan (ed.), *Atatürk'ün Yazdığı Yurttaşlık Bilgileri* [Civics (Manual) Written by Atatürk] (Istanbul, 1994), p.23.

87. *Türk Tarihinin Ana Hatları* [An Outline of Turkish History], reprinted in 1996 with an introduction by Doğu Perinçek (Istanbul), p.289.
88. Law No.2510, published in *Resmî Gazete* [Official Gazette] on 21 June 1934.
89. *ASD*, Vol.II, p.328.
90. İhsan Sabri Çağlayangil, *Anılarım* [My Reminiscences] (Istanbul, 1990), pp.46–55.
91. Özel Şahingiray (ed.), *Atatürk'ün Not Defteri* [Atatürk's Logbook] (Ankara, 1955), pp.672–4.
92. *ASD*, Vol.IV, pp.678–9.
93. Asım Us, *1930–1950 Hatıra Notları* [Notebooks 1930–1950] (Istanbul, 1966), p.234. İsmet İnönü says in his memoirs that, on the contrary, he had concentrated on education in Dersim and that by 1950, when he left the office of president, it had more primary schools than any other Turkish province. In the end, says İnönü, railways solved the problem of Dersim. Roads were later built to link the area to the rest of the country (İsmet İnönü, *Hatıralar* (Ankara, 1987), Vol.II, p.269.)

Kosovo Revisited: Sultan Reşad's Macedonian Journey of June 1911

ERIK-JAN ZÜRCHER

For the Young Turks of the Committee of Union and Progress (CUP), whose movement started in Macedonia in 1906,[1] the situation in that rich but unruly region of the empire[2] in 1910–11 was all but reassuring. Although the constitutional revolution of July 1908 caused a wave of rejoicing and reconciliation between the ethnic communities in Macedonia, this had proved short-lived and agitation and small-scale guerrilla warfare by Serb, Bulgarian and Greek bands recommenced. More worrying from the point of view of the CUP was the attitude of the Albanians. After all, the Committee had originally been an organization of Ottoman Muslims[3] who aimed to strengthen the Ottoman state and the position of the Muslims within it. Most Albanians were Muslims and Albanians, such as the famous Niyazi Bey of Resne [Resen/Resnja][4] played leading roles both in the revolution of 1908 and in the suppression (by military units from Macedonia which had stayed loyal to the CUP) of the counterrevolution of April 1909 in Istanbul.

Nevertheless, the attempts by the constitutional regime to strengthen the hold of the state, to make taxation more effective, and to standardize education (in the Ottoman language and script)[5] soon led to disenchantment on the part of the Albanians. The Unionists' drive to enforce military conscription (and at the same time disarm the population) caused great resentment among the Albanians. There were revolts in Northern Albania and Kosovo even in 1909, but in early April 1910 twelve Albanian tribes from the province of Kosovo rose up in arms, led by two tribal chiefs: Isa Boletin, who controlled the Mitrovica area, and Idris Sefer, a chief from Skopska Crna Gora. Led by Idris, 5,000 Albanians cut off the railway between Priştina and Üsküp (Skoplje) at Kacanik, while Isa Boletin led 2,000 rebels against Firzovik (Verisovic/Ferisaj) and Prizren. The insurrection was suppressed with some difficulty by 16,000 Ottoman troops under Şevket Turgut Paşa[6] and by August order was reestablished.[7] The government now took harsh measures to ensure that the area remain under control: all men between the ages of 15 and 60 were registered (with a view to conscription); Albanian men were disarmed and those who were eligible were conscripted into the army. A new tax on livestock was introduced; farmers were ordered to widen the windows of their homes (to make them less suitable as loopholes) and almost 150,000 guns were confiscated.

Nevertheless, the rebellion flared up again in February 1911, this time in the area of Dibra. On 24 March, Albanian refugees in Montenegro attacked over the border into Skutari (Üsküdar/Skhoder) district. Again Şevket Turgut Paşa was ordered to suppress the rebellion and he arrived with 8,000 strong Anatolian troops in Skutari on 17 April.[8] After a difficult campaign the rebels were forced back, but when war with Montenegro threatened, the government ordered the Paşa to declare a ten-day armistice on 17 June. In the meantime, yet another rebellion flared up, this time of Catholic Albanians more to the south.[9]

The CUP was deeply worried about the situation in Macedonia. One of the reasons they unleashed the constitutional revolution when they did, in July 1908, was their fear that European powers were threatening to intervene directly in Macedonia, and the danger certainly had not passed. The committee therefore decided on a campaign of counter-propaganda built around the most powerful symbol of national unity at their disposal: the figure of the Sultan himself.

Tours of the provinces were not a part of the Ottoman monarchic tradition. Of course, until the seventeenth century, sultans had personally conducted military campaigns which took them through the length and breadth of their domains. Later sultans had largely restricted themselves to hunting trips. Otherwise, their visibility was restricted mainly to the capital. The nineteenth century sultans who oversaw the process of institutional and legal reforms known as the *Tanzimat*, Mahmud II (1807–39), Abdülmecit (1839–61) and Abdülaziz (1861–76) left their palace with increasing frequency and travelled outside the capital. Sultan Abdülmecit visited Izmir and Bursa in 1845 and Salonica in 1859, a visit during which he was accompanied by his sons, among them the young Prince Reşad – the protagonist of this story.[10] Sultan Abdülaziz had visited Bursa in 1861, Egypt in 1863, and the most famous imperial voyage of all was, of course, his visit to the Paris World Exhibition in 1867.

During the long reign of Sultan Abdülhamit II (1876–1909), the Sultan only rarely ventured outside the palace of Yıldız, situated on a hill overlooking the Bosphorus and quite isolated from the capital. He never made any effort to acquaint himself directly with the situation outside the capital or to get in personal touch with the population in the provinces. Instead, Abdülhamit relied on his bureaucracy and his extensive network of informers for his intelligence and on propaganda through the printed media and through the pulpits of the mosques for the projection of his image as just ruler and defender of Islam.[11] The Sultan certainly used modern propaganda techniques to promote his image abroad,[12] but he did not do so by personally boarding ship and going there. So, by 1909, when Abdülhamit was finally deposed, the memory of sultans actually going out to meet their flock was quite a distant one.

Prince Reşad,[13] on the other hand, had already made two very symbolic journeys outside his capital since he had ascended the throne as Mehmet V[14] in April 1909. He visited the old Ottoman capitals of Bursa and Edirne. But these expeditions were minor ones compared with the one now undertaken.

The expedition to Macedonia was planned meticulously, not only by the government, but also by the palace, especially the palace kitchens, the stables and, of course, the privy purse. It was foreseen that for the Sultan and his entourage to move, eat, drink and dress according to their custom, everything would have to be catered for by the palace and everything would be brought along for the trip, from kitchen utensils to carriages.[15] The visit was originally planned for April, but the unrest in Albania and the complexity of the preparations necessitated a postponement.

The Sultan left Istanbul on 5 June 1911 amid great pomp and circumstance and watched by a large crowd on the banks of the Bosphorus. He travelled aboard the battleship *Hayrettin Barbaros* with part of his entourage, escorted by the battleship *Turgut Reis*[16] and the steamer *Gülcemal*. After a short stop in Çanakkale, during which the Sultan paid homage at the tomb of Yazıcıoğlu Mehmet Efendi, a famous fifteenth-century mystic, the imperial flotilla arrived before Salonica on the morning of 7 June, a day of continuous rain. There seem to have been worries whether Reşad would be able to withstand the exhaustion of the long trip, particularly the sea voyage to which he was unaccustomed, but according to his private secretary, once at sea he seemed rejuvenated and relaxed and altogether changed from the person he was in Istanbul. He even spoke fluently in public, whereas in Istanbul he had been notoriously shy.[17]

The flotilla was met at sea by a squadron of warships carrying dignitaries, such as the governor of Salonica, the inspectors of the 4th, 5th, 6th and 7th Army corps and the secretary-general of the CUP, Haci Adil (Arda). A special delegation composed of representatives of all parts of the empire had put to sea aboard the steamer *Midhat Paşa* to greet the Sultan. The fleet greeted the monarch with a 21-gun salute, after which he watched naval manoeuvres. The flotilla then moved into Salonica harbour escorted by the naval squadron. After a second 21-gun salute, the *Hayrettin Barbaros* anchored off the quay and the official reception committee, consisting of representatives of the town and of parliamentarians hailing from Macedonia and representing different communities, went on board.[18]

The Sultan stayed aboard the battleship overnight, but within an hour of his arrival he dispatched his secretary, Halit Ziya Bey (Uşaklıgil),[19] and the inspector of the armies of Rumelia (the European provinces), Hadi Paşa, on a very delicate mission. They were instructed to go to the villa of the Alatini family of Salonica industrialists, just outside Salonica, where the former Sultan Abdülhamit lived under strict house arrest. Reşad apparently felt it necessary to enquire after the ex-Sultan's health because he was afraid the latter might see the tour of Macedonia as an affront. For Halit Ziya, meeting the man who had ruled Turkey for 33 years and who had been the hated enemy of the Young Turks for 20 of them was an awesome experience, but the interview proved easier than expected. The ex-Sultan politely wished his brother success on his trip and used the occasion for some personal requests. He asked for his son Abid to be allowed to study and to live in Istanbul and he enquired after a bag full of jewellery which had disappeared when he was moved from the Yıldız palace to Salonica.

The next morning, the Sultan disembarked, supported by Grand Vizier Hakkı Paşa. Two sheep were sacrificed and the *müftü* of Salonica led the prayers. Then the Sultan, dressed in full military uniform, drove to the main government building (the *Konak*) in an open carriage. The streets, which had been newly paved with the houses along the route freshly painted[20] and ceremonial arches erected in many different spots, were lined with schoolchildren singing Greek and Turkish national songs. By all accounts, the monarch was greeted warmly (although, according to the British consul 'much less so than in the West on such occasions').[21] The afternoon was filled with audiences. During these, Evrenos Bey, a local notable and a scion of the most famous Christian *gazi* dynasty[22] was singled out for praise by the Sultan, who pointed out how his family had served his own forefathers back in the fifteenth century – a clear call for loyalty from the contemporary Ottoman Greek community. Then Reşad received a delegation from the garrison, whom he greeted saying that 'the army was the soul of the nation' and from the schools of Salonica.[23] The Sultan also gave audiences to delegations from all over the empire (Skutari/Üsküdar, Janina, Erzurum, Trabzon, Crete and Lebanon), who had come to Salonica especially for the occasion.[24]

Right from the start the CUP made it its business to associate itself as closely as possible with the imperial visit. Rahmi Bey (Arslan), one of the founder members of the CUP in Salonica, thanked the Sultan for his exertions, to which the latter answered that he was grateful for the opportunity to get in touch with his people. The famous CUP orator Ömer Naci addressed the representatives of the province on behalf of the committee and later the Sultan visited the CUP club, where top Unionists like Talât Bey, Cavit Bey and Midhat Şükrü (Bleda) as well as the historian Abdürrahman Şeref were present to welcome him.

FIGURE 1
THE SULTAN'S ARRIVAL IN SALONICA

FIGURE 2
ARCH ERECTED BY SALONICA INDUSTRIALIST ALATIMI
(NOTE THE CHIMNEYS)

FIGURE 3
PRIŞTINA STATION DECORATED FOR THE OCCASION

FIGURE 4
'HEROES OF THE REVOLUTION' IN MONASTIR

Niyazi Bey is second from the left, front row.

On the morning of 9 June, the Sultan received the *mücahit-i muhterem* (honoured fighter) Niyazi Bey, who in his dual capacity as hero of the constitutional revolution and revered (although politically marginal) member of the CUP on the one hand, and ethnic Albanian on the other, was a key figure throughout the whole Macedonian tour. Niyazi Bey was reported as having come to town in the company of 600 'well-built young men' from his native Resne.[25] After the Friday prayers in the Aya Sofya mosque of Salonica, the Sultan distributed 4,500 Lira in largesse to benevolent societies, to the poor and to students.[26] In the late afternoon Cavit Bey gave a speech in the public gardens of Beşçınar, which was attended by a large crowd (10,000 people according to the Unionist newspapers) in which he called for unity between the communities and praised the Committee.

On Saturday, 10 June, the Sultan first received a delegation from Izmir. This was yet another in the series of audiences to delegations from all over the empire. Thereafter leading officials and Unionist politicians were presented with decorations (*Mecidiye* order first class), gold watches and – in the case of the editor of the local paper *Rumeli*, Yunus Nadi (Abalıoğlu – later to become famous as the founder of the newspaper *Cumhuriyet* in Istanbul in 1924) – with a ruby ring.

The programme continued with a visit to the army barracks, where the foundation stone was laid for a monument commemorating the visit. The Sultan then received Haci Adil (Arda) and through him praised the CUP for its work. In the afternoon, the Sultan attended a *sema* (religious ceremony) in the *Mevlevihane*, the local headquarters of the Mevlevi Dervish order, of which the Sultan was a devoted member.

In the meantime, an auction in support of the Ottoman Fleet Society (Donanma Cemiyeti – modelled after Germany's Flottenverein) had been organized in the Beşçınar gardens. Among the items being auctioned were carpets and the Sultan, at the request of the organizers, agreed to walk over them in order to increase their value.

The Sultan's departure for the interior was on 11 June. The trip to Üsküp was made by train – a seven-hour journey as the train moved at a slow pace. A pilot train carrying part of the entourage and also Niyazi Bey preceded the imperial train and it was announced that anyone attempting to come near the tracks between the two trains would be shot on sight. The Sultan boarded the train (on which the director-general of the Oriental Railways, Mr Müller, acted as conductor)[27] in the company of CUP grandees Haci Adil and Ömer Naci and the governors of Salonica and Kosovo provinces. The military commander and mayor of Üsküp also joined the company. Along the route five stops were made. One of just three minutes to take on water at Karasulu Kimence, one of ten minutes at Gevgili, one of 11 minutes at

Strumitza, one of 12 minutes at Krivolak and one of 15 minutes at Köprülü (Velez). During all of these stops the train was received with a guard of honour and military music and at the last stop an 'old and historic banner' [*sancak*] was presented to the Sultan, who took it in his hand and prayed that 'God make the Ottoman banner ever honoured'. The theme of 'unity of the elements' was again expressed at the ceremonies at the station: a Bulgarian girl made a moving speech and a Muslim girl recited a poem. Both were rewarded, the Bulgarian Christian girl being offered an education at the Sultan's expense. Four sheep were sacrificed, after which the governor of Salonica officially handed over responsibility for the Sultan's well-being to his colleague of Kosovo.

On his arrival in the capital of Kosovo province, Üsküp, the Sultan was driven in a four horse carriage (brought from Istanbul) from the station to the government *Konak*, but he was lodged in the arts and crafts school, because that was the most comfortable building around. Then he addressed the local dignitaries, repeating the central themes of his visit. He stated that his aim was the 'mutual understanding of the [ethnic] elements' and that the CUP deserved the gratitude of the fatherland for its services. The Sultan was enthusiastically received by the Albanian population. Albanians performed folk dances after which each of them received a Lira. Some 5,000 Albanians had come to the town from villages up to 20 kilometres away, but considerable effort seems to have gone into 'engineering' this Albanian enthusiasm. According to one report, the district governor (*mütesarrıf*) of Prizren had given Albanian villagers five days food supplies to enable them to make the trip.[28]

Reconciliation with the Albanians still had the highest priority, especially now that the Sultan was getting close to the areas with an Albanian majority. Two Albanian chiefs, Süleyman Batusha and Hasan Aga of Plevlje (Pljevlja), came to swear fealty to the Ottoman throne and were pardoned, but the notorious Isa Boletin, who had been expected, did not show up. Largesse was again employed as a means to win support for the throne, this time not only in the form of donations to his favourite Dervish order, the Mevlevis (200 Lira) and to charitable institutions (for instance a promise to build a *medrese* in Priştina and 300 Lira towards the cost of building a school in Firzovik), but also in the form of blood-money, distributed to pay off blood-feuds. A sum of 30,000 Lira is reported to have been spent for this purpose.[29] Another instrument for reconciliation was the granting of amnesties. There had been high hopes among the Christian communities of a large-scale or even general amnesty, but during the visit to Salonica nothing had materialized. Now an amnesty for all except convicted murderers was announced and 107 Albanians and 134 Bulgarians were released from Üsküp prison.[30]

As in Salonica (and later in Priştina) the Sultan made a conscious and very visible effort to get in touch with the population, inviting the people into the garden of his residence and showing himself on the balcony a number of times.

After the visit to Üsküp, the time came for what was meant to be the climax of the whole imperial visit: the Sultan's pilgrimage to the 'Meşhed-i Hüdavendigâr', the tomb of Sultan Murad I on the old battlefield of Kosovopolje near Priştina. The visit had been widely publicized beforehand. On the day the Sultan left for Salonica, Haci Adil, the secretary-general of the CUP in a statement reminded the population that in the battle of Kosovopolje in 1389, the crusading Christians, 'numerous as locusts', had wanted to throw the Ottomans out of Europe, but that, thanks to the sacrifice of Sultan Murat and his warriors, they failed. Muslims were called upon to come to Kosovo in great numbers to show their determination to follow Murat's example and expectations about the number of people attending were very high. In the newspapers, 150,000 or even 200,000 Albanians were reported to be assembling in the plain. The British consul in Üsküp expected 100,000 to turn up.[31]

On 15 June the Sultan left Üsküp for Priştina by train. During short stops in Kacanik and Firzovik, sheep were sacrificed and prayers offered. After three and a half hours, the Sultan arrived in Priştina, where the mass of people awaiting him was reported by the Unionist press as having grown to 300,000. Four sheep were sacrificed and an amnesty declared for those who had taken part in the rebellions of 1910 and 1911.

In Priştina an interesting role was played by the local Serbian community. A visit by a direct descendant of Sultan Murat I to the battlefield of Kosovopolje, which played (and still plays) such a vital part in the national identity of Serbia, might be expected to meet with strong Serbian resistance, but in fact at this time the Serbs saw the Ottomans as less of a danger than the Albanian and Macedonian/Bulgarian nationalists and were supportive of Young Turk policies to a certain extent. The Serbian Crown Prince had even been originally expected to come to Üsküp, but that visit did not materialize, as he had to attend King George V's coronation in London.[32] In Priştina, however, the Sultan was serenaded by the choir of the Serbian Orthodox seminary and the Serbian vice-consul Rakić had gathered a large Serb crowd.[33]

The next day the royal entourage left for Kosovopolje where it arrived at 10 a.m. Reports on what actually happened there vary widely. The pro-CUP press depicted the meeting as an enormous success and stated that 300,000 Albanians attended and Sir Edwin Pears gives a number of 80,000 in his memoirs,[34] but according to Halid Ziya, who was present in Kosovopolje, there were about 50,000 people. He says that many more had wanted to come, but that they were stopped for fear of overcrowding[35] According to British consular reports however, the Ottomans had real trouble gathering a credible number of people. The Grand Vizier made a personal request from local notables such as Hasan Bey (a representative for Priştina) and Beytullah Bey of Gilan and most of the villagers came from their areas. From places such as Ipek (Pec), Djakova and Prizren, where resentment against the repression by the Ottoman army was strongest, only a few official representatives appeared.[36] Indeed, photographs taken during the ceremony seem to show an attendance of 20,000 people at most.

Facing the mausoleum of Murat I, a historic tent originally belonging to Sultan Selim I (1512–20) had been erected for the Sultan's use. To the right of the tent there stood the Mihrab and the pulpit. After the communal prayer (in which the Sultan took part), the traditional Friday sermon was delivered by a local notable who was at the same time an *âlim* and an Ottoman senator, Manastırlı İsmail Hakkı Efendi. According to one report[37] the Imam Reşit Ibrahim Efendi 'walked through the ranks of the believers, exhorting them to be brothers and reminding them that the late Sultan Murat I, in his testament, had ordered Muslims to love Christians and Jews as their brothers'. Then a declaration by the Grand Vizier was read out. According to Halid Ziya, this was supposed to be translated into Albanian by Manastırlı İsmail Hakkı Efendi, who, however, turned out to have no Albanian. The ceremonies were ended with a military parade and with the laying of the foundation stone for a new university.

After this high point of the visit the Sultan returned via Priştina and Üsküp to Salonica. *En route*, he was again greeted with parades and military music. In Salonica he stayed for three days (17–19 June), during which time he again showed himself to the public in an open carriage and hosted an official dinner in honour of the Serbian delegation which had come to pay its respects. On the morning of 20 June, he boarded a train for Monastir (Bitola), the main base of the Third Army. The Sultan's visit of three and a half days to the garrison town was again depicted as a great success by the Unionist press, but according to the British consul he was 'rather coolly received'.[38] The town was again illuminated (sadly, the arch erected by the Serbian community burned to the ground) and there were the usual presentations by the different communities and the schools. As during his earlier visits to the provincial capitals, the Sultan received the local notables, delegations from the outlying parts of the province and the consular corps. Military matters moved to the fore in this garrison town. Mahmud Şevket Paşa, who as commander of the First, Second and Third armies was the military strong man of the empire. He had joined the Sultan's entourage on 15 June and used the visit to this military centre to give a speech in which he asked the officers not to meddle in politics. The factionalism of the officer corps was by now seriously undermining the discipline of the Ottoman army. In Monastir, too, an amnesty was declared which again fell short of the expectations of the local Christians: 104 prisoners were pardoned, but 12 others (among them leading Bulgarian nationalists) were banished to Anatolia and the status of 12 others remained unclear.

An interesting event was the reenactment, for the Sultan's benefit, of scenes from the constitutional revolution, notably the entry into town of the constitutional forces on 10 July 1908, by troops under the command of Niyazi Bey.[39]

After his visit to Monastir, the sultan returned to Salonica and thence after only a very short stop to Istanbul, where he was greeted by large and enthusiastic crowds, as the surviving photographs show. The whole town was illuminated to celebrate the return of the monarch and a torch parade was held from Sirkeci to the palace of Dolmabahçe and back. Newspaper editorials commented that many Ottoman sultans had in the past returned to their capitals with the keys of conquered cities, but that this Sultan returned with the keys to the hearts of the people of Rumelia.[40]

What was the Sultan's Macedonian voyage meant to achieve and what did it accomplish? I think we can say that Sultan Reşat's Macedonian journey served four distinct – but interconnected – political purposes. In the first place it was meant to cement ties with the Albanian Muslim population, which was regarded by the CUP as a crucial factor in retaining its hold over the area. After the insurrections of the previous year, reconciliation with the Albanians was the most urgent issue on the agenda. The high profile role played by Niyazi Bey during the whole visit and the Sultan's visit to Kosovo served this purpose, as did the amnesties which were declared during the visit and the paying of blood-money. The second, more general political aim was to strengthen the policy of *İttihad-i Anasır* (Unity of the Elements or 'Ottomanism') by the organization of demonstrations of inter-ethnic solidarity in the most ethnically mixed area of the empire. Hence the demonstrations of loyalty by Bulgarians and Greeks and references to Gazi Evrenos.

Thirdly, the journey served to strengthen the political position of the Committee of Union and Progress, which had been losing public support and political power over the past year, through the close and very visible association of the Sultan with leading committee members. Top people of the Committee, such as the orator Ömer Naci and Haci Adil, constantly accompanied the monarch, and the latter expressed his gratitude to the CUP in all four towns he visited. Fourthly, the visit, and in particular the ceremonies on the battlefield of Kosovopolje, served the more general purpose of strengthening Ottoman (and more specifically Ottoman-Muslim) national consciousness through reference to historically significant symbols. In this sense, the visit to Kosovopolje was a logical sequence to the earlier imperial visits to Bursa and Edirne – the first and second Ottoman capitals. The use of relics, such as Sultan Selim's tent and the 'old and historic' banner should be seen in this context.

Apart from its political and ideological content, the Sultan's journey is an interesting phenomenon in its shape. It is an example of something quite novel: attempts of the regime to promote the ruler as a popular figure, highly visible and close to his people. Hence the constant emphasis on the way the Sultan tried to get in touch with his people, showing himself to them and inviting them to join him. Reşad was projected as the 'father of the nation' and he was, of course, very suitable, both physically and mentally, for this role. The years until Reşad's death in 1918 would show many more examples of this use of the monarchy.

It is however no exaggeration to say that in the end the tour failed in at least three of its four objectives. In 1912 the Balkan War, the immediate cause of which was the Porte's rejection of Greek, Serb, Montenegran and Bulgarian demands for far-reaching reforms in Macedonia, put paid to any hopes of achieving the 'Unity of the Elements'. After the collapse of the Ottoman defence, the Albanians finally opted for complete independence and severed their ties with the Ottoman throne; and the CUP failed to increase its popularity. It lost political power in 1912 and only managed to regain it through a *coup d'état* in January 1913. The efforts to strengthen Ottoman-Muslim consciousness on the other hand may be termed successful. There can be no doubt that in the ten years between 1912 and 1922 Ottoman-Muslim nationalism became the most important factor in the mobilization of the Muslim population, first during the Balkan War, then in the First World War (with its attendant inter-ethnic conflicts with the Greeks and Armenians of the Empire) and finally in the struggle for independence. Turkish nationalism was adopted as state ideology only after the establishment of the Republic of Turkey in 1923.[41]

NOTES

1. It was founded as the 'Ottoman Freedom Society' in Salonica in that year, but merged with the much older (founded in 1889) Committee of Union and Progress based (known between 1905 and 1908 as the Committee of Progress and Union) in Paris under the latter's name in 1907. Cf. Erik-Jan Zürcher, *The Unionist Factor. The Role of the Committee of Union and Progress in the Turkish National Movement 1905–1926* (Leiden, 1984).
2. It is perhaps useful to point out that 'Macedonia' was not an Ottoman administrative unit. The area so described comprised the provinces (*vilâyets*) of Selânik, Kosovo (capital: Üsküp) and Monastir.

3. This is evident from Kâzım Karabekir, *İttihat ve Terakki Cemiyeti 1896–1909* (Istanbul, private, 1982 [written in 1945]), p.176.
4. Erik-Jan Zürcher, Niyâzî Bey, Ahmed, in *Encyclopaedia of Islam. New Edition* (Leiden, 1995), Vol.8, pp.67–8.
5. In November 1908 a so-called Pan-Albanian conference in Monastir (Bitola) had endorsed a plan to use a modified Latin alphabet for the Albanian language and to introduce it in schools in Albania.
6. Officer of Circassian descent. Commanded the Kosovo army corps during the 1908 revolution and after. Commander of the Thracian army corps in the Balkan War. After the First World War he held the position of Minister of Supplies and of War under Damad Ferit Paşa, but had to resign because of his nationalist sympathies. After his retirement from the army in 1919 he worked as a trader until his death in 1924.
7. Noel Malcolm, *Kosovo: A Short History* (London, 1998), pp.239–43. Malcolm gives the number of Albanians who blocked the railway at Kacanik as 9,000.
8. Malcolm gives the total number of Ottoman troops involved in the campaign as 40,000. *Kosovo: A Short History*, p.242.
9. Peter Bartl, *Die Albanische Muslime zur zeit der nationalen Unabhaengigkeitsbewegung (1878–1912)* (Wiesbaden, 1968), p.176.
10. In 1911, the newspapers stated that Mehmet Reşad's earlier visit with his father had taken place in 1863, but that must be a mistake as his father died in 1861.
11. François Georgeon, 'Le Sultan caché. Réclusion du souverain et mise en scène du pouvoir à l'époque de Abdülhamid II (1876–1909)', *Turcica*, Vol.29 (1997), pp.93–124.
12. Selim Deringil, *The Well-protected Domains. Ideology and the Legitimation of Power in the Ottoman Empire, 1876–1909* (London, 1998).
13. Prince Reşad was born as son of Sultan Abdülmecit in the Çiragan Palace in Istanbul on 2 Teşrin-i Sani/16 November 1844. He succeeded his brother Abdülhamit as Sultan on 27 April 1909 and reigned until his death on 3 July 1918. For a biography see Enver Ziya Karal, 'Mehmed V' in *İslam Ansiklopedisi*, Vol.7 (Istanbul, no date), pp.557–62.
14. That Prince Reşad took the official name of 'Mehmet V' on his accession was also an act of historic symbolism. The name Mehmet had not been used by rulers since the late seventeenth century and its revival on this occasion was meant to evoke memories of Mehmet II, the conqueror of Istanbul in 1453. Reşad was portrayed as a 'second conqueror' because his accession was the result of the taking of the city by the 'Action Army' which suppressed the counterrevolution known as the *Otuz bir Mart vak'ası*.
15. The Sultan's private secretary at the time, Halit Ziya Uşaklıgil, describes the preparations in detail in *Saray ve Ötesi. Son Hatıralar* (Istanbul, 1965, second edition, two volumes in one binding), pp.238–9, 260–1.
16. The *Turgut Reis* and *Barbaros Hayreddin* were the largest capital ships of the Ottoman navy in 1911. They were built in Germany in 1890–91 as the *Weissenburg* and *Kurfürst Friedrich Wilhelm* of the Imperial German navy. In August 1910 both ships were sold to the Ottoman navy. The *Barbaros Hayrettin* was sunk by a British submarine in 1915, while the *Turgut Reis* went on to serve as a stationary school ship at Gölcük and was finally broken up in 1950. (Bernd Langensiepen and Ahmet Güleryüz, *The Ottoman Steam Navy 1828–1923* (London, 1995).
17. Uşaklıgil, *Saray*, p.245.
18. Unless otherwise stated, the facts are given as reported in *Senin* (the temporary name of the newspaper *Tanin* when the latter was banned by the government). Many of the reports are by Hakkı Tarik (Us). The reporting in the newspaper is detailed, but it should be kept in mind that it was the unofficial organ of the CUP and strongly biased in favour of that organization.
19. Halit Ziya (1869–1945) was a scion of a prominent trading family from Izmir, the Uşakizadeler, to which Atatürk's wife, Latife Hanim, also belonged. He first worked in the tobacco monopoly and then served Sultan Reşad as secretary for four years. Thereafter, his career was an academic one. Halit Ziya is best known as one of Turkey's most successful novelists, famous for his exquisite use of the language.
20. PRO/FO 195/2381/54 Consulate in Salonica (Lamb) to Embassy in Istanbul. Report of 11 June 1911.

21. Ibid.
22. Evrenos Bey (d. 1417), a Greek convert to Islam, was an Ottoman military commander under both Sultan Murat I and Sultan Bayezit. His son and grandsons also served with distinction in the Ottoman army.
23. Among these was Şemsi Efendi, the founder (in 1870) of the first private primary school for Muslims in the empire. His was the primary school attended by Mustafa Kemal (Atatürk). In 1879 the school was renamed Terakki Mektebi (Progress School) when it received *Rüşdiye* (middle school) status. In 1919 the school was moved to Istanbul, where it continues to exist today. Since 1994 it has been located in Levend.
24. *Lloyd Ottoman* 134, 10 June 1911, p.4
25. *Lloyd Ottoman* 131, 7 June 1911, p.4. Whether this report (based on rumours circulating before the Sultan's arrival) is actually correct is unclear.
26. *Senin* of 10 June 1911; PRO/FO 195/2381/54.
27. *Lloyd Ottoman* 136, 13 June 1911, p.4.
28. PRO/FO 195/2381/25 Report from consul Üsküp (Hugh) to consul Salonica (Lamb) of 19 June.
29. Ibid.
30. PRO/FO 195/2381/26 consul Üsküp (Hugh) to consul Salonica (Lamb), report of 22 June.
31. PRO/FO 195/2381/27 consul Üsküp (Hugh) to consul Salonica (Lamb), report of 19 June.
32. *Senin*, 2/15 June 1911 (report of 1/14 June). *Lloyd Ottoman* 137, 14 June 1911 (reprot of 'Agence Ottomane').
33. Noel Malcolm, *Kosovo: A Short History*, p.244. Malcolm bases himself on the memoirs of Rakić.
34. Sir Edwin Pears, *Forty Years in Constantinople. The Recollections of Sir Edwin Pears 1873–1915* (London, 1916), p.308.
35. Halit Ziya Uşaklıgil, *Saray ve Ötesi. Son Hatıralar* (Istanbul, 1965), p.266.
36. PRO/FO 195/2381/27: consul Üsküp (Hugh) to consul Salonica (Lamb). Report of 26 June.
37. *Lloyd Ottoman* 139, 16 June 1911 (from 'Agence Ottomane').
38. PRO/FO 294/47 (political correspondence Monastir)/38 Report of 27 June 1911 by Arthur Geary (consul) to Sir C.M. Marling, Chargé d'Affaires, Constantinople.
39. *Lloyd Ottoman* 145, 23 June 1911 (from 'Agence de Constantinople').
40. Quotation from *Senin* in *Osmanische Lloyd* 148 (27 June 1911), p.1, 'Pressestimmen'.
41. Erik-Jan Zürcher, 'Muslim nationalism: the missing link in the genesis of modern Turkey', *Hamizrah Hehadash. The New East*, 39 (1997–8), pp.67–83.

An Ottoman Warrior Abroad: Enver Paşa as an Expatriate

ŞUHNAZ YILMAZ

There are few characters in Turkish history whose rise and fall have been as rapid and as dramatic as those of Enver Paşa. Starting out as an unknown graduate of the Imperial War College, he was only in his mid-twenties when he became the 'hero of freedom' after the Young Turk Revolution of 1908. Thus started his meteoric rise from the ranks of a lieutenant-colonel to a virtual dictator during the rule of the Triumvirate in 1913. Within a year, when he married an Ottoman princess, he also joined the royal family as the son-in-law of the Sultan. Rapidly achieving the power and titles he sought, Enver became the Minister of War as battle clouds were gathering over Europe. Hence, at the outset of the First World War, he emerged as one of the most important Ottoman political and military leaders who determined the fate of a crumbling empire, which in return shaped his own destiny.

The fall and dismemberment of the Ottoman Empire at the end of the War also meant the beginning of the end for Enver. He was forced not only to give up his political and military position, but also to leave the country. His expatriate years were marked by his persistent efforts to redeem himself, by attempting to resume a leading role first in the nationalist struggle in Anatolia and, failing to achieve that, in the Basmachi movement in Central Asia. In the end he died on the battlefield at the age of 41 trying to lead an indigenous movement of which he had rather limited control and insight. This was the last ring in the life-chain of an Ottoman warrior fighting to restore the glory of a diminishing Empire.

Enver Paşa has also been one of the most controversial figures in Turkish history. He was first glorified as the 'hero of freedom', but was then demonized for his deeds during the rule of the Triumvirate and was blamed as a key actor in dragging the Ottoman Empire into the First World War alongside the Central Powers. Moreover, the last phase of Enver's life (1918–22), starting with his flight after the Mudros Armistice, has been eclipsed for a long time by the 'orthodox' Turkish historical interpretation of this period. The underlying reasons for this perspective could be found in the perceived threat of potential competition by the former Unionists for political leadership in general, and the personal rivalry between Enver and Mustafa Kemal in particular. Thus, the activities of the Unionist émigrés and especially those of Enver have barely been mentioned and often discarded as mere 'adventurism'. Only recently, with the dissolution of the Soviet Union and the establishment of contacts with the Turkic Republics of Central Asia, Enver Paşa is receiving more attention because of the 'pan-Turkic' and 'pan-Islamic' ideas he promoted during the last years of his life.

This essay presents a study of Enver Paşa by evaluating his rapid rise and the period during which he was in power as one of the most influential figures who shaped the last decade of Ottoman history. However, the major emphasis of this work is on Enver's often neglected activities during his émigré years. The study of this later period, starting with Enver's expatriation in 1918 and ending with his death in Central Asia in 1922, is crucial for understanding Enver's important role in the initial stage of Turco-Soviet relations, his attempts to regain power in Anatolia, and the motives for and the results of his joining the Basmachi resistance.

Enver was born in Istanbul on 22 November 1881. His family was originally from Monastir and their ancestry can be traced back to the 'Gagavuz Turks'.[1] The family moved back to Monastir when Enver was a boy in primary school. He completed his secondary schooling there, after which he headed once again to Istanbul in order to enter the Imperial War College (Mekteb-i Harbiye-i Şâhâne). In the military academy, he completed both the regular officers' training and the advanced general staff courses and he graduated second in his class on 5 December 1902.[2]

As a young general staff captain, he was now ready to assume his first military post in the Third Army in Macedonia. He worked for three years in the military operations against Macedonian bands fighting against the Ottoman rule. These operations, which were simply called 'brigand chase' (*eşkiya takibi*), entailed much more than following and fighting with random brigands, since these groups were actually well-organized and well-equipped Serbian, Macedo-Bulgarian, Greek and sometimes even Albanian nationalists who often received support from the small Balkan governments. At this post, Enver Paşa performed outstandingly, taking part in one successful chase after another. In the meantime, he was becoming increasingly aware of the existence and the strength of the nationalist movements in the Balkans,[3] which he perceived to be more of a reaction to the despotic rule of Abdülhamid II and the corruption of the Ottoman state, rather than a manifestation of nationalism *per se*.

In September 1906 Enver was promoted to the rank of major in the Third Army headquarters in Monastir, where he would serve until his rebellious flight to the Macedonian hills in 1908. The most significant impact of this period in Monastir was that Enver became acquainted with and joined the Committee of Progress and Union (CPU), the conspiratorial nucleus of the Young Turks, and helped to spread its activities with his strong organizational skills.[4] The members of this secret organization were ready to defend the Empire. Before doing that, however, they demanded the restoration of parliament and the constitution of 1876 which would limit the absolute powers of the Sultan.

Rumours about the activities of the Committee of Progress and Union disturbed the Sultan greatly and an inspection committee was sent to inquire into the situation. As the Sultan's agents assiduously worked in Macedonia, denunciations of the committee members and assassinations of the Sultan's agents and officials working against the CPU took place. After the assassination attempt on Nazım Bey,[5] Enver knew he would soon be under suspicion for being among the group of conspirators, so he refused to accept a reassignment to Istanbul. Instead, in June 1908, he escaped with a group of followers to the Macedonian hills, where he joined an adjunct-major, Ahmet Niyazi, and his men. This action, which served as the prelude to the Young Turk revolution of July 1908, was also in line with the CPU decision 'to come out in the open in an effort at self-preservation'[6] in response to the constant threat of exposure by the Sultan's agents. The initial attempts of Abdülhamit II to suppress the insurrection failed when Şemsi Paşa, who was in charge of government troops, was assassinated in Monastir on 7 July. There was strong public support for the CUP[7] which demanded a constitutional government. In addition to this issue, one of the major tools used by CUP for instigating popular support was the appeal to nationalistic ideas. The rumours about a secret decision of the Russian Tsar and the British King to end Ottoman rule in Macedonia, and appeals to the Albanians by Firzovik to unite against an imminent Austrian attack to protect their religion and fatherland, proved quite successful in mobilizing the people.[8] Finally, the Sultan yielded and restored the constitution that had been suspended in 1877. With the restoration of the constitution and parliament, brotherhood among all Ottomans, regardless of religion and race, was stressed, and the Christian, Jewish and Muslim religious leaders celebrated the declaration of the constitutional government together.[9] Hence the Second Constitutional Period (which would last until 1918) began, and Enver was widely acclaimed as the 'hero of liberty and revolution'.

This incident proved to be a turning point in Enver's life, the first step on his rapid rise in less than a decade from his rank as major to the rank of Paşa and Minister of War, eventually leading the Ottoman Empire into the First World War. When Atatürk was asked when his birthday was, he responded that it was 19 May 1919, the day he reached Samsun and started the Turkish War of Independence. If Enver had had a chance to choose a birthday for himself, it would probably have been 23 July 1908, the day when he became the 'hero of freedom' and claimed to have saved 'the sick man' of Europe.[10]

Owing to his significant role in the restoration of the constitution, Enver's fame kept increasing: his pictures appeared everywhere, babies were named after him[11] and even his moustache style known as '*Enver bıyığı*' became very fashionable. People had very high hopes for the Young Turk victory and the era of impending change. However, the honeymoon with the Young Turks would not last long, for history would witness the emergence of the very 'hero of freedom' as a leading autocrat during the rule of the Triumvirate.

In 1909, Enver was sent as a military attaché to Berlin, where he established personal contacts with some German academics, journalists, high level government officials and even the Kaiser himself. This period was also significant in that it was during Enver's posting in Berlin that the seeds of his lifelong admiration for German culture and military power took root.[12] His adoration of things German is clearly reflected in a postcard which he sent to his sister Hasene Hanım from Germany: 'Yesterday I watched the parade of one of the German army corps with 33,000 soldiers marching. It is so excellent that it makes one's mouth water.'[13]

During April 1909, Enver made a brief return to Istanbul, in order to join the Action Army (Hareket Ordusu) in the suppression of a conservative counter-revolution[14] against the constitutional government. This incident consolidated the position of the CUP, dethroned Abdülhamit II, and brought about his replacement by his brother Mehmet V. Real power was concentrated in the hands of the CUP leaders with Enver being among them. It is also noteworthy that starting with the period after the revolution of 1908 and the suppression of the counter-revolution, Enver (together with Kemal Bey) would play an increasingly important role in army–Committee relations.[15]

The next place where Enver would greatly increase his fame and prestige was Tripoli of Barbary. In the autumn of 1911 Enver volunteered for service in the Libyan War against the Italians, where he successfully organized Arab tribes in resistance and fought with distinction. Consequently, he earned a double promotion to the rank of a lieutenant-colonel. The defence of Benghazi (Cyrenaica) enabled Enver greatly to utilize his organizational skills by forming effective defensive units from Arab tribes.[16]

A series of letters Enver wrote to the sister of Hans Humann, the German naval attaché in Istanbul, during his stay in Tripoli presents detailed information about his life and activities in this area.[17] The letters also reveal Enver's complicated ideas and feelings towards Europe. On the one hand he felt disgusted with European tactics aimed at dismembering the Ottoman Empire, while on the other hand he appreciated and admired European culture. He wrote in one of his letters, 'your civilization is a poison, but a poison that awakens people'.[18] Just like the story of Goethe's *Faust* that Enver was reading on his way to Benghazi, in which Doctor Faust bet against the devil, Enver perceived himself to be in a struggle against all the Great Powers. Enver's remark in response to an article in a European newspaper is a good indicator of his approach to the issue and how he took all the developments so personally: 'the Italians are furious with me'.[19] As stressed by Haley, 'In his mind, the entire conflict was between his own person and various scheming European nations, not between Italy and the Arab tribes, not even between the Ottoman state and the Europeans. He had been personally dispatched to right the situation.'[20] Enver's letters are full of comments like, 'This time I will show them that patriotism in Turks had not died, and that we know how to make enemies pay'.[21]

As Enver's frustration with the lack of supplies and money grew worse, so did his expression of disgust at the European powers, especially at the Italians and the British. After a while, he stopped reading European newspapers and built himself a 'palace', which S. Aydemir nicely describes as 'an oriental general's tent' having neither windows nor door because of the lack of glass and wood.[22] Adapting very well to his role as the ruler, Enver went as far as to print paper money bearing the signature of the 'New Saviour of Tripoli of Barbary, Enver Bey'. The new currency sold so well that Enver wondered whether the Ottomans had ever got a better rate.[23]

Enver's aspirations, however, could not be confined to ruling a distant land of the Ottoman Empire. He sought the grandeur of a world leader. He had great admiration for Napoleon Bonaparte whose portrait would eventually decorate his office by the Bosphorus. Kemal Bey had compared Enver to Napoleon after Enver's first public speech in 1908. 'Unfortunately for the Ottoman army, Enver took the comparison to heart and was never able to be saved from its effects.'[24] Thus, when the developments in the Balkans and the outbreak of the First Balkan War shifted the attention of the Ottoman Empire from distant North Africa to this much closer threat, Enver left Benghazi to be once again at the centre of attention and to fulfil his aims for greater power.

Enver criticized severely the government's passive policies throughout the Balkan Wars. He was especially against the plans to cede Edirne[25] (a former capital of the Ottoman Empire which had strategic importance as well as symbolic significance for the general public), as part of the peace settlement. He condemned the influential senior bureaucrats in the government for 'signing the will of the fatherland with their shaking hands'.[26] He was also very frustrated with the conservative and defeatist attitude of the senior commanders in the army.[27]

On 23 January 1913, shortly after his return to Istanbul Enver led an attack by a small group of Unionist officers on the Sublime Porte. The Grand Vizier was forced to retire at gunpoint and the Minister of War was killed. The stated aim of this *coup d'état*, known as the 'Sublime Porte Incident', was an energetic resumption of the Balkan War and a halt to the loss of territory. However, the complete loss of Macedonia, most of Thrace and even Edirne would indicate how far the leaders were from achieving their aims.

The coup resulted in the establishment of a Union and Progress Party cabinet with Mahmud Şevket Paşa as the Grand Vizier. After the assassination of Mahmud Şevket on 11 June 1913, the triumvirate formed by Enver, Talât and Kemal Paşas started ruling the country. Thus, the transformation from the constitutional monarchy of 1908 to the rule of a military and partisan CUP triumvirate which would last until 1918 was completed.

Given the fact that Enver played a major role in the restoration of the constitution and the parliament in 1908 and was glorified as the 'hero of freedom', such a transformation might seem surprising. However, Hanioğlu points out that 'Except for its value as a "modern" symbol and a mechanism for preventing Great Powers' intervention, "parliament" as well as "representative" government meant little to the Young Turks ... Their stalwart adherence to Le Bon's theories shaped their attitude toward parliament as an institution.'[28] Such an approach was shared by Enver Paşa and a number of influential junior officers of his generation. Thus, although this group emerged with the claims of establishing a parliamentary system as their primary goal, the underlying motives of their action seem to be determined more by a desire to limit the absolute powers of the Sultan while promoting Turkish nationalism and a more active and militaristic approach in response to the dismemberment of the Ottoman Empire.

In line with this more active and militaristic policy, during the Second Balkan War Enver led the troops which recaptured Edirne and thus greatly enhanced his power and prestige. Aware of his popularity and clearly revealing his excessive self-confidence, he wrote, 'I am as happy as a child, not because the entire Islamic world admires me, but because I am pleased with myself. I was the only person who could enter Edirne in a single night.'[29] In the ensuing two years, Enver promoted himself again and again, resulting in his meteoric rise from the rank of a lieutenant-general to the rank of deputy commander-in-chief and the Minister of War. He further accelerated his rise in 1914 when he married an Ottoman princess, Naciye

Sultan, and became a member of the royal family and the son-in-law of the caliph. Thus, at the outset of the First World War, Enver emerged as one of the most important political and military leaders who would determine the fate of the Empire.

One of the major determinants of the outlook of the CUP in international affairs, especially after the severe Ottoman defeat in the First Balkan War, was the effort to deal with the trauma of rapid and continual territorial disintegration. The commonly agreed-upon panacea was to seek a powerful European ally, though there were different shades of opinion within the CUP about who this ally should be. The perception was that any one of the European Great Powers could prevent further encroachments on the Ottoman territories by Russian attacks, as well as by powers of lesser strength which were seen as especially dangerous, such as Italy and Greece. Consequently, different members of the CUP made desperate attempts to approach all the Great Powers of Europe and even Russia in search of an ally.

In the meantime, war was brewing in Europe. When the efforts of Kemal Paşa in Paris and Talât Paşa in Bucharest, and the appeals to Britain, proved fruitless in securing an alliance for the Ottomans, Enver approached the German ambassador, Freiherr Hans von Wangenheim, for a secret alliance. The negotiations, which resulted in a defensive alliance against Russia on 2 August 1914, were conducted mainly by Enver Paşa himself, who informed only a few of the other CUP members about them.[30] During the first days of August, in fact, many of the cabinet ministers were still totally unaware that a secret alliance had been made with Germany. Moreover, even those involved in the negotiations with Germany, except for Enver, seemed to be having second thoughts about the suitability of rapid intervention.[31]

Enver Paşa was strongly in favour of Ottoman participation in the Great War and worked assiduously to accomplish it. He was greatly inspired by German military success against the Russians at the Battle of Tannenberg and anticipated joining the camp of the victors as soon as possible.[32] He thought that otherwise the Germans would win the war without Ottoman help and it would be too late to get a share of the pie. His policies, initially shaped by the fear of Russian expansionism, were gradually being replaced by the expectations of Ottoman victory which would put an end to the territorial disintegration and the long existing Russian threat.

In the events leading to the Ottoman entry into the First World War Enver emerged as a very important actor. Especially in the extremely crucial period during which the two German cruisers, *Goeben* and *Breslau*, fleeing from the Royal Navy were permitted to enter into the Straits through a fictitious purchase by the Ottomans and ended up bombarding Russian ports. During this period marking the end of Ottoman neutrality, he played a key role in shaping the developments through his mostly secret contacts with the Germans.[33] Hence he led the Ottoman Empire to fight its last great war with dreams of glory, resulting, however, in the death of the 'sick man' of Europe on the battlefield.

During the course of the First World War, with the aim of encircling and destroying the Russian forces by a surprise offensive, Enver took personal command of the Third Army on the Russian Front during December 1914. He thought such a victory would greatly increase his power and fame, while opening the way for more conquests in the east. Liman von Sanders wrote in his memoirs, 'Before Enver left for the Caucasus while he was explaining me his plans, at the end of our discussion he told me about his magnificent, but rather strange ideas. After the Caucasus, he was intending to go on to (the conquest of) India and Afghanistan.'[34] The offensive was also encouraged by the Germans who did not share Enver's overwhelming optimism, but nevertheless wanted to divert the attention of the Russians from the Polish front as soon as possible.

The military campaign in the Sarıkamış region turned out to be a disaster, because Enver failed to take the terrain and the weather conditions into consideration. Far from fulfilling the initial plan of encirclement of the Russian forces, most of the Third Army was destroyed through cold and hunger even before reaching the battlefield. Out of 90,000 soldiers, the estimated casualties were around 80,000.[35] After this incident, Enver returned to Istanbul and tried unsuccessfully to cover up the extent of the disaster. Armenians served as a convenient scapegoat for this purpose. In response to the ensuing Russian offensive in spring, the efforts of Enver and other the CUP leaders to undermine the Armenian support for the Russians by deporting them out of the war zone to Syria also proved to be disastrous. The deportations were marked by cold, illness and massacres, and most of the Armenian population of this region perished.[36]

Although there were some important military successes in the following years, notably the victory in Gallipoli owing to the brilliant skills of Mustafa Kemal as a military tactician and the advances in the Caucasus front after the collapse of the Russian Empire, by the autumn of 1918 the military situation became untenable. On 14 October 1918, the Grand Vizier Talât Paşa resigned with his Unionist cabinet in order to facilitate the armistice negotiations. Immediately after the signing of the Mudros Armistice on 30 October 1918, in response to their constantly deteriorating situation, on 2 November, Enver, Talât, Kemal and other leading Unionists left Istanbul aboard a German submarine, going to Odessa from where they went to Berlin. In the meantime, in Istanbul the court-martial proceedings resulted in death sentences *in absentia* for the fugitive CUP leaders including Enver.

When the CUP leaders left Istanbul, reflecting on their future Talât Paşa concluded, 'Our political life is over'.[37] The flight of the triumvirs, however, by no means meant an end to their political activities. Enver's intentions, in particular, were far removed from the idea of withdrawing to a quiet corner leaving the political and the military arena. He viewed the situation only as a temporary setback: a tactical retreat to resume fighting after gathering some strength.

In the last meeting of the CUP members before their departure, Enver clearly revealed his determination to fight what he perceived as 'the second phase of the war'. He optimistically reminded his colleagues, 'Don't forget, in the past we won the Balkan War in its second phase.'[38] Enver initially intended to leave directly for the Caucasus, which was to be his new base to lead an anti-Entente struggle. He wrote, 'The last developments are evident. We lost the war. In accordance with the Armistice, the British will be coming to Istanbul. Rather than seeing the British in Istanbul like this, I am determined to go to the Caucasus to serve Islam.'[39] It was not coincidental that Enver Paşa specifically wanted to start the struggle from the Caucasus. Before the surrender in 1918 he had already assembled a considerable military force there, which he had placed under the control of his brother Nuri and uncle Halil Paşa.[40]

Owing to an illness and the failure to reach the Caucasus in a *taka* (small sailing boat) which was wrecked off the shore in a storm, he had to postpone his plans. Moreover, upon the news that the military unit in the Caucasus had been disbanded and his relatives in command arrested,[41] he decided to join the other CUP leaders in Europe. He thus set off for Germany.

During the winter of 1918–19, which Enver spent in Berlin, he tried to contact the British agents there for a settlement.[42] When he realized that nothing would come of these contacts, he turned his attention once again to the East. His most important activity during this period was to visit the Bolshevik Comintern Secretary Karl Radek in prison and to propose to him a Muslim-Soviet alliance against the British. In the meantime, his numerous efforts to reach Russia were marked by a series of catastrophes. Enver later wrote to Mustafa Kemal, 'With the realization that the aid for Anatolia would be provided only by the Russians, I agreed with the people here [meaning the CUP leaders in Germany] to leave for Russia accompanied by Baha Bey. However, during the course of one year, I was detained twice and spent five months in prison. I survived six plane crashes.'[43]

Enver Paşa finally arrived in Moscow in early 1920. He was politically very active during his stay in the Bolshevik capital. He established contacts with the Soviet Foreign Office and with Lenin. At the same time, he was in touch with the Turkish Nationalist delegation visiting Moscow, which was headed by Bekir Sami.[44] During this period, Enver emerges as an important intermediary in establishing the initial contacts among the nationalists in Anatolia and the Soviets.

Although the Ankara government's plenipotentiaries initialled a friendship treaty with the Soviets, the diplomatic bargaining for financial and military aid was deadlocked owing to Soviet demands for the cession of Van and Mush districts to Armenia.[45] Taking advantage of these developments, Enver got involved in the diplomatic parley. According to the final decision reached during the negotiations, the Soviets agreed to provide the Turkish mission with a substantial amount of weapons and ammunition.[46] The extent of Enver's contribution during the negotiations is unknown. However, after this meeting Enver flattered himself that the successful conclusion of the negotiations was due mostly to his timely intervention. Enver had also written to Mustafa Kemal enthusiastically informing him about his meeting with Chicherin accompanying the plenipotentiaries from Ankara, and his participation to the preliminary meetings among the Turkish diplomats.[47] Mustafa Kemal's response to this letter was not matched with a similar degree of enthusiasm with respect to Enver's activities. He was rather sceptical about Enver's intentions of acting as an intermediary and trying to present himself as a genuine representative of Turkey. Moreover, Mustafa Kemal feared that overemphasis on pan-Islamism by Enver might alienate the Bolsheviks against the nationalist struggle in Anatolia. His conviction was that the anti-British aspect of the Turco-Soviet alliance should be emphasized. Thus he wrote to Enver Paşa that in order not to arouse Soviet suspicion and apprehensions, it was necessary to present their aims and activities as a struggle for independence and maintenance of survival against British oppression, 'which tries to lower all the Muslim and non-Muslim peoples of the East to the level of farm animals'.[48] He stressed once again that Enver should refrain from over-emphasizing pan-Islamism.[49]

The Soviets, however, rather than being apprehensive of Enver's pan-Islamic intentions, thought that his prestige in the Islamic world could be manipulated in two ways: (i) to provide the unity and the support of the Islamic domains under Soviet rule in particular;[50] (ii) and to provoke resistance against the British yoke in the Islamic world in general.[51] Thus, with the encouragement of the Soviet authorities, Enver proclaimed the formation of a 'Union of Islamic Revolutionary Societies' (İslam Cemiyetleri İttihadı) which was intended to be a Muslim Revolutionary international. In addition to this party, its Turkish affiliate 'People's Council's Party' (Halk Şuraları Fırkası) was also established.[52] The Young Turk émigrés even envisaged a division of labour among themselves in promoting anti-imperialist revolutionary movements in different areas of the Muslim world: Enver Paşa was to be in charge of Turkestan, Kemal Paşa of Afghanistan and India, and Halil Paşa of Iran.[53]

Between 1 and 9 September 1920, Enver attended the Soviet-sponsored 'Congress of the Peoples of the East' in Baku. His participation was separate from the Kemalist Turkish delegation. He had the status of a special guest with the title of the representative of 'the Union of the Revolutionary Organizations of Morocco, Algeria, Tunisia, Tripoli, Egypt, Arabia, and India'. Apparently, this title was created to depict Enver's ties with various Muslim leaders of the local movements, which actually did not go much beyond having conversations with them in Berlin. Enver Paşa's speech during the Baku Congress was a juxtaposition of Bolshevik terminology with Unionist ideas, emphasizing their common anti-Imperialist and anti-British struggle. In his speech, Enver made extensive use of Bolshevik jargon, frequently using expressions such as 'oppressed peoples', 'national self-determination', and 'struggle against capitalism and imperialism'.[54] He also tried to justify the Ottoman entry into the First World War on the side of imperial Germany, arguing that when compared with the British and the Russian Empires, Germany was a lesser evil which at least accepted the Ottoman Empire's 'right to survival'. He claimed that he had always fought against imperialists and never pursued a goal other than preserving his state's independence.[55]

It was rather difficult, however, for the other members of the Conference to accept these arguments at face value. Moreover, there were not many incidents in the Unionist record which revealed them as the champions of oppressed nations or the proletariat.[56] Enver's important role in the Ottoman entry into the First World War on the side of the Germans and in the decision for the Armenian deportations and massacres aroused further suspicions as to the sincerity of his remarks. Yamauchi points out that 'At the Baku Congress, Enver was mistrusted by the majority of the communist deputies, especially those who were principally composed of non-Muslims, and they undoubtedly did not offer him a platform for further political ventures. It appears that the objects of his Bolshevik sponsors, Zinoviev and Radek, were entirely defeated.'[57]

A great degree of confusion and chaos dominated the Congress. As a British agent reported:[58]

> The majority of the 1,500 delegates who arrived in Baku for the Congress, ...[were] illiterate and the wildest confusion characterised the proceedings. Not the faintest notice was taken of most of the numerous speeches made, the delegates being far more interested in each others' swords and revolvers. There was a constant coming and going throughout the sessions, and the proceedings were always interrupted for the 'Namaz' or prayers.

Moreover, the delegates from the Gandje and Kokand districts (although not allowed to complete their speeches) were spreading information about the misdeeds of Bolsheviks and the massacres of Muslims.

During his stay in Baku, Enver established contacts with various Muslim groups, most significantly with the Volga Tatars and Sultangaliev. The ideas of 'Muslim National Communists', as represented by Sultangaliev, Ryskulov and Khodzhaev (who propagated support for all revolutionary movements in the colonial world and communism with a nationalistic and Islamic undertone)[59] seem to have had a significant impact on Enver Paşa. Enver's already existing inclination for pan-Islamic and pan-Turkic ideas would strengthen, and combined with the impact of communist ideology would evolve into his unique blend of communism, nationalism and Islam (as reflected in the political programme he prepared entitled *Mesa* [Labour]).

By the end of the Baku Congress, the Russians had to admit their failure in terms of meeting the Bolshevik interests, and Zinoviev even sent a telegram to this effect to Lenin. Moreover, Enver's personal meetings with numerous Muslim delegates, especially with those from Turkestan, were making the Russians quite anxious. 'The general opinion in Baku' was that 'he was "advised" by the Soviet authorities to return to Moscow at his earliest convenience'.[60] Thus, the Baku Congress, which was symbolically the highest point of Enver's collaboration with the Bolsheviks, in terms of its results was more functional in bringing about a realization of conflicting interests on both sides, rather than enhancing their co-operation.

Enver spent the period between October 1920 and February 1921 in Europe in order to promote the inauguration of the Islamic Revolutionary Societies. In the meantime he established contacts with the Germans and the Italians for arms and ammunition sales to the Soviets. During this period, he was trying to preserve an uneasy balance. On the one hand, he was acting as a loyal supporter of the Turkish Nationalist cause. On the other hand, he was trying to persuade the Bolsheviks to provide military support for an expedition in Anatolia.[61] He intended to present himself as a better and more reliable leftist alternative for the Soviets than the Nationalist government of Ankara.

Enver was very eager to retrieve his lost position, which Mustafa Kemal had 'usurped'. Thus, his *rapprochement* with the Bolsheviks was marked by hopes of utilizing Soviet financial and military aid for the rehabilitation of his political power and of regaining control over the national resistance movement in Anatolia.

Enver had several conversations with Ali Fuat Cebesoy (the newly appointed ambassador of the Ankara government) and even with Chicherin, and both of them tried to prevent him from interfering in the Anatolian movement.[62] Bekir Sami Bey tried to persuade Enver Paşa that he should struggle for his fatherland and for Islam outside Anatolia in the east.[63] In response to these appeals, Enver sent a lengthy letter to Mustafa Kemal assuring him of his loyalty and his contentment in supporting the nationalist movement from abroad. However, when Major Naim Cevad, whom Enver had sent from Russia to Anatolia, was arrested by the Kemalists with large quantities of propaganda material for the Peoples' Councils Party,[64] it became clear that Enver had no intention of abandoning his former plans.

Enver's plans of initiating a national guerrilla resistance based in Anatolia dated from as far back as 1915, and was instigated by the fears of an Allied breakthrough at the Dardanelles.[65] The most important actor at the institutional level that was responsible for the implementation of such plans both during and after the First World War was the 'Special Organization' (Teşkilât-ı Mahsusa), which has been created by Enver in 1914. Teşkilât-ı Mahsusa was the Ottoman version of a military secret service, combining an intelligence and propaganda service with a guerrilla organization.[66] It is noteworthy that prominent members of the inner circle of the CUP, such as Dr Bahattin Şakir and Mithat Şükrü also formed the political core of this organization. Teşkilât-ı Mahsusa propagated pan-Islamic themes, and later on increasingly pan-Turkic ones.

In 1918, the activities of Teşkilât-ı Mahsusa were supplemented by the formation of another organization, namely the Guard (Karakol). The Guard, which sheltered former Unionists, benefited greatly from the resources and expertise of Teşkilât-ı Mahsusa. It played a crucial role for the national resistance movement by smuggling men and materials to Anatolia and establishing clandestine resistance networks. In addition to this, in the provincial centres of Thrace and Anatolia, the local branches of the CUP instigated the national agitation. In their struggle, the national activists made extensive use of the secret depots of arms and ammunitions, which had been established by Teşkilât-ı Mahsusa.[67]

Enver tried very hard to maintain his contacts with these organizations and a group of former Unionists in Anatolia, who were supportive of him. At the initial stages of the nationalist struggle, Mustafa Kemal's position seemed far from being secure, especially since Enver was very willing to be in charge of Anatolian developments once again. There were reports that 'Baku, the Unionist stronghold, at the center of the Oriental intrigue' was becoming 'the rival of Angora'.[68] The US High Commissioner in Constantinople was stating that Enver, who was cast out of Turkey, was regaining his prestige and influence.[69] The British at this point even considered Enver and his followers to pose a more serious threat than the Kemalists. According to them, there were '...two parties in Anatolia, not only one. The weaker is that of Mustafa Kemal and the Nationalists... They have failed and their adherents are going over to the other far more dangerous party, that of Enver, Talât and the CUP–Jew–German–Bolshevik combination'.[70] About one third of the Nationalist Assembly of Ankara was inclined towards or supportive of Enver.[71] Even if Enver might not have been as powerful as the British sources indicate, it is certain that he was making intense efforts to capture the Nationalist movement and was steadily gaining strength.

At this period, when it was still unclear who would eventually capture the leadership of the Nationalists, the Bolsheviks maintained their contacts with and provided support for both sides. On the one hand, Nationalist delegations were visiting Moscow[72] and Mustafa Kemal was corresponding with the Soviet Foreign Commissar Chicherin.[73] On the other hand, the Soviets were said to be 'finding the money for the Unionist campaign'.[74] Mustafa Kemal was seriously disturbed by the challenge presented by Enver to his authority at home and abroad. To prevent Enver's return, the Turkish Grand National Assembly issued a decree on 12 March 1921 to the effect that Enver and Halil Paşa were prohibited from returning to Anatolia 'since this would be detrimental to the internal politics and external relations' of the Ankara government.[75] Enver, however, had no intention of giving up.

The peak of Enver's efforts and expectations to regain control in Anatolia occurred at a time when the Greek offensive towards Ankara was in full progress. Nationalists were withdrawing and were even considering temporarily moving the Turkish Grand National Assembly to another city further away from the war zone.[76] Enver's letter written on 16 July 1921 to Mustafa Kemal is very significant in indicating his intentions. He wrote:[77]

> If you consider us [the Unionists] as a rival, you are making a big mistake....We are not after any titles or positions. As far as I am concerned, I will follow my ideals. That is to incite the Muslims to struggle against the European beasts which trample upon Islam.... By the news which you have been sending through my friends I understand that you do not want us to return.... For the time being since we are being helpful to our motherland in Moscow, we are not coming back.... However, when we start to feel that... our staying abroad becomes useless and even dangerous for Turkey... and the Islamic world, we will return to Anatolia.

On 30 July 1921, Enver went to Batumi, where he met with other Unionists and started waiting for an opportunity to enter Anatolia. It is noteworthy that the Congress of the People's Councils Party meeting, held in Batumi on 5 September 1921, revived and used the name 'Union and

Progress Party' and demanded the Ankara government to abandon its hostility towards the émigré Unionists. In this period, Enver not only had support among the émigré Unionists, but was also closely linked with a number of influential people within the resistance movement in Anatolia, thus posing a serious challenge for Mustafa Kemal. Rustow points out that 'The Trabzon Defense of Rights Society was openly supporting Enver, and in the Ankara Assembly a group of about forty ex-Unionists are said to have been working secretly to replace Kemal with Enver'.[78] However, Mustafa Kemal's decisive victory at the Sakarya battle (2–13 September) consolidated his political position and authority, while sweeping away the expectations of Enver and his supporters.

When the Bolsheviks shifted their support from Enver Paşa to Mustafa Kemal in the aftermath of the Sakarya battle, Enver had to abandon his Anatolian plans, marking a final break in his flirtation with Moscow. Moreover, he was increasingly becoming aware of the discouraging prospects of his hybrid ideology in striving to promote a version of Bolshevism compatible with Islam. Developments in Russian Turkestan had been signalling the incompatibility of Bolshevism and Islam for a while now.

While the Baku Congress was in progress, on 2 September 1920 the Red Army stormed Bukhara City and proclaimed a People's Soviet Republic.[79] The new reformist government of Young Bukharans which replaced the Emir in collaboration with the Soviets was soon to be disillusioned. It assumed that Bukhara would be at least semi-independent. However, the increasing Russian overlordship, the pressure from the Red Army and the removal of the State treasury were indicating otherwise. In the meantime, the fugitive Emir of Bukhara, Alim Khan, was still trying to hold out in eastern Bukhara[80] with the support of a sporadic Muslim resistance movement composed of 'Basmachi'[81] bands.

When the Soviet government sent Enver Paşa to Central Asia in the early days of November 1921, it had a number of motives. First of all, Enver, an unwanted ally to the Nationalist leaders of Anatolia, would be prevented from intermingling in the Anatolian affairs where he was no longer needed. Instead, the Soviets were planning to exploit his popularity among the Muslims in an effort to curtail the support for the Basmachis. Moreover, Enver could be useful in counteracting a possible bid by the Afghans (with British support) to interfere in the Central Asian affairs under the banner of Islam and pan-Islamic ideas. The unfolding events would soon indicate, however, that Enver had quite different motives of his own.

Enver had the intention of leading a pan-Islamic and pan-Turkic battle in Turkestan, about the realities of which he had very scarce knowledge. He had received some news about the developments in Central Asia through the Muslim delegates he met during the Baku Congress. Moreover, the distorted information, most of which he obtained through Hacı Sami, seemed quite promising. Hacı Sami claimed, 'In 1916, as a simple and unassuming Turk I raised all of Kirgizistan against the Russians. Given your [Enver Paşa's] great fame and popularity nothing can stand in our way in Turkestan.'[82] In addition to the idealistic motives, there were also important (and frequently overlooked) practical considerations shaping Enver's decision to leave his communist allies. Ever since it became clear that Enver would not have a significant role in Anatolia, his relations with the Russians were becoming more and more ambiguous. There was also an increasing degree of distrust on both sides. Enver was very disturbed when the Bolsheviks did not permit Kemal Paşa to stop in Bukhara on his way from Afghanistan to meet him. The response he got upon asking the Russian Consul Jurinev about the time of Kemal's return to Afghanistan was even more alarming for Enver. Jurinev said, 'The return of Kemal Paşa to these areas? Forget about it. We are also well aware of the kinds of activities you are engaged in here.'[83] In his memoirs, Zeki Velidi Togan[84] reports that Enver perceived this remark as an outright threat and was thinking that the Russians would eventually kill both Kemal Paşa and himself.[85]

When Enver revealed his intentions to join the Basmachis to Togan in their secret meetings in Bukhara, Togan warned him a number of times about the problems associated with his decision. He argued against any overt collaboration with the traditionally-minded ex-Emir and the Basmachis and a direct military confrontation against the Bolsheviks. Togan recommended Enver to support the movement from Afghanistan and he even started to make some arrangements towards this end upon Enver's request.[86] In this period, Enver also briefly considered returning to Berlin via Moscow to rejoin his wife Naciye Sultan, whom he appeared to love passionately.[87] In the end, however, Enver's idealistic motives and Central Asian dreams weighed more heavily.

Twenty-three days after his arrival in Bukhara, Enver used the pretext of going on a 'hunting expedition' to get out of the city in order to defect to the Basmachis. He sent news to the ex-Emir in Afghanistan that he was willing to fight on his side; and set out to meet with İbrahim Bey, a loyal supporter of the ex-Emir and one of the major leaders of the Basmachi movement in his absence.

After Enver's changing sides, there was also a radical change in how the Soviets depicted him. They accused their disloyal partner Enver as 'an adventurist, to whom Turkey and afterwards Bukhara were indebted for some of the most tragic and bloody pages of their history'.[88] According to the Soviet accounts, 'That adventurist, not staying idle for a moment, while the better sons of Turkey were fighting for the freedom of their motherland, arrived in Bukhara as a visitor and decided to take advantage of the difficult situation and laid his blood-stained hands on the Bukharan Revolution.'[89]

How much Enver would have been willing to fight along, actually to lead 'those better sons of Turkey', if he were once again admitted in that exclusive club! However, not surprisingly, yet very astonishingly and frustratingly for him, its doors had been slammed shut in his face. The unwanted guest was now seeking a new home with which he could identify and dreamed to make it the base of his future glory. Hence, deprived of his Anatolian plans, Enver once again started to promote pan-Islamic ideas and pan-Turkism and joined the Basmachi movement in Central Asia against the Russians.

The initial response of the Basmachis to Enver Paşa was very far from a cordial embrace. When Enver and his companions entered the Lokay tribal territory, which was controlled by İbrahim Bey, they were distrusted as previous Bolsheviks and were disarmed. In the following three months, as revealed by numerous letters addressed to his wife scribbled in microscopic letters on tiny pieces of paper, Enver would be a virtual prisoner in the hands of İbrahim.[90] During this period, he would have better insight into the movement into which he had rushed with very little knowledge about its nature. First of all, he became aware of the bigotry of many of the Basmachi bands, who perceived the Jadidist Young Bukharans, rather that the Russians, as their biggest enemy. Not to be a target, Enver even had to burn his family photographs. He wrote in despair to his wife: 'After the morning prayer in Göktaş, I cried while burning the photographs of you and our children. The people of this area are extremely conservative. There is constant propaganda against me. In order to destroy everything that would cause a reaction from these bigots, I also had to burn the books that I had with me…'[91] Humiliated and frequently robbed (not only of his belongings but also of his ideals and dreams), even Enver himself at one point admits that it was a big illusion for a foreigner like him to think that he could accomplish something with the people of this area.[92] İbrahim Bey released Enver only after receiving a letter from the ex-Emir conferring on him the title of '*ghazi*' and ordering that he should be allowed to fight for the cause of Islam as the son-in-law of the former Sultan-Caliph.[93] Hence, finally freed from detention, Enver set off to fight.

Just as the paths of Enver and the Soviets were diverging, relations between the Kemalists and the Bolsheviks were becoming even more cordial. There were 'several signs of a détente between the Angora government and Moscow…' and little was now heard of open Bolshevik support to Enver Paşa and his party.[94] In September 1921, Mustafa Kemal ordered the delivery of 40 per cent of the produce in the Black Sea region to the famine-struck Soviet Union as an indication of Turkey's goodwill and friendship.[95] Soon after the Turkish victory at Sakarya, the Soviets resumed supplying the Turks with financial aid and some arms and ammunition. On 19 December 1921 General Frunze, the Commander of the Ukrainian Red Army and a member of the executive committee of the Communist Party in Ukraine, came to Ankara to sign a Treaty of Friendship between the Turkish Nationalists and his government.[96] It is ironic that this was the very same General Frunze who headed the Red Army in Turkestan and overthrew the Emir of Bukhara in collaboration with the Young Bukharans. Moreover, Mustafa Kemal gave a speech to welcome the Soviet Bukhara Commission visiting Ankara and spoke pointedly 'of the statesmen of revolutionary Russia as men who had recognized, not merely in theory but in fact, the right of peoples to dispose of their own destinies'.[97]

While Enver was trying to gather some military strength to fight against the Bolsheviks in eastern Bukhara during the early days of March 1922, Comrade Aralov, the new Russian Ambassador in Anatolia, was raising his glass to the strong bond of friendship between Ankara and Moscow. Aralov expressed his wish that this friendship would be as pure as the water in his glass. To which Mustafa Kemal replied, 'I desire that we shall be bound as tightly together as the hydrogen and oxygen of which that water is composed'.[98] Relations between the Kemalists and the Bolsheviks were not always as cordial as this sounds and there was a considerable degree of suspicion and mistrust in how they perceived each other. Nevertheless, in their international isolation and respective solitary struggles, the bonds between the Turkish nationalists and the Bolsheviks were getting stronger. As for the ties of Enver with Moscow, by this time they were completely broken. Enver now had the extremely difficult mission of uniting various groups of Basmachi, who fought under different leaders for different aims, to fight against the Red Army.

Achieving this goal was certainly not an easy task. The Basmachis were very far from being a monolithic unit and having a unity of purpose. As reflected by British intelligence reports:[99]

> It is necessary to distinguish between two classes of Basmachis in Ferghana. The genuine political Basmachis, the original Soviet rebels against Soviet rule, are represented by Sher Mohammed and his following of 5,000–6,000 men.... He is at present practically powerless, owing to lack of ammunition, but he and his men do little looting and are in fact popular among the inhabitants, who feed them and otherwise keep them supplied. On the other hand, there are the purely bandit Basmachis, under such leaders as Ahmad Pahlawan (circ. 2,000 men), who terrorise the countryside. These men originally

> went out, like others, from hatred of the Bolsheviks, but shortage of food and other necessities was too much for them and the patriot became merged in the brigand.... The latter Basmachis are hated by the people of the towns and by the militia.

The Basmachis, nevertheless, often enjoyed the support of the local people oppressed by the Red Army and had 'almost as many spies out as their enemies'. For instance, at Kokand on 21 June some 20 youths of the town sang a song in the bazaar abusing the Basmachis. Next morning everyone of those 20 men was found with his throat cut, and his body hanging from a hook in one or other of the butcher's shops in the town.[100] There were many similar incidents indicating the support of the people for the Basmachi movement.

Enver Paşa strove, without great success, to unite all the rebel leaders under his command. Despite the factionalism of the Basmachi and difficulties confronting him, he had considerable military achievements by the middle of spring of 1922, when his forces controlled the whole of the eastern part of Bukhara. The Soviets were quite worried and perceived this situation to be more complicated than some military victories won by Enver:[101]

> What will be the outcome of this enterprise? From a military point of view, there can be only one opinion, that the large Soviet Federation which knew how to contain the English and the French attack when fighting Denikin, Kolchak and Wrangel, is strong enough to destroy the enterprise of Enver Paşa.... It is not the military aspect of this affair which makes us worry, it is more the political aspect... In effect, the past glory of Enver as man of the Muslim state, can still attract crowds of ignorant *dehgans* in some remote regions today.

Soviet authorities, who at this point seemed to be more concerned with Enver's prestige in the Muslim world than with his military capabilities, tried to negotiate with their 'former Comrade' in April 1922. Enver's response was, however, much more ambitious than they could imagine and would be willing to take.

Enver not only refused to negotiate a truce with the Soviet Government, but also sent them an 'ultimatum' (dated 19 May 1922) through his friend Nariman Narimanov, the chairman of the government of Soviet Azerbaijan. He demanded an immediate withdrawal of Soviet troops ('generously' allowing them 14 days for carrying it out) from Turkestan, which he described as being 'under the heels of a regime of brute force dragged in from abroad by demagogues and anarchists'.[102] In his ultimatum, Enver did not fail to mention that if the Soviets refused to comply with his demands, his wrath would be upon them. He threatened, 'In the event of Soviet Russia finding it unnecessary to respect the wishes of the Muslim peoples, who are under the oppressive yoke of dishonest Commissars, and who have sprung to arms to free their territory from the alien power of Moscow, I must warn you Mr. Commissar, that two weeks after the handing over of the present memorandum from the Supreme Council, I shall act according to my own judgement.'[103] The response of the Russians was to declare Enver an agent of the British and to send Red Army reinforcements to the region.

Enver's position began to deteriorate rapidly after this point. He was not only fighting against the Russians, but also struggling with numerous other problems. A major source of weakness for the Basmachi movement was the rivalry among individual chieftains and tribal feuds. In addition to this, 'Basmachi units of different ethnic origin were at times as busy warring with each other as they were fighting with the Communists'.[104] There were bitter hostilities especially between the Turkmens and Uzbeks and Kirghiz and Uzbeks. Moreover Enver, with his pan-Turkic and pan-Islamic ideas and a history of collaboration with the Soviet authorities, was still considered to be an 'outsider' by many of the Basmachi leaders. They viewed him with suspicion and were hostile towards him. Ibrahim Bey, who was a significant source of trouble for Enver from the beginning, was not only uncooperative, but was also becoming aggressive. Enver actually had to send some of his forces against him in July 1922.[105] The limited scope of Enver's power and the untenable nature of his position were indicated by the fact that of the 16,000 rebels active in Eastern Bukhara at most 3,000 owed him allegiance.[106]

Enver's problems were not limited to the factionalism of the Basmachis. When he assigned himself as 'Commander in Chief of all Islamic troops, son-in-law of the Caliph and the Representative of the Prophet' and started issuing decrees concerning civil life in Bukhara, he was already stepping on the toes of the ex-Emir. Uneasy and suspicious about the activities of Enver, the ex-Emir began to withhold his support. Enver, who had high hopes of obtaining substantial military aid via Afghanistan, was to be disappointed. Consequently, he lacked the arms and especially the ammunition which he desperately needed to fight against the Russians. He even tried to produce his own ammunition at Baysun; however, the results were not encouraging. The high lead content in the cartridge cases made them useless when rifles became heated.[107] Enver placed himself in an even more difficult situation by frequently engaging in open battles against the Russians, as opposed to guerrilla warfare in which the Basmachis were more experienced and in a relatively advantageous position.

In this period, during which facts merged with rumours, it becomes very difficult to trace Enver. As a bewildered British agent reported, 'Regarding

Bukhara and the career of Enver, I have been able to obtain very little trustworthy information. Feeling runs high in Ferghana between pro- and anti-Bolsheviks, and each side spreads "the news" it would like to be true'.[108] Then he gave an example that one of his informants heard in the middle of June at Uzgend that Enver had conquered Katta Kurghan and Bukhara. Upon the agent's arrival to Samarkand to verify this information, however, he was told that Enver had fled to Mezar-ı Şerif without fighting at all.[109]

The truth was that Enver's already weak forces were rapidly melting away. Brief successes were increasingly followed by defeats and heavy losses. Enver, nevertheless, kept on fighting until he was killed on 4 August 1922, by machine-gun fire while leading a cavalry counter-charge against a superior Russian force.[110]

Just like his life and previous activities among the Basmachis, Enver's death was also surrounded by a cloud of intentional and unintended pieces of misinformation, rumours and an odd combination of myth and reality. For one thing, according to many accounts he lived much longer than he actually did. There was a deliberate effort on the side of the Turkestan Committee to keep Enver's death a secret. Qadir gives an account of how Hacı Sami sent a special messenger to Togan informing him of Enver's death and warning him about the necessity of suppressing the truth: 'Sami Bey suspected treachery. He said that the Committee must give out that Enver was not dead; simply that he had disappeared. This was necessary in order to keep the movement going; if it were known that Enver were dead it would collapse altogether.'[111] This effort to hush up the news, combined with the vivid imagination of the people, seems to have been quite successful in keeping Enver alive well after his death.

The Red Army troops did not realize that they killed Enver during this battle. The announcement of his death was made as late as 11 October in *Pravda* and many papers in Turkestan continued to report on the activities of Enver.[112] Even the Russians realized that they could benefit from keeping Enver alive and using his name for propaganda purposes. The communist journal *Siren,* published on 29 October in Turkestan, claimed that finally peace had been established between Enver Paşa and Moscow. According to this article, Enver was to command the Muslim troops, who would help Mustafa Kemal in the occupation of the neutral zone of Chanak.[113]

Liman von Sanders wrote about the activities of Enver Paşa in Turkestan referring to an article published in *Le Temps* on 5 August 1922 (the day after Enver Paşa's death): 'The "Temps" for the 5th August publishes an interesting telegram from Constantinople, according to which an agreement has been reached between the governments of Moscow and Angora and that of Enver Paşa, whereby Enver is to be nominated general representative of

Russian and national Turkish interests in Bukhara. If this news is true, it constitutes another failure of the British anti-Turkish oriental policy in the Near East.'[114] In September, already a month after he died, it was strongly believed in Ferghana that Enver was hiding somewhere in Bukhara and would be able 'if only further assistance is given him, to raise all Turkestan against the Bolsheviks'.[115] As late as November 1922, the British Foreign Office received Meshed Intelligence reports 'full of news of renewed rebellions under Enver's direction'.[116] Though there was also a newly emerging doubt about the trustworthiness of these reports.[117]

Towards the end of October, Afghan papers were, however, already publishing alleged eyewitness accounts of Enver Paşa's end. According to the *İttihad-ı Islam* of Mezar-ı Sharif:[118]

> Enver had allowed his forces to disperse to their homes for the 'Id-ul-Zuha. On August third, the eve of the 'Id, he told his officers and followers that he had dreamt that he would die a martyr's death. Next day, after the 'Id prayers, the few remaining troops went off to join the general feasting and a party of Russians surrounded the camp at Baljiwan and rushed it. Enver is said to have put up a gallant resistance and routed one party of Russians with the few followers who hurriedly came to his assistance, but was then hit three times and fell. His body was recovered and buried with all honour.

There were also dramatic details added of the devotion and death of his companion-in-arms Davlet, who immediately rushed to his aid. In the Afghan and Basmachi versions of Enver's last battle and death, the martyrdom aspect was strongly emphasized. If Enver was killed, it had to have been a martyr's death!

After Enver's death the Basmachi resistance did not survive very long either. In this period, the Soviet tactic of combining repression with a degree of appeasement (especially in religious matters) proved to be very effective. They restored *waqf* land to mosques, reopened Sharia courts and Koranic schools. At least temporarily they seemed to compromise with Islamic values and institutions in its traditional forms and to withdraw their support from Islamic reformists. Consequently, the popular support for the resistance movement declined sharply starting with the second half of 1922. Deprived of their popular base, the Basmachis were confined to dispersed bands in mountainous areas. The resistance movement would emerge once again during the Stalin era as a reaction to the compulsory collectivization of agriculture, which entailed a direct assault on the traditional way of life in Turkestan.[119]

Enver's venture to Central Asia exhibited a number of problems from the beginning. First of all, Enver had very little knowledge about the realities of the situation in Turkestan. His idealistic motives and apprehensions about his uneasy relations with the Russians, combined with the boldness of his entire career, gave way to his hasty involvement in an indigenous movement with very little insight and planning.[120] This lack of information and understanding was clearly revealed when Enver tried to juxtapose his pan-Islamic and Turanian ideals to a resistance movement which had nothing to do with them. Even though religion played a very important role for the Basmachis, they were merely fighting against the oppressive policies of the Russians and had neither the power nor the intention of uniting the Islamic world. As for pan-Turkic ideals, 'The people knew little, and cared less, about Osmanlı dreams of Central Asian hegemony, if such exist; certainly Pan-Turanism did not figure on the Basmachi programme, whether inspired by Enver or not.'[121] Moreover, Enver was once again unable to assess his capabilities and limits realistically. His ultimatum to the Russians, unwise handling of the ex-Emir, and engagement in open warfare rather than partisan resistance were just some of the indicators of this deficiency. Even Enver, however, was aware that his situation was not as promising as Hacı Sami made it sound. Muhittin Bey, one of his aides-de-camp, recalls that while Enver Paşa was leaving Bukhara he said, 'It is necessary to struggle for Turkestan. If you are afraid of the death that you deserve, you are doomed to live like a dog. You would be cursed by past and future generations. However, if we are ready to die for independence, we can provide those who are following us with free and happy lives.'[122] He had hopes for success. If he could not be victorious, however, he wished to die on the battlefield just like the Ottoman Empire. Although he was unable to realize his Central Asian dreams, he managed to achieve his last wish.

In order to have a better understanding of Enver's goals and actions marking his rapid rise and fall, it is important to place him within the wider context of his society and time. This is crucial for a genuine understanding of the dynamics of the rendezvous of a man with his historical role, which requires him to be at the right place at the right time, as well as having the willingness and capability to be 'that man'. In the case of Enver, the setting was the Ottoman Empire of the late nineteenth century. The Empire, whose glory had been fading away since the seventeenth century, was now considered the 'sick man of Europe'. It suffered enormous financial losses and numerous territorial defeats on all fronts. The Ottomans were especially threatened in the Balkans, where the impact of the rise of various nationalisms was strongly felt in this multi-national empire which was quite far from being a 'melting pot'. The despotic rule of Abdülhamit II and the extreme corruption at all levels of the state apparatus were making the situation even worse. Thus, by challenging this despotic and corrupt rule, Enver emerged as the 'hero of freedom'. The dethronement of Abdülhamit II created an opportunity for Enver to attain more power and attention which he desperately sought and a vacuum of leadership which he did not hesitate to fill. Enver, however, would be transformed in a very short time from the 'hero of freedom' to a despotic ruler playing a major role in shaping the last decade of Ottoman history.

Enver's prestige and public support were mostly based on his military successes and his demands for a more active rather than a merely responsive and incremental policy-making, while confronting the challenge of dismemberment. His successes, especially in Tripolitania and during the reconquest of Edirne in the Second Balkan War, stood out in a period marked by the despair of successive defeats; his military reputation endowed him with great power and authority, beyond the general strength of the CUP.[123] Enver, along with Kemal Paşa, was a leading figure in the army-Committee relations. His position at the intersection of the political and military spheres enabled him to acquire and consolidate his power. Thus, at the outset of the First World War, Enver emerged not only as the leader of a group in the CUP, but also as a major decision-maker for the country.[124]

'War is the surest vehicle through which great historical figures accrue guilt or fame.'[125] In the case of Enver it was both. His rise was determined by military successes, and his fall would also be closely tied to the defeat of the Ottoman Empire fighting on the side of the Germans during the First World War. While Enver's power was rapidly increasing while Minister of War, his dreams of greater glory clouded his ability for reality-testing at an even faster rate. Hence, the Sarıkamış campaign against the Russians, during which he failed to assess the capabilities of his army realistically, marked the beginning of the end for Enver. His defeat in a way echoed the fall of his great hero, Napoleon. When the Ottoman Empire lost the War, he had to leave not only his military and political position, but also his country.

There is a lot of insight that Enver's expatriate years can provide. Although Enver was out of his country, during this quite neglected chapter of his life he was definitely not out of the political scene. His activities were influential at the initial stages of Turco-Russian relations and to a certain extent for Russian–German relations as well. Moreover, Enver presented a serious challenge to Mustafa Kemal as the leader of the nationalist struggle, which was mostly shaped around and built on Unionist organizations and initiatives. Enver's close ties with the former Unionists both in Anatolia and abroad enhanced his position and determination to regain control of the nationalist struggle, an idea which he would only give up after Mustafa Kemal's decisive victory against the Greeks at Sakarya.

The shift of Soviet support to the Kemalists marked the end of Enver's honeymoon with the Bolsheviks. The collaboration between the Bolsheviks and a group of émigré Unionists led by Enver – two groups who shared only a common enemy, Western imperialism in general and Britain in particular– proved to be ephemeral. The disillusioned Enver then joined the anti-Soviet Basmachi resistance in Central Asia. At this stage, Enver's pan-Islamic and especially pan-Turkic ideas gained ascendance. The last phase of Enver's career among the Basmachis was marked by the incongruous dreams of Enver and his followers. Throughout his struggle in Central Asia, he was unable to arouse the support of the masses to his pan-Islamic and pan-Turkic ideals. Nevertheless, he tried to co-ordinate and lead an indigenous struggle against the Russians with very limited means and even less insight. This would be Enver's last battle, concluded by his death on the battlefield.

In evaluating Enver's activities, the final point which needs to be stressed is the necessity to revise official Turkish historiography, especially with respect to Enver's activities during his émigré years. The trend has been to disregard them as insignificant and to view these actions as merely those of an adventurer. However, there are two important points which need to be re-evaluated:

(i) Enver's (and former Unionists') relations with the nationalist struggle in Anatolia;
(ii) his contacts with the Soviets and his role at the initial stage of Turco-Soviet relations.

As E.-J. Zürcher points out, 'Turkish history and biography accentuate the antagonism between the Kemalists and Unionists (these two groups being regarded as two distinct entities), emphasizing the role of the former and belittling that of the latter. They present the Turkish nationalist movement as an original creation of Mustafa Kemal and disregard the existing continuity between the Young Turk and Turkish nationalist periods and the role played by the CUP in the national resistance movement.'[126] However, there was a significant continuity in terms of the cadres and institutions that formed the base of the nationalist movement, some factions of which shaped and assisted Enver's ambitions to regain control in Anatolia.

In evaluating Enver's relations with the Bolsheviks, it is necessary to place him once again within a historical context. The collapse of the Russian Empire created new dynamics in the region, opening up new horizons in the East. Not only Enver, but also a number of his contemporaries (for example, Kemal Paşa in Afghanistan), perceived the rising Bolshevik power and the predominating revolutionary atmosphere as an opportunity to respond and counterbalance the challenge of the West. Thus, their *rapprochement* with Bolshevism and their promotion of pan-

Islamic and pan-Turkic ideas should be evaluated by taking into consideration these drastic changes in the international scene.

Enver Paşa wrote in one of his letters, 'The other day I read a German book, and one sentence inspired me: "When we can't realize our ideals, we can at least idealize our reality."'[127] Just like the sentence in the German book which inspired him, Enver Paşa during his military and political career constantly strove towards either realizing his ideals or, more often, idealizing reality. In many instances, however, engulfed by his ambitions, he was unable to draw realistic limits around his aspirations and this led to his downfall. He spent his entire life in a perpetual battle in both the political and the military fields in order to restore the long-lost glory of an Empire which no longer existed.

NOTES

1. Gagavuz Turks are a Turkish tribe of Christian faith which settled around the banks of the Danube river. Şevket Süreyya Aydemir, in the first volume of his monographic work *Makedonya'dan Ortaasya'ya Enver Paşa*, discusses the origins of the Gagavuz Turks and also presents a family tree of Enver Paşa for seven generations. For detailed information on Gagavuz Turks see: B. Lewis, C. Pellat and J. Schacht (eds.), *Encyclopaedia of Islam*, Vol.2, No.38 (1965), pp.971–2.
2. Enver Paşa, *Enver Paşa'nın Anıları (1881–1908)*, ed. Halil Erdoğan Cengiz (Istanbul, 1991), p.44.
3. Şevket Süreyya Aydemir, *Makedonya'dan Ortaasya'ya Enver Paşa*, Vol.II (Istanbul, 1970), pp.437–8.
4. The details of how he became a member are extensively covered in his memoirs. Enver Paşa, *Enver Paşa'nın Anıları*, pp.57–61.
5. Nazım Bey, the commander of the Salonica garrison, was well known for his activities against the CPU. It is also noteworthy that he was Enver's brother-in-law and the assassination attempt took place in the house where Enver lived together with his family. Enver discusses this incident in detail in his memoirs: Enver Paşa, *Enver Paşa'nın Anıları*, pp.79–84.
6. Norman Itzkowitz and Vamık Volkan, *The Immortal Atatürk* (Chicago, 1984), p.59.
7. The Committee of Progress and Union (CPU) was renamed as the Committee of Union and Progress (CUP) after the Young Turk Revolution of 1908.
8. Şükrü Hanioğlu, *Kendi Mektuplarında Enver Paşa* [Enver Paşa in his Own Letters] (Istanbul, 1989), pp.20–21.
9. Enver Paşa, *Enver Paşa'nın Anıları*, p.123.
10. Ibid.
11. Some of these babies who were to become important political leaders include Enver Hoca of Albania and Anwar Sadat of Egypt.
12. S. Aydemir, *Makedonya'dan Ortaasya'ya Enver Paşa*, Vol.II, p.209.
13. Ibid., p.210. The original form of the card in Turkish is 'Dün burada 33,000 kişilik bir Alman kolordusunun geçit resmini seyrettim. İnsanın ağzının suyu akacak derecede mükemmel'.
14. This incident is known as 'The Event of 31 March' (31 Mart Vakası) in Turkish history because of the difference in calendars.
15. Şükrü Hanioğlu, *Kendi Mektuplarında Enver Paşa*, p.11.
16. For a detailed account of Enver's activities in Tripoli see: Friedrich Perzynski, *Enver Pasha um Tripolis* (Munich, 1918); Ernst Bennett, *With the Turks in Tripoli* (London, 1912).

17. These letters are published in 'Section II: Letters about the Tripoli Resistance' in Şükrü Hanioğlu, *Kendi Mektuplarında Enver Paşa*, pp.73–211.
18. Charles Haley, 'The Desperate Ottoman: Enver Paşa and the German Empire – I', *Middle Eastern Studies*, Vol.30, No.1 (Jan. 1994), p.13.
19. Hanioğlu, *Kendi Mektuplarında Enver Paşa*, p.191.
20. Charles Haley, 'The Desperate Ottoman', p.5.
21. Hanioğlu, *Kendi Mektuplarında Enver Paşa*, p.91.
22. The quotation marks also exist in Enver's memoirs reflecting Enver's sarcasm. S. Aydemir, Vol.2, p.234.
23. Haley, p.11.
24. Ibid., p.9.
25. Edirne, the first significant Ottoman conquest in Europe (1361), was perceived to be one of the symbols of Ottoman military greatness.
26. Hanioğlu, *Kendi Mektuplarında Enver Paşa*, p.222.
27. Consequently, when Enver eventually became the Minister of War, replacing these senior commanders with enthusiastic and reform-minded junior officers formed the essence of his reforms in the army. Alfred Nossig, 'Die Reform der türkischen Armee', in *Die neue Türkei und ihre Führer* (Halle, 1916), pp.24–9.
28. Le Bon discarded the assemblies as 'a type of mob that could be hazardous to any society'. S. Hanioğlu, *The Young Turks in Opposition* (New York, 1995), pp.31–2.
29. Hanioğlu, *Kendi Mektuplarında Enver Paşa*, p.249.
30. Ulrich Trumpener, 'Turkey's Entry to World War I: An Assessment of Responsibilities', *The Journal of Modern History* (Chicago, 1962), pp.378–9.
31. For example, on 3 August 1914, Said Halim Paşa reported to Wangenheim that he was against any overt action until the mobilization had been completed and the willingness of Bulgarians to be on the side of the Central Powers had become clear.
32. For a more detailed account see: Ulrich Trumpener, *Germany and the Ottoman Empire (1914–18)* (Princeton, 1968).
33. For a more detailed account see Ulrich Trumpener, 'Turkey's Entry to World War I', pp.380–3; David Fromkin, *A Peace to End All Peace* (New York, 1989), pp.56–61.
34. Aydemir, op. cit., Vol.III, p.133.
35. Dan Rustow, 'Enver Pasha' in Lewis, Pellat and Schecht (eds.), *The Encyclopaedia of Islam* (London, 1965), p.699.
36. The number of deaths cited differ drastically between 500,000 and 1,500,000 and it is still a significant issue of controversy especially among Turkish and Armenian historians.
37. S. Aydemir, op. cit., Vol.III, p.497. During this discussion, Talât Paşa underlined that considering their present conditions and the current dynamics of world politics, they should withdraw to a corner in Europe keeping a low profile and should refrain from active involvement in politics. However, he also noted, 'if an opportunity arises it is natural that we will make use of it'.
38. Masayuki Yamauchi, *The Green Crescent under the Red Star: Enver Pasha in Soviet Russia 1919–1922* (Tokyo, 1991), p.9. In this book, Yamauchi publishes numerous documents from the Turkish Historical Association Archives, which hereafter will be indicated as THAA.
39. Letter from Enver Paşa (in Crimea) to his uncle Kamil Bey dated 12 Nov. 1918 (THAA Klasör 2/Fihrist 732) in Yamauchi, *The Green Crescent under the Red Star*, p.79. It is interesting to note that in this letter Enver expresses his intention to serve Islam, instead of mentioning the fatherland or the Turks.
40. Halil Paşa, *Bitmeyen Savaş: Kütülmare Kahramanı Halil Paşa'nın Anıları*, M.T. Sorgun (Istanbul, 1972), pp.247–8.
41. Ibid., pp.267–77.
42. Yamauchi, *The Green Crescent under the Red Star*, p.13.
43. Enver's letter from Moscow to Mustafa Kemal (Ankara), undated, ca. 21 May (THAA Klasör 7, Mustafa Kemal Dosyası, Fihrist 5), in Yamauchi, *The Green Crescent under the Red Star*, p.229.
44. Dan Rustow, 'Enver Pasha', *The Encyclopaedia of Islam*, p.700.

45. Turkish Parliamentary Library (T.B.M.M. Kütüphanesi), *Minutes of Meetings of Turkish Grand National Assembly*, 'Reports and Discussions on the Relations with the Russian Bolshevik Republic' İ.84, C.3, 16 Oct.1920; İ.85, C.1, 10. *Gizli Oturumlarında Sorunlar ve Görüşler* 17.1920. Also see: Mustafa Kemal, *Türkiye Büyük Millet Meclisi*, 1920–1923 (Problems and Opinions in the Confidential Meetings of the Turkish Grand National Assembly), Raşit Metel (Ankara, 1990), pp.141–55. These parliamentary discussions are very significant in indicating how the nationalist Turks viewed their relations with the Bolsheviks.
46. The Soviets promised to provide 15,000 Austrian rifles with 2,000 cartridges each, French guns for three batteries with 1,000 shells each and one million cartridges. Yamauchi, op. cit., p.120.
47. Kazım Karabekir, *İstiklal Harbimizde Enver Paşa ve İttihat ve Terakki Erkanı* (Istanbul, 1967), p.21.
48. Letter from Mustafa Kemal to Enver dated 4 Oct. 1920, in Ali Fuat Cebesoy, *Moskova Hatıraları* (Istanbul, 1955), p.56.
49. Ibid.
50. It should not be forgotten that this was the period of Civil War and Soviet rule was being seriously challenged in the Caucasus and especially in Central Asia.
51. Especially in strategic places like India and Iran.
52. Dan Rustow, 'Enver Pasha', *The Encyclopaedia of Islam*, p.700.
53. Kazım Karabekir, *İstiklal Harbimizde Enver Paşa ve İttihat ve Terakki Erkanı*, pp.10–17.
54. From the original text of the speech delivered by Enver Paşa at the Baku Congress (THAA Klasör 32/Fihrist 1168), in Yamauchi, *The Green Crescent under the Red Star*, pp.318–21. Cebesoy, *Moskova Hatıraları*, pp.25–9.
55. Ibid.
56. Within this context, Enver tried to emphasize his contributions to the struggle in Tripoli.
57. Yamauchi, p.33.
58. [P]ublic [R]ecords [O]ffice FO 371/ 5178 (E 13412/345/44).
59. For further information on this issue see Richard Pipes, *The Formation of the Soviet Union: Communism and Nationalism* (New York, 1968), p.260–62.
60. PRO FO 371/ 5178 (E 13412/345/44).
61. Yamauchi, op. cit., p.33–4.
62. Dan Rustow, 'Enver Pasha', *The Encyclopaedia of Islam*, p.700.
63. Bekir Sami Bey (Moscow) to Enver Paşa (Berlin), Nov. 1920 (THAA Klasor 28/Fihrist 439), in Yamauchi, op. cit., p.125.
64. Dan Rustow, 'Enver Pasha', *The Encyclopaedia of Islam*, p.700.
65. Eric Zürcher, *The Unionist Factor* (Leiden, 1984), p.169. At that time, even abandoning Ankara and establishing a base in Konya or Eskisehir was under consideration.
66. For additional information on Teşkilat-ı Mahsusa see Philip Hendrich Stoddard, 'The Ottoman Government and the Arabs, 1911–1918: A Preliminary Study of the Teşkilat-ı Mahsusa' (unpub. Ph.D. diss., Princeton University, 1963).
67. Ibid., p.168.
68. *Political Report on the Caucasus*, Constantinople, 7 Sept. 1920 (confidential) PRO FO 371/5178 (E 14638/345/44) .
69. *Bristol to Secretary of State*, Constantinople, 2 Jan. 1920, National Archives, Records of the Department of Navy, Record Group 45, Box. 831.
70. S.I.S., 2 Sept. 1920, No.CX/ 676/V, PRO FO 371/5178 (E 11702/345/44).
71. Ibid.
72. Turkish Parliamentary Library (T.B.M.M. Kütüphanesi), *Minutes of Meetings of Turkish Grand National Assembly*, 'Reports and Discussions on the Relations with the Russian Bolshevik Republic', İ.84, C.3, 16 Oct. 1920.
73. Robeck to Curzon, 12 June 1920, No.695, PRO FO 371/ 5178 (E 6346/345/44), see also attached the article 'Tchicherine et Mustapha Kemal Pasha' in *La Cause Commune*, the Russian weekly newspaper published in Paris, sent by the British Embassy in Paris.
74. S.I.S., 2 Sept. 1920, No.CX/ 676/V, PRO FO 371/5178 (E 11702/345/44).
75. Turkish Republican Archives, Decree of the Parliament concerning Enver and Halil Paşa, 3 Dec. 1921, No.731/ 385.

76. K. Gürün, *Türk-Sovyet İlişkileri (1920–1953)* (Ankara, 1991), p.46.
77. Ibid., pp.46–7; A.F. Cebesoy, *Moskova Hatıraları,* p.231.
78. Dan Rustow, 'Enver Pasha', *The Encyclopaedia of Islam*, p.700.
79. *Istoria grazhdanskoy voyny u Uzbekistane*, Vol.2 (Tashkent, 1970), p.152.
80. When his situation became totally untenable, he took refuge in Afghanistan and continued to support the Basmachi movement across the border.
81. In Richard Pipes, *Formation of the Soviet Union: Communism and Nationalism (1917–1923)* (Cambridge, 1954), p.178 there is a discussion on the origins of the word *Basmachi* being obscure. Pipes states that Zeki Velidi Togan traces the word from 'basmak' meaning 'to press' and Basmachi being 'the oppressed'.
82. Zeki Velidi Togan, *Hatıralar: Türkistan ve Diğer Müslüman Doğu Türkleri'nin Milli Varlık ve Kültür Mücadeleleri* (Istanbul, 1969), p.390. These claims of Hacı Sami were of course grossly exaggerated.
83. Aydemir, op. cit., Vol.III, p.633.
84. Zeki Velidi Togan was a well-known and respected figure in Turanian circles and played a key role in the Bashkirian struggle for independence.
85. Togan, *Hatıralar*, p.391.
86. Ibid., pp.387–9.
87. Arı İnan (ed.), *Enver Paşa'nın Özel Mektupları* (Ankara, 1997). This book is a collection of the private letters of Enver Paşa written to his wife Naciye Sultan and Halil Paşa. Frequent letters of Enver Paşa (written almost every day) to his wife Naciye Sultan usually have a very romantic and passionate tone. However, even his love for her and the birth of his youngest son were not enough to make him quit the battlefields.
88. Soloveichik, 'Revoliutsionnaia Bukhara', *Novyi Vostok*, No.22 (1922), p.281.
89. Ibid., p.283.
90. Aydemir, op. cit., Vol.III, pp.641–58.
91. Ibid., p.652.
92. Ibid., p.658.
93. Said Alim Khan, *La Voix de la Boukharie Opprimée* (Paris, 1929), pp.36–7.
94. Rumbold to Curzon, 24 Jan. 1922, No.95, Foreign Office Confidential Print (E 1107/27/44), Vol.3, p.36.
95. Mustafa Kemal to Turkish Embassy in Moscow (letter to be presented to Chicherin), 3 Sept. 1921, No.2705, in Turkish Ministry of Culture (ed.), *Atatürk'ün Milli Dış Politikası: Milli Mücadele Dönemine Ait 100 Belge (1919–1923),* Vol.I (Ankara: Kültür Bakanlığı, 1981), p.353.
96. Kamuran Gürün, p.76. The Treaty of Friendship was signed on 2 Jan. 1922.
97. Rumbold to Curzon, Constantinople, 24 Jan. 1922, no.95, Foreign Office Confidential Print (E 1107/27/44), Vol.3, p.37.
98. Rumbold to Curzon, Constantinople, 7 March 1922, No.229 (confidential), Foreign Office Confidential Print (E 2755/5/44), Vol.3, p.47.
99. PRO FO 371/ 8075 (N 10281/6/97).
100. Ibid.
101. I. Sol'ts, 'Anglo-Envreskaia avantiura i osvobozhdenie narodov vostoka' (The British-Enver Venture and the Liberation of the Peoples of the East), *Kommunist* (Apr.-May 1922), p.8 quoted in Helen Aymen De Lageard, 'The Revolt of the Basmachi According to Red Army Journals (1920–1922)', *Central Asian Survey*, Vol.6, No.3 (1987), p.8. In her interesting article, De Lageard presents a comprehensive study of three journals published by the Red Army in Tashkent for the period 1920–22, which corresponds with the arrival of Turkommissiia in Turkestan, as well as the most powerful moments of the revolt of the Basmachi.
102. Joseph Castagné, *Les Basmachis* (Paris, 1925), pp.49–50; Glenda Fraser, 'Basmachi-II', *Central Asian Survey*, Vol.6, No.2 (1987), pp.37–8.
103. Ibid.
104. Richard Pipes, op. cit., p.257.
105. Glenda Fraser, 'Basmachi-I', *Central Asian Survey*, Vol.6, No.1 (1987), p.61.
106. K. Vasilevskii, 'Fazy Basmacheskovo dvizheniia v Srednei Azii'. *Novyi Vostok*, No.29 (1930), p.134.

107. Glenda Fraser, 'Enver Pasha's Bid for Turkestan, 1920–1922', *Canadian Journal of History*, Vol.22 (1988), p.207.
108. PRO FO 371/ 8075 (N 10281/6/97).
109. Ibid.
110. For a detailed account of Enver's death see: S. Aydemir, op. cit., Vol.III, pp.683–6; and E. Kozlovskiy, *Krasnaya Armiya v Srdeney Azii* (Tashkent, 1928), p.37.
111. India Office 1920/73, Statement by Qadir, autumn 1923, quoted in Glenda Fraser, 'Basmachi-I' *Central Asian Survey*, Vol.6, No.1 (1987), p.61.
112. *Pravda Turkestana* was one of the sources which reported Enver's death relatively early, on 15 Aug. 1922.
113. India Office Library, IS Meshed, 20 Nov. 1922, quoted in Fraser, 'Enver Pasha's Bid for Turkestan, 1920–1922', p.211.
114. Lord D'Abernon (Berlin), 21 Aug. 1922, No.646, PRO FO 371/ 8074 (N 7819/6/97) Lord D'Arbernon enclosed to his report on the activities of Enver Paşa in Turkestan transmits the summary of a related article by Liman von Sanders in *Vossische Zeitung* dated 12 Aug. 1922.
115. PRO FO 371/ 8075 (N 10281/6/97).
116. Meshed Intelligence Diary, India Office, 25 Nov. 1922, No.P 4635 (confidential) FO 371/ 8080 (N 10497/173/97). Part of the reason that the news about Enver's death arrived at the Foreign Office so late was the long delays in the tranmission of the copies of the Meshed Intelligence Diaries. For example, the cited document transmits copies diaries form periods ending 25 Sept. and 2 Oct.
117. Ibid.
118. North West Frontier Province Intelligence Bureau Diary, India Office, 1 Dec. 1922, No.P 4716 (confidential) PRO FO 371/8080 (N 10675/173/97). This report transmits a copy of diary No.40 for the week ending 19 Oct. 1922. But as can be seen from the dates the British Foreign Office received the news of the death of Enver as late as December. Copies were also sent to Director of Military Intelligence and Air Ministry.
119. Geoffrey Hosking, *The First Socialist Society: A History of the Soviet Union from Within*, 2nd ed. (Cambridge, 1993), pp.113–14.
120. In his memoirs Togan states that during their secret meetings in Bukhara he realized that Enver was 'an idealist out of touch with real life and incidents. He has not read any of the European or Russian publications concerning the geography or statistics of Turkestan. Without any doubt he decided on what he was going to do in Turkestan during his stay in Bukhara' (p.392)
121. *Extracts from Despatch no.101 of 14 Sept. 1922, from acting British Consul General*, Kashgar, to Government of India (Communicated to Foreign Office, 16 Nov.) India Office, 16 Nov. 1922, no.P 4536 (confidential), PRO FO 371/ 8075 (N 10281/6/97). A copy of this report was also sent to the Director of Military Intelligence.
122. Muhittin Bey, *Vakit*, 25 Nov. 1923, quoted in Togan, p.395.
123. Hanioğlu, *Kendi Mektuplarında Enver Paşa*, p.13.
124. Ibid.
125. Hailey, p.244.
126. Eric Zürcher, *The Unionist Factor*, p.172.
127. From the letter written by Enver Paşa, 20 Aug. 1912, in Şükrü Hanioğlu (ed.), *Kendi Mektuplarında Enver Paşa*, pp.167–8.

Turkey's Participation in the Middle East Command and its Admission to NATO, 1950–52

BEHÇET K. YEŞİLBURSA

The object of this article is to detail and analyse the gradual stages in the formation of the British Middle East Command and the admission of Turkey to NATO. After first examining the Anglo-American compromise which permitted Turkey's admission into NATO while committing it to supporting the British initiative to form a Middle East Command, the article analyses the way in which this support was given, the failure of the Middle East Command project and the admission of Turkey to NATO. It deals with Turkey's campaign for NATO membership and the origins of her involvement in the Middle East Command. It also examines Turkey's role in the abortive attempt to implement the Middle East Command. It identifies the linkage between Turkey's participation in the Middle East Command and her admission to NATO. The article is based on British and American archival material as well as primary sources in English and Turkish.

After the Second World War, the idea of some kind of a Middle East defence pact, in which Britain and the United States and one or more of the Middle East countries would participate, had been considered by Britain. However, the British government realized that the Arab–Israeli dispute and inter-Arab frictions such as those between the Hashemite Kingdoms of Iraq and Jordan on the one hand, and Egypt and Saudi Arabia on the other, would render the formation of such a pact problematic. The prospect of the Arab countries and Israel joining together in such a pact was remote. The British government also realized that the United States was not willing to join such a pact in the near future, and without United States participation it would be of doubtful value. In these circumstances, the British government was not so sure about whether a Middle East defence pact would assure Britain of the strategic facilities which she possessed or required in the Middle East. It was thought, therefore, that better results might be obtained through separate approaches by the Western Powers to individual states, and by co-ordinated arrangements by the Western Powers to defend the Middle East, particularly Egypt, Turkey and Israel, against Soviet aggression, both in peace and war. After the war, a collective defence pact in the Middle East was therefore not a real alternative, since neither Britain nor the United States were prepared to develop one. Britain continued to pursue its military objectives in the Middle East by its bilateral treaties with Jordan, Iraq and Egypt. However, Britain's ultimate object in the Middle East remained a comprehensive defence pact among all Middle East countries, backed by Britain and the United States.

In early 1950, the British government was beginning to think more seriously of the potential value of a regional defence pact in the Middle East, primarily as a way of stimulating the talks with Egypt over the Suez Canal base. The talks with Egypt had bogged down in 1946, and all subsequent attempts to restart them had proved unsuccessful. At the beginning of the same year, Egypt renewed its demand for a total evacuation of British troops from the Suez Canal base. The British considered this unacceptable, since the maintenance of their forces and of their base in Egypt was in their view a strategic necessity, not only for Britain but also for its allies. The British government sought to find some way of bringing the Egyptians to accept this position. They thought of an international approach to Egypt. What they had in mind was that Egypt would be invited to take its part as an equal with the Western Powers (namely the United States, Britain and France) in establishing an 'Allied Middle East Command' in Egypt. There would thus no longer be British troops in Egypt as such, but Allied troops under an Allied Military Organization in which Egypt would participate on an equal footing. In short, Britain wanted to convert the British base in Egypt into an allied base, and by offering Egypt equal partnership in a Middle East Command, to put an end to its trouble in Egypt.[1]

However, the United States was still unenthusiastic about a regional defence pact in the Middle East. The United States Chiefs of Mission in the Middle East, at their meeting in Cairo in March 1950, reaffirmed their conclusion, reached in Istanbul in November 1949, that 'it would be impractical and undesirable for the United States to encourage any Near Eastern regional defense pact'. The Pentagon was also hesitant.[2]

In May 1950, however, the issue was brought up by the British Foreign Office during the tripartite London meeting of foreign ministers from Britain, France and the United States. On 7 May State Department officials were told that the Foreign Office was considering setting up a Middle East defence pact on the lines of NATO (including Turkey, Egypt and the Commonwealth countries, notably Australia, New Zealand and South Africa). This was a significant beginning for a 'Middle East Command'.

However, the State Department considered this unworkable and untimely, warning that the United States commitments in Europe and elsewhere made it impossible to consider extending them. They would neither encourage nor discourage arrangements in the Middle East.[3] The United States Joint Chiefs of Staff also remained opposed to any military commitment in the Middle East. They believed that it would be incompatible with United States security interests and detract from United States responsibilities elsewhere and 'must be viewed as the probable genesis of a series of otherwise unacceptable United States deployments in the Near East'.[4]

In contrast, the British Chiefs of Staff still thought that in the Middle East some kind of multilateral defence pact to prevent possible Soviet aggression was necessary. They recommended a 'mutual security system' that would include Britain, the Arab League states, Israel, Turkey, Iran and possibly Greece, with Egypt providing the base facilities. Although the proposal faced obvious political difficulties, the Chiefs of Staff thought that it might be 'interesting' for Egypt.[5]

In June 1950, Field Marshal Sir William Slim, the Chief of the British Imperial General Staff, went to Cairo to offer the Egyptian government a defence pact as a way to stimulate the Anglo-Egyptian talks over the future of the Suez Canal base. Slim's offers included the following points: (a) the British should completely abandon any idea of the 'occupation' of Egypt; (b) a complete new approach to defence based on equal alliance between Egypt and Britain on the lines of the Atlantic Defence Pact (NATO) should be made. This was the first serious proposal for a Middle East Command. However, the Egyptian government refused to consider any defence pact until Britain withdrew its forces from Egypt completely.[6]

However, in June 1950, the outbreak of war in Korea undermined the confidence among American policy-makers in Washington that Britain alone could protect the Middle East against Soviet aggression. They accepted that there was no substitute for the Suez base, which now appeared as the anchor of the Western security in the Middle East. Hitherto, the United States had seen the Middle East more as a part of the southern flank of Europe or as a transit area to the Far East than as an area of strategic importance in itself, and having become engaged in Europe and in the Far East, had regarded the defence of the Middle East as a British responsibility. However, after the outbreak of the Korean war the United States accepted the necessity for collective defence schemes in the Middle East and Britain's inability to defend the region on its own against possible Soviet aggression. This increased awareness of the need for collective responsibility gave continued British military presence in Egypt more validity, and propelled the United States towards closer ties with Britain in an effort to strengthen the defence of the Middle East against the growing

Soviet threat. Strategic concerns, principally the Suez base but also Persian Gulf oil, reduced slightly the United States reluctance to share the Middle East responsibilities of a weakened Britain. However, the United States was still reluctant to accept any military commitments in the region. Meanwhile, the British argued that just as Britain stood behind the United States in Korea, the United States should stand behind Britain in the Middle East.[7]

The United States believed that the Korean war was merely the opening stage in the worldwide struggle between West and East, and that the Middle East would be the next region where the Soviets would start problems. As a sensitive point on the periphery of Soviet influence and power, Iran was considered as a possible next object of Soviet designs. The United States was concerned with the Communist challenge in Iran and the growing strength of the Communist Tudeh Party in that country. It was also concerned with the rich oil reserves in Iran. On 26 June President Truman told his assistant, George Elsey, that the Soviet Union might advance into the Middle East to secure the oil needed for its Far East venture. Iran, he said, 'is where they will start trouble if we aren't careful'. He told Elsey that 'Korea is the Greece of the Far East. If we are tough enough now, if we stand up to them like we did in Greece three years ago, they won't take any steps. But if we just stand by, they'll move into Iran and they'll take over the whole Middle East. There is no telling what they'll do, if we don't put up a fight now.'[8]

On 25 July the National Security Council concluded that 'the danger of Soviet resort to war, either deliberately or by miscalculation, may have been increased by the Korean war'.[9] As a result, policy-makers in Washington concluded that the United States had to play a more active role in the Middle East in containing the Soviet Union along its southern frontier. One immediate consequence was a softening of the United States' attitude towards the notion of a Middle East defence pact.[10] The Korean war and Britain's inability to solve the Suez Canal base dispute with Egypt on a bilateral basis created an environment in which American opposition to multilateral defence arrangements in the Middle East became less feasible. The State Department was beginning to think that a multilateral approach might be the effective answer to the Anglo-Egyptian dispute and to the security of the Middle East. However, although the United States maintained its assessment that the security of the Middle East was mainly a British responsibility, and Britain's military presence in the Middle East was an assurance to the security and stability of the region, it was aware of declining British power in the region, which posed a problem for the policy of containment against Soviet aggression. The United States also realized that the Anglo-Egyptian dispute over the future of the Suez Canal base created an obstacle to the consolidation of an anti-Soviet alliance in the Middle East.[11]

In the light of the Korean war, Anglo-American defence talks on the Middle East were held in Washington at the end of July. The talks highlighted differences between American and British strategic preoccupations in the Middle East. The United States, obsessed with containment of the Soviet Union and concerned about oil areas, was in favour of a wider Middle East defence system based on the 'Outer Ring' of the Middle East, that is, primarily Iran and Turkey. However, this, from the British point of view, was logistically too difficult. The British were in favour of the 'Inner Ring' defence strategy based on Egypt. Although the British representatives accepted the importance of Iran and Turkey to the security of the Middle East and the risk of a Soviet attack on Iran and Turkey, they pointed out Britain's inability to defend the 'Outer Ring' of the Middle East on her own without American military aid. These Anglo-American differences regarding the defence of the Middle East forecast a later American preference for what would become known as the 'Northern Tier'.[12]

Further talks between Foreign Office and State Department officials were held in London in September, and the two sides agreed on the supply of arms to Turkey, military co-operation with Israel, the retention of bases in Egypt, and the redeployment of military forces throughout the area to create positions of strength. They also agreed that the two countries' Chiefs of Staff should hold high level military talks in October. During these military talks in Washington in October, the British Chief of Staff was told that the United States was now prepared to endorse a joint Anglo-American approach to Egypt, leading to a Middle East defence pact. This implied a significant shift in American policy in favour of a regional defence pact. However, the United States Joint Chiefs of Staff still remained reluctant to commit any American forces to the Middle East. They considered the defence of the Middle East to be a British and Commonwealth responsibility, and warned their British counterparts that the United States would not provide reinforcements for the region for at least the first two years of a global war. They also rejected the British 'Inner Ring' defence strategy since it defended only Egypt, not the Middle East as a whole. In their view, a Soviet attack should be held on the 'Outer Ring', in Turkey and Iran. The British agreed to examine the possibility of defending the 'Outer Ring' of the Middle East.[13]

In the meantime, the attention of British and American policy-makers was also being drawn to the Middle East by Turkey and Greece, which were making approaches to Britain and the United States in the hope of joining NATO.[14] Turkey's exclusion from the Atlantic Pact had been a severe blow to the Turkish government, in spite of the assurances about Turkey's position which accompanied the signature of the pact.[15] However, these assurances had not satisfied the Turks. Turkish foreign policy had hinged on fear of Russia and a desire to secure either the inclusion of Turkey in NATO, or some form of direct United States security guarantee in addition to the guarantee afforded by the Anglo-French-Turkish Treaty of 1939.[16] This desire had been consistently presented to the United States, Britain and France. It had been the policy of successive Turkish governments to secure an American guarantee equivalent to that of the British and French, and they had in particular sought to do this by obtaining admission into the Atlantic Pact. In this respect the policy of the new Turkish government, which came into office in May 1950,[17] was identical with that of its predecessors, and was set out in a statement of foreign policy made by the Prime Minister, Adnan Menderes, to the Turkish Parliament on 29 May. Menderes emphasized the importance of the security of the Eastern Mediterranean and referred to his government's intention to seek closer relations with Middle Eastern countries. Hitherto, Turkey's relations with the Middle Eastern countries had been characterized by an attitude of indifference on the part of the Turks and resentment and distrust on the part of the Arab states, which had been caused by long-present historical factors, Turkish support of Western Powers in opposition to Arab positions, especially on the Palestine question, and suspicion in some countries, such as Iraq, of a possible recrudescence of Turkish territorial ambitions. Menderes' Democrat Party government therefore attached great significance to the development of closer relations between Turkey and the Middle Eastern countries, and began to follow an active policy in the Middle East. The United States and Britain encouraged Turkey in the pursuit of this policy. They felt that if Turkey could gain the Arab states' confidence, she could exercise a constructive influence over them.[18]

At the end of May, the new Turkish government renewed in a more pressing form Turkey's appeal to the United States and Britain for admission to NATO. However, this appeal was rejected by Britain and the United States. The reasons why it had not been possible for Britain to agree to the inclusion of Turkey in the Atlantic Pact were given by William Strang, Permanent Under Secretary of State at the Foreign Office, to the Turkish Ambassador in London in conversation on 31 May and 1 June. They were as follows:

(1) the United States was not in a position to enter into further political commitments at present;

(2) it was not possible for the United States to enter into military understandings in the absence of political commitments;

(3) military undertakings and staff talks between Britain and Turkey would be meaningless without the participation of the United States since British and American plans for the area were dovetailed together.[19]

Britain wanted Turkey to be associated with her Middle East defence plans, which would in turn be connected to NATO through the NATO Standing Group (the permanent NATO steering body, with American, British and French membership). From the British point of view, a Middle East defence pact under NATO (including Turkey, Greece, Britain and the United States) would be an ideal way to attract Middle East states. The Ministry of Defence conceded that Turkey's membership in NATO would improve Middle East defence planning between Britain, the United States and Turkey, but a formal United States guarantee to Turkey could achieve the same thing. The Foreign Office agreed. Similarly, the State Department thought that if Turkish and Greek membership in NATO were refused, a regional defence pact of Turkey, Greece and Iran might be possible with American, British and French support. The difficulty was that the United States was not prepared to give Turkey any direct American security guarantee.[20]

In the summer of 1950, particularly after the outbreak of war in Korea, the Turks again began to put strong pressure on the United States and Britain for some kind of security guarantee or Turkey's admission to NATO. At the end of July, shortly after the announcement of its decision to send troops to Korea on 25 July, the Turkish government officially renewed its application to be admitted to the Atlantic Pact. The Turkish government hoped that the decision to send troops to Korea would strengthen Turkey's case for admission to NATO.[21] However, from the British point of view, there remained three main reasons against admitting Turkey into the Atlantic Pact. These were:

(1) it would destroy the conception of the Atlantic Pact as a basis for building an Atlantic Community as a political and economic association of nations having common traditions, etc.;

(2) it would spread the security risks, introduce military problems which had no relation to the main European defence theatre and would generally disturb the organization which was just beginning to find its feet;

(3) many of the existing members would be strongly opposed to any extensions of their obligation to go to war.[22]

Moreover, if Turkey were accepted into the Atlantic Pact, Greece would have to be accepted too. Although the Greek government was not pressing for admission, it would certainly do so if the Turks were admitted, and it would be difficult to exclude it without causing offence. As a result, the Foreign Office concluded that it would be better that the United States should undertake a direct commitment to Turkey than that Turkey should be taken into the Atlantic Pact. However, as noted, the United States was not prepared to undertake a direct commitment and preferred to undertake commitments within a general framework such as the Charter of the United Nations or the Atlantic Pact.[23]

As a result, at its meeting in New York in September 1950, the North Atlantic Council rejected the admission of Turkey and Greece into NATO, but it accepted them into NATO as 'associate members'. It was thought that this would partly satisfy the demands of Turkey and Greece and allow them to be involved in NATO defence planning in the Mediterranean area.[24]

By the end of 1950, a multilateral defence pact in the Middle East was being seriously considered by Britain. The Korean War and the Turkish attempts to join NATO offered an opportunity for Britain to bring about her long-range goal of a Middle East pact. Although the United States was still averse to involving itself directly in the Middle East, and still gave priority to Europe and the Far East, it was now more willing to support British initiatives in the Middle East. At the end of December 1950 George McGhee, Assistant Secretary of State for Near Eastern, South Asian and African Affairs at the State Department, sent the Secretary of State, Dean Acheson, a memorandum on American Middle East policy. Britain, he wrote, lacked the resources and manpower, and was unable to defend the oilfields in the Middle East, the loss of which would be a major blow to the West. In view of this, he proposed a more positive United States approach to the Middle East. He believed that the United States should state publicly its interest in the security of the Middle East, and suggested a combined Anglo-American command structure in the Middle East, which would stimulate co-operation between Middle Eastern countries and the Western powers, and make the idea of a multilateral defence pact much more attractive to the Arab states. In his view, the United States now had to turn away from the concept of primary British responsibility towards the concept of combined Anglo-American responsibility and active Anglo-American co-operation in the development and implementation of plans in the Middle East.[25]

Acheson supported McGhee's ideas up to a point. On 27 January 1951, he wrote to the Secretary of Defense, George Marshall, that 'more affirmative United States action' was needed to safeguard vital security interests in the Middle East, but reiterated that this did not mean joining a security pact or committing American forces. The security of the Middle

East would still primarily be a British responsibility. He added that the United States strategic, political and economic interests in the Middle East could be defended best 'through the co-ordination of American, British, and indigenous efforts under a concept of the defense of the Middle East as a whole'.[26]

However, a State-Joint Chiefs of Staff meeting on 6 February disclosed differences of opinion. McGhee stressed the need for a 'regional effort' under US–UK sponsorship in addition to American reliance on Turkey, but not a command organization. He proposed creating a US–UK co-ordinating mechanism for the Middle East as a whole. McGhee also pointed out that the State Department was not looking for a commitment of forces but only for an insurance policy against Soviet aggression. He believed that a modest military aid programme to Syria, Lebanon and Israel, involving a maximum of $10 million and administered by a very small advisory mission, would be useful as a 'small insurance payment'.[27] However, the Joint Chiefs of Staff doubted the wisdom of making even so small a commitment. They refused to support any defence arrangement that would commit American forces to the defence of the Middle East. They wanted to concentrate first on the defence of Western Europe and not to relieve the British of their overall responsibility for the Middle East. They also wanted to keep the defence of Greece and Turkey separate from the rest of the Middle East. The Joint Chiefs of Staff would accept nothing more than the proposal first made by the British, to establish some link between NATO and the Middle East. They thought that this could be done by bringing Greece and Turkey into NATO. In their view, it would require indirect and limited American commitment and thus be easier to obtain the approval of Congress. It would also satisfy British demands for a Middle East Command and facilitate an Anglo-Egyptian settlement.[28]

Soon after his meeting with the Joint Chiefs of Staff, McGhee went to Turkey to attend the conference of the United States Middle East Chiefs of Mission. On his way he stopped in London and had talks at the Foreign Office, at which he said that in the Middle East Britain should have the primary responsibility. He said that no common planning for the Middle East was possible, but the Middle Eastern countries could be strengthened through the supply of arms. At their meeting in Istanbul on 14–21 February the United States Middle East Chiefs of Mission concluded that the United States should clarify its military responsibilities with Britain, but there should be no attempt to organize a security pact. However, they urged that the United States should publicly announce its willingness, in association with Britain, to assist Middle Eastern states in strengthening their defence capabilities. McGhee returned from his Middle East tour convinced that a regional approach to the defence of the Middle East was necessary, and that

British and American policies in the Middle East should be closely co-ordinated. He reaffirmed the need, which he had expressed to the Joint Chiefs of Staff on 6 February, for a more positive United States security policy towards the Middle East by providing limited material assistance and small military missions to Syria, Lebanon and Israel to create a regional stability, and by creating a US–UK co-ordinating mechanism for the Middle East as a whole.[29]

Meanwhile, a division of opinion had emerged between the British and American military planners over the role of Turkey. General Sir Brian Robertson, Commander-in-Chief of the British Middle East Land Forces, and Admiral Carney, the United States Sixth Fleet Commander and Commander of NATO's Southern Flank, met in Malta on 22–24 January 1951. General Robertson argued that Turkey was essentially a part of the Middle East, and should be under the British Middle East Headquarters. The British wished to attract Turkey to their Middle East Command idea because of Turkey's manpower resources and strategic position in the Middle East. On the other hand, the Americans saw Turkey as a Mediterranean power, useful for the support of NATO's southern flank. Admiral Carney argued that as the United States was the main supplier of arms to Turkey, Turkey should be under his command in the Mediterranean. He said that Turkey was anxious to join NATO, but was unwilling to participate in a Middle East defence pact or place her forces under a British command in the Middle East.[30]

After his talks with Admiral Carney in Malta, General Robertson visited Turkey from 22 to 25 February. His object was to find out to what extent and on what basis the Turks would be prepared to plan with Britain in the defence of the Middle East. Although the Turks showed interest in co-ordination and liaison on strategic planning with the British in the Middle East, they were unwilling to commit themselves in any way at that stage. However, they assured the British that once the question of the admission of Turkey into NATO had been settled, Turkey would be ready to play her part in Middle East defence.[31]

On 12–13 March, Admiral Carney and General Robertson again met in Malta to discuss the position of Turkey in relation to Middle East defence. Admiral Carney maintained his view that Turkey should play a dual role in her association with the West and be co-ordinated with both Europe and the Middle East, which clashed with the British view that Turkey was primarily a Middle Eastern country. It was clear that no planning could take place with Turkey until Britain and the United States had worked out their differences.[32]

Meanwhile, American opinion both in Congress and in the State Department was moving towards the idea of bringing Turkey and Greece fully into the Atlantic Pact. Congress was very hesitant about any extension of direct American commitments, but was prepared to extend a guarantee to Turkey and Greece in the context of NATO, that is, by full Turkish and Greek membership of the Atlantic Pact. The State Department felt that Iran, who would receive no equivalent guarantee, would be less disturbed by Turkish and Greek membership of NATO than by direct United States guarantees to Turkey and Greece. The State Department believed that the best solution on balance would be Turkish and Greek membership of NATO. The United States was also anxious to obtain the right to use Turkish bases, and considered that it would be more likely to obtain these bases if Turkey was a member of the Atlantic Pact.[33] On the other hand, the British government still remained opposed to the admission of Turkey and Greece to full membership of the Atlantic Pact, and preferred a direct United States guarantee to Turkey equivalent to that made by the British and the French in 1939.[34]

Meanwhile, the British government was attempting to reopen negotiations with Egypt. At the end of March 1951, the Chiefs of Staff proposed a phased withdrawal of British forces from Egypt up until 1956, after which the Suez base would be run by civilians, though it would be defended by an integrated Anglo-Egyptian air defence system, requiring 10,000 RAF personnel in Egypt. On 5 April, the Cabinet approved the proposals, and decided to reopen negotiations with Egypt on the lines that the Chiefs of Staff had proposed.[35] The proposals for the revision of the Anglo-Egyptian Treaty of 1936 were presented to the Egyptian government on 11 April, but the Egyptian government rejected them, demanding the evacuation of all British troops from Egypt within one year, the withdrawal of British officials from the Sudan within two years, and 'self-government under the Egyptian crown' for the Sudanese. The Egyptian government conceded only that British troops might return to Egypt in the event of direct aggression upon Egypt or her Arab neighbours.[36]

During Anglo-American talks in Washington on 16 May, the British Chiefs of Staff realized that the United States would not give a unilateral American guarantee to Turkey and would only proceed by means of Turkish membership of NATO. They also assumed that Turkish membership in NATO would draw the United States more towards the Middle East, that this would make Turkey less reluctant to enter a defence pact for the Middle East, and that if Britain succeeded in attracting American support for the Middle East, the advantages of Turkish membership in NATO would outweigh any disadvantages. However, in their view, Turkey and Greece should not be a part of Eisenhower's European Command (SACEUR), but under a Supreme Allied Commander Middle East (SACME), who would be British, with his headquarters under the NATO Standing Group. They thought that even if it did not want to commit forces, the United States should be part of this integrated command. The State Department approached the notion of a Middle East Command (MEC) more cautiously. It thought that the Middle East states would be 'most unlikely' to enter MEC 'during the Cold War', but believed that it might prove possible to engender a 'co-operative relationship' for military planning and assistance. On the other hand, the United States Joint Chiefs of Staff accepted the idea of a Middle East Command, but remained non-committal about its details. They suggested that Turkey and Greece should be brought into NATO. President Truman and Acheson accepted the Pentagon's proposal, and decided to invite Turkey and Greece to join NATO.[37]

The British followed suit. On 22 May, at a Cabinet meeting, Emanuel Shinwell, the Defence Minister, said that Greece and Turkey were pressing strongly for admission to NATO, and they would be affronted if Britain obstructed their admission. Their goodwill was essential for the effective defence of the Middle East. If Turkey were brought into NATO, Britain would be in a better position to press for a Supreme Allied Command, Middle East (SACME), with a British Supreme Commander, in which Turkey would play a vital part. The Chief of the Imperial General Staff, Field Marshal Slim, also supported Turkey's admission to NATO. He said that arrangements for the defence of the Middle East could not be made fully effective without Turkish co-operation since in a general war the Turkish forces would be urgently needed to meet any Soviet threat against the Middle East. The new Foreign Secretary, Herbert Morrison, indicated that the admission of Turkey and Greece to NATO might be the only way in which the United States government could persuade Congress to accept further United States commitments in the Middle East. The Cabinet noted that a Middle East regional pact itself had little attraction for Turkey, since it would afford her no effective increase in security. The Cabinet therefore agreed in principle to support the admission of Turkey and Greece to NATO and in return to ask the United States to support a Middle East Command under British auspices.[38]

On 24 May, the State Department informed the Foreign Office that the United States was now prepared to support a Middle East Command in some form, though the details would be worked out during further talks. The State Department now considered a Middle East Command system as a possible solution for the defence of the Middle East. In their view, it would meet Britain's need for a command structure, protect NATO's southern flank, integrate Turkey into defence plans, attract the support of Middle East states and integrate Anglo-American Middle East interests. They suggested that the British should arrange a 'Middle East Cooperative Defence Board' with United States, French, Turkish and Commonwealth adherence. This, in their view, would create an alternative to the old bilateral defence agreements, and would be co-ordinated with NATO through Turkey.[39]

On 4 June, the British Chiefs of Staff agreed on a Middle East Command under a British SACME linked to NATO; the association of Turkey and possibly Greece with the Middle East Command; and a Middle East Defence Board under SACME chairmanship. On 7 June they presented these views to the Cabinet Defence Committee, which decided that British agreement to the American proposals should be conditional upon the United States accepting a British SACME and the inclusion of Greece and Turkey within a Middle East Command.[40] On 19 June, at Anglo-American talks in Washington, Air Chief Marshal Sir William Elliot, who headed the British delegation, presented the British proposal for a Middle East Command under a British commander as SACME and linked to the NATO Standing Group. Below the headquarters would be a Middle East Defence Board consisting of a British chairman and members from the United States, France, Turkey, Greece and Italy, but not from any of the Middle East countries. The Americans, however, wished Middle East Command to be a NATO command so that the United States could join. They also suggested that Turkey should join MEC and NATO at the same time. Moreover, they suggested that the Headquarters of the MEC should not be located in Egypt. Although they agreed that the West should retain control of the Middle East Defence Board, they wanted to use it as a way to bring Middle East countries into the defence arrangements with the West.[41]

On 24 June, the British Chiefs of Staff agreed to the admission of Greece and Turkey into NATO, on the understanding that Turkey would take her place in a Combined Allied Middle East Command, since the Turks would not join MEC unless they joined NATO at the same time. The Chiefs agreed that MEC should in effect be a NATO operational command under the NATO Standing Group. They also decided that a Middle East Defence Board was necessary, though full membership should be restricted to those countries who were willing to contribute forces to Middle East defence. The Chiefs were doubtful about the practicality of a Middle East Defence Board that included all the Middle Eastern countries. In their view, the Middle Eastern countries should be associate members. These proposals were approved by the Cabinet in late June.[42]

In early July, Sir William Elliot, Chairman of the British Joint Services Mission in the United States and British Representative on the Standing Group of the Military Committee of NATO, and Sir Oliver Franks, the British Ambassador to the United States, met with the United States Joint Chiefs of Staff and told them that the British would now accept Greek and Turkish membership in NATO on the condition that they should join MEC at the same time. However, the United States Joint Chiefs of Staff opposed the British condition. They also disagreed with the British on the composition of the Middle East Defence Board. They preferred a loose arrangement, with emphasis on planning rather than fully-fledged military command, and with no restrictions on membership. The British preferred a more functional defence-oriented body, with membership restricted to countries which would contribute forces to Middle East defence. Meanwhile, the State Department decided that MEC should not be a NATO command, since it was intended to defend the Middle East, which was not appropriate for NATO. As a result of American pressure, the British eventually dropped the condition that Turkey should join NATO and MEC at the same time. They also accepted that MEC should not be a NATO command, though the two should be closely associated.[43]

Meanwhile, the Foreign Secretary, Herbert Morrison, informed the Egyptian government that the British government was working on a new approach to the Anglo-Egyptian dispute. Egypt should join the MEC in return for providing base facilities. Once again, however, the Egyptian government refused to join any Middle East defence arrangement until the Canal Zone was completely evacuated by British troops.[44]

At the end of July, Stevenson, the British Ambassador in Cairo, urged the Foreign Office that the British government should make up its mind on a policy for the Middle East in conjunction with the Americans. He said that Britain no longer possessed sufficient economic and military strength to consider the Middle East as a purely British sphere of influence and that Britain would have to rely on the United States for economic and military help. He stated that reliance on *ad hoc* arrangements, which might have served when Britain could act alone and unchallenged over a great part of the world, would be foolish, particularly when such arrangements seemed now to be the cause of misunderstanding, impatience and irritation in Anglo-American relations. Stevenson concluded that Britain's future Middle East policy should be devised in conjunction with the United States, combining their high level policy planning for the Middle East.[45]

On 15 August Morrison wrote to Acheson that Egypt was not and would never be able to defend herself against aggression by a major power, but that since Egypt had rejected the British proposals of April and June 1951 without discussion, and declared the negotiations closed, Britain should be ready for an abrogation of the 1936 Treaty. He believed that MEC offered the best solution to the Anglo-Egyptian dispute over the Suez Canal base. He asked for United States support both as regards working out one more line of approach to the Egyptians and, if that failed, in resisting attempts to dislodge Britain, whether they be made in the Security Council of the United Nations or elsewhere.[46]

On 21 August Acheson wrote to the Secretary of Defense, George

Marshall, that Anglo-Egyptian discussions had reached 'an impasse with dangerous potentialities'. The pressure of public opinion, he wrote, might compel the Egyptian government unilaterally to abrogate the 1936 Treaty. Accordingly, Acheson asked the Joint Chiefs of Staff to reassess the relative strategic importance of the Suez Canal base, and the conditions for maintenance and terms of re-entry that would allow 'immediate use of the bases' upon outbreak of hostilities. The Joint Chiefs of Staff reaffirmed the importance of access to Suez Canal base facilities in the event of war in order to preserve the security of the Middle East. They suggested that the United States should support Britain politically in preserving her rights to maintain strategic facilities in such conditions as to allow their quick and effective utilization, and to re-enter and make full use of these bases when necessary. On 22 August the State Department circulated a position paper prepared for use at the forthcoming Washington Foreign Ministers' meeting between the United States, Britain and France. This paper echoed the Joint Chiefs of Staff recommendations regarding the importance of continued use of the Suez Canal base facilities. Within that framework, the State Department concluded, Britain should be encouraged to go along with the MEC proposals.[47]

Meanwhile, the British Chiefs of Staff had warned their government that Egypt would not be impressed by a change of name, from 'British' to 'Allied'. In their view, Egypt would have to be given a major role within the organization. They proposed an Egyptian Base Area Commander, who would look after base security and command the base's air defence organization.[48] However, Morrison was convinced that MEC was the only solution, and he carried the rest of the Cabinet with him. On 4 September the Cabinet agreed that Morrison should seek allied agreement on the MEC proposals during the forthcoming tripartite talks in Washington and the NATO Council meeting in Ottawa.[49]

During US–UK working level discussions on 6–8 September, British representatives strongly defended their position. They insisted that solutions must lie in Egyptian acceptance of (1) the concept of the MEC and (2) the right of the Sudanese to decide for themselves whether they wanted a union with Egypt or not. In the British view, establishment of the MEC and internationalization of the Suez Canal base would afford an opportunity for a fresh negotiating approach. McGhee's efforts to extract concessions from the British proved unavailing. However, both sides finally reached agreement on the formal structure of the MEC, which would consist of an integrated allied headquarters and a Middle East Defence Board. Above the Middle East Defence Board there would be a Chiefs of Staff Committee consisting of representatives of the United States, Britain, France and Turkey, which would in turn report to a Steering Committee (similar to the

NATO Standing Group) of the same four powers. As the United States wanted, the Middle East Defence Board, which would act as an advisory committee, would include all Middle Eastern countries interested in regional defence. The Board would be under the control of SACME, which would include a military and a political representative from each country. The commander of SACME would be British, but a Turkish officer would be Deputy SACME since Turkey would contribute most of the land forces. The United States, though not contributing forces to the MEC, would be represented on the headquarters staff, since it would provide carrier forces in the Mediterranean and arms for Turkey. In peacetime the command structure would be very small, consisting only of SACME and a small headquarters staff.[50]

Both sides also adopted a timetable for presenting the MEC proposals to Egypt, which was as follows:

(a) when the concurrence of Turkey and the Commonwealth countries has been obtained, the Egyptian government would be approached concerning the MEC;

(b) at an appropriate time, Iraq, Jordan, Lebanon, Syria and Saudi Arabia would be informed of the general terms of the MEC plan;

(c) as soon as consultations with Egypt reached a point where a public announcement would not prejudice the negotiations, a statement regarding the command structure would be issued.[51]

On 10 September Morrison and Acheson met in Washington, and Morrison outlined the British proposal for a MEC in which Egypt would be a full partner. Acheson agreed with him, and said that the United States supported the British position in Egypt. However, on 12 September, at a tripartite meeting, Robert Schuman, the French Foreign Minister, said that he could only accept the proposed command arrangement on two conditions. First, a French officer should be given a high profile at the Supreme Commander's Headquarters. Second, in order to balance the British naval command in the Eastern Mediterranean, a French admiral should be given the naval command in the Western Mediterranean. There was general agreement on the first French condition. On the second, there was a prolonged argument between the French and the Americans. The Americans were not prepared to give the French an area command in the Western Mediterranean. They thought that the French should have a functional command, which would be confined to the task of maintaining north and south communications in the Western Mediterranean. On 14 September, during another tripartite meeting, Morrison suggested that at the Ottawa meeting of the NATO Council on 14–20 September, Greece and Turkey should be asked to join NATO. Afterwards, Turkey would be approached regarding MEC. Once Turkish approval was secured, Britain would present the MEC proposals to Egypt. Simultaneously the Australian, New Zealand and South African governments would be informed by the British government of the MEC proposals. Acheson and Schuman agreed.[52]

In Ottawa, the British hoped to obtain agreement on MEC before allowing Greece and Turkey into NATO, but this appeared to be difficult because of the opposition of the United States and France, and also of the smaller NATO powers such as Denmark, Norway and Holland, which disliked the whole idea of bringing Turkey into NATO, fearing it would alter the character of NATO. They also knew that the United States was not entirely convinced about MEC, and did not share the British view that Turkey belonged primarily to the Middle East and was essential to its defence.[53]

However, in Ottawa, the British were successful in convincing the United States and the other NATO members of the importance of MEC and Turkey's participation in it. At the end of the Ottawa talks, the United States agreed to join with Britain in presenting the MEC proposals to Turkey, and appointed General Bradley, Chairman of the Joint Chiefs of Staff, to proceed with Field Marshal Sir William Slim, Chief of the British Imperial General Staff, to Ankara. The United States also agreed to join with Britain in presenting the MEC proposals to Egypt. In return, Britain agreed that as far as the defence of Turkey was concerned, the Supreme Allied Commander would be responsible to the NATO Standing Group. The North Atlantic Council agreed in principle to a British-led MEC, and to admit Greece and Turkey to NATO.[54]

However, neither in Washington nor in Ottawa were the British and the Americans successful in obtaining French agreement to the MEC proposals, and it was therefore decided that Field Marshal Slim and General Bradley should visit Paris on their way to Ankara. Schuman accepted this proposal on the understanding that the French government must reserve its final attitude with regard to the MEC until after the proposed talks in Paris. At the beginning of October, General Bradley and Field Marshal Slim arrived in Paris, where after considerable discussions, the French accepted that a French admiral would be appointed to a naval command in the Western Mediterranean under Admiral Carney, with responsibility for the communications between France and North Africa. They also agreed to two principal naval commands in the Mediterranean: one, American, in the West under SHAPE, and one, British, in the Eastern Mediterranean under SHAPE, each responsible for the support of their respective supreme commanders.[55]

On 12 October, Field Marshal Slim and General Bradley, together with General Lechères of France, went on to Turkey to invite the Turkish government to join with them in presenting the MEC proposals to Egypt. On 13 October, the Turkish government agreed to participate in MEC on an equal footing and to join with the United States, Britain and France in presenting the MEC proposals to Egypt. At the same time, the Turkish government insisted, as part of Turkey's admission to NATO, on being included in a European NATO Command. They hesitated very much at the idea of coming under a British Commander. The solution which the Turks favoured was that Turkey should be placed under Admiral Carney's Southern European Command. The entry of Turkey into NATO and the establishment of a MEC were, in their view, two separate questions which should not be linked together. They did not accept that Turkey was a Middle Eastern country, they considered Turkey to be part of Europe. However, although it wanted to be under SHAPE for both military and political reasons, the Turkish government finally agreed to be under SACME, which for this purpose would be responsible to the NATO Standing Group. The British Chief of Staff commented that the Turks did not grasp the organization of NATO or of the proposed MEC, since Turkey would have a dual role which would call upon it to perform in relation to NATO on the one hand and the Middle East on the other.[56]

Knowing that Egypt might abrogate the Anglo-Egyptian Treaty of 1936 at any time, the British government wanted to act quickly and use the MEC proposals to prevent an abrogation. Under the pressure of urgency, the British government did not heed the warnings sent from its own Embassy in Egypt. On 3 October, the British Embassy in Cairo warned the Foreign Office that Egypt was only interested in terminating the 1936 Treaty. MEC would be seen as 'putting the cart before the horse' and Egypt would not co-operate until the 1936 Treaty was abrogated.[57] Despite this warning, at a Cabinet meeting on the following day, Morrison said that Egypt might abrogate the 1936 Treaty before 10 October, so it was necessary to make a new approach to Egypt without delay. They would propose an allied MEC consisting of Britain, the United States, France, Turkey and Egypt as equal partners. MEC would replace the 1936 Treaty, all British forces that were not assigned to the MEC would be evacuated, and the Suez base would become 'allied' instead of British. If Egypt rejected the proposals and abrogated the 1936 Treaty, Britain would condemn the action and stand on her existing treaty rights. On 6 October, Morrison informed the Egyptian government that he would shortly submit new defence proposals.[58]

However, on the following day, the Egyptian Prime Minister, Nahas Pasha, submitted a bill to the Egyptian Parliament calling for the abrogation of the 1936 Anglo-Egyptian Treaty and the 1899 Sudan Condominium

Agreement. Under the pressure of the threatened abrogation, the Foreign Office was anxious to present the MEC proposals to Egypt without delay. However, on 9 October, Stevenson, the British Ambassador in Cairo, warned the Foreign Offfice that no further approach should be made to Egypt, as it would be rejected immediately and would give the Egyptian government the chance to make additional capital out of their action. Stevenson argued that the MEC proposals would cause stupefaction in Egypt. They would undermine the confidence of Britain's friends and would be generally regarded as further evidence of Britain's weakness. The proposals would not satisfy Egypt's national aspirations, since they did not immediately offer a step towards Egypt's accomplishment of these greater than the conditional offer to withdraw a portion of British troops.[59]

On the same day, Morrison sent a telegram to Stevenson, warning that the British government would not be deterred by the Egyptian government's manoeuvres from presenting the MEC proposals as they stood to the Egyptian government. He noted that the chances of the Egyptian government accepting them had been greatly reduced but nonetheless Britain's position, if it was obliged to stand on its treaty rights, would have been strengthened by the presentation and publication of the MEC proposals.[60]

On 10 October, the American, British, French and Turkish Ambassadors met at the British Embassy in Cairo and agreed with Stevenson that to proceed with the proposals would only invite rejection. They suggested that the four governments should issue statements regretting that Egypt's attitude made it impossible to proceed with the new proposals, which should at least wait until after the British general election, due to take place on 28 October.[61] Morrison remained firm: on the same day, he wired back that Britain would continue to stand on her existing treaty rights pending agreement on the MEC proposals. He stated that he knew that there was little chance of acceptance at that time, but the situation might not improve later. He pointed out that Britain's position of standing on the 1936 Treaty would be justified if the MEC proposals were rejected by Egypt. He added that MEC would be set up whether Egypt wanted it or not. The Foreign Office was also afraid of losing the support of the United States, Turkey and France, if the proposals were not presented at once.[62]

On 12 October, Morrison, in a letter to Acheson, said that the British government was still determined to proceed with MEC, and had reached the limits of its concessions to Egypt. He said that Britain would stand on her rights under the 1936 Treaty and continue to stay in the Canal zone no matter what pressure Egypt brought to bear, and that if things did not work out, MEC would be set up without Egypt, and its headquarters established on Cyprus. At the same time Britain would hold the Suez Canal base for allied use until an agreement was reached with Egypt.[63]

On 13 October, the four powers' Ambassadors in Cairo invited Egypt to join MEC as a founder member on a basis of equality and partnership with the other founder members. The wording was made as attractive as possible, emphasizing Egypt's role in the Free World and the benefits which Egypt would gain by participating in MEC. According to the MEC proposals, British forces which were not allocated to the Allied Middle East Command would be withdrawn from Egypt. The British base in the Suez Canal Zone would become an Allied base within the Allied Middle East Command, with full Egyptian participation in the running of this base in peace and war. The proposals also provided for the setting up of an air defence organization, including both Egyptian and Allied forces, with joint responsibility to the Egyptian government and to the Allied Middle East Command. The proposals were considered to provide a possible solution to the Anglo-Egyptian dispute over the status of the Suez Canal base, and it was hoped that through this device it would be possible to satisfy Egyptian national aspirations while maintaining the extensive installations at the Canal base, considered essential for the Middle East defence. It was also hoped that the Arab states, although they might hesitate to participate fully in MEC, might, through a liaison organization, be brought into an association with the Western Powers.[64]

However, the Egyptian government was in no mood to consider any defence proposal until British troops evacuated the Suez Canal base. On 15 October it rejected the invitation and abrogated the 1936 Treaty and the 1899 Sudan Condominium Agreement. Egypt considered the MEC proposals by far worse than the 1936 treaty itself, since, it argued, a provisional and limited occupation by one state was to be replaced by an occupation of four or more states without any limitation as to time or number. Egypt maintained her demands that British troops should be evacuated from the Canal Zone, and that Britain should recognize the unity of Egypt and Sudan under the Egyptian Crown. As long as there were British forces of occupation in Egypt and the Sudan, Egypt would not consider the MEC proposals or any other proposals.[65]

The four sponsoring powers (the US, the UK, France and Turkey) declined to accept Egypt's initial refusal as a conclusive rejection. Britain stated that the action of the Egyptian government was illegal and without validity, since the 1936 Treaty contained no provision for unilateral denunciation at any time. Britain regarded the 1936 Treaty as remaining in force and declared her intention to stand on her rights under the Treaty and the 1899 Agreement. The United States expressed regret. Acheson sent a general message to the United States Middle East missions that Egypt's rejection of MEC would not prevent the four powers from setting up MEC, and that the United States would continue to support the British position as the Egyptian action was not legal. The State Department suggested that, since the MEC concept had become public knowledge, the sponsoring powers should proclaim openly at an early date the basic political philosophy and principles of the command 'with a view to developing pro-MEC sentiments in the Arab states and Israel'. While generally approving the State Department's view, the Joint Chiefs of Staff believed that creation of the MEC 'would be most difficult under current conditions in the Middle East, and that considerable departure from original concept may have to be made'.[66]

Despite Egypt's rejection, the four sponsoring powers intended to proceed with MEC, and to set it up with or without the participation of Middle East states. This policy was pursued, mainly by Britain, in 1952–53, though the United States remained interested. On 10 November 1951, the four sponsoring powers issued a statement of principles upon which MEC would be based. Significant segments of this declaration were as follows:

(a) The task of the Middle East Command at the outset will be primarily one of planning and providing the Middle East States on their request with assistance in the form of advice and training …

(b) The Supreme Allied Commander Middle East will command forces placed at his disposal....However, the placing of forces under the command of the Supreme Allied Commander Middle East in peacetime is not a prerequisite for joining in the common effort for the defense of the Middle East …

(c) ...All states joining in this enterprise will be individually associated with the Command on the basis of equality through a Middle East Defense Liaison Organization …

(d) The sponsoring states....do not regard the initial form in which the Middle East Command will be organized as unchangeable …[67]

However, this statement had no discernible effect on Egypt. The MEC idea existed on paper, but it proved to be difficult to bring it into reality. The United States was not willing to commit forces. The Turkish government was still reluctant to join MEC, preferring NATO as they believed they would receive more American military aid. Moreover, there was lack of enthusiasm among Middle East states to participate, and Anglo-Egyptian relations rapidly worsened.[68]

On 14 November, General Bradley met the British Chiefs of Staff and proposed an Aegean Command which Turkey and Greece would join and an

MEC which would be established separately; the two commands would be gradually linked together. The British Chiefs of Staff wanted the two commands to be set up simultaneously.[69] During the NATO Council meeting in Rome on 27 November, the United States, Britain and France agreed that Greece and Turkey should join either an Aegean or an Eastern Mediterranean Command under SHAPE. An MEC under British command should be set up on Cyprus, and the two commands should be closely linked. 'The higher direction of MEC would come from the US, UK, French and Turkish Chiefs of Staff, and Britain would be responsible for setting it up.'[70]

By the end of 1951, the United States was beginning to realize that Britain was losing the initiative in the Middle East, and that the United States should prepare a more forward Middle East policy. On 12 December, State Department officials met with the Joint Chiefs of Staff to discuss Britain's position in the region. They concluded that 'the [military] bases can no longer be regarded as operational bases. This puts us in a precarious position in the Middle East.' They therefore suggested that the MEC idea should be redrafted to make it more acceptable to Egypt. At the end of December, the National Security Council concluded that the rapidly declining capabilities of Britain in the Middle East made it necessary for the United States to review its policies. On 29 December, Acheson wrote to the new Secretary of Defence, Robert Lovett, that an MEC headquarters should be established on Cyprus no later than April 1952, with staff officers from the participating countries. He pointed out that the MEC idea should be made a physical entity, since it had been announced publicly.[71]

However, in early 1952, from the British point of view, to set up MEC still seemed to be possible. The Conservative government, which came in office in October 1951, was even more enthusiastic than the previous Labour government. In January the Prime Minister, Winston Churchill, and the Foreign Secretary, Anthony Eden, went to Washington to work out the Anglo-American differences over the MEC and to obtain American support for the British position in Egypt. At his meeting with President Truman on 9 January, Churchill said that Britain was keeping troops in Egypt to protect the Suez Canal, not for imperial designs. In his view, this should be an international task, and he suggested that the four powers should send token forces to Suez, which would allow Britain to evacuate most of her troops from Egypt. Churchill argued that Egypt would adopt a more positive attitude if she was confronted by an allied approach. Furthermore, the British desired a British General in command of the MEC and of the Eastern Command of SACEUR and preferred that he be the same person, wearing two hats. The British wished to obtain an agreement on the relationship between the two commands.[72]

The United States position involved a more political approach, and was based on bringing as many Arab states as possible into the MEC. The United States sought through the MEC to gain active Middle Eastern co-operation with the West in the defence of the Middle East. The MEC would also offer a possible solution of the Anglo-Egyptian problem. However, the United States was not inclined to take preparatory steps towards the establishment of the MEC until Turkey and Greece had entered NATO and full agreement had been reached on these two states' relationship to the NATO Command structure. The State Department made it clear to the Foreign Office that the United States did not envisage any further extension of its military commitments in the Middle East, and its participation in the MEC should not involve the commitment of American troops. United States participation should be limited to participation in the integrated command staff and to the provision of some military aid.[73]

By the end of January, the British government had concluded that there was no immediate prospect of getting Egypt to join the MEC as a founder member, and in a memorandum dated 28 January it informed the United States that there should be no further delay in taking the first step to establish the MEC. The British government proposed to set up a nucleus Middle East Command Organization in Cyprus in accordance with the principles set out in the Quadripartite Declaration of November 1951.[74]

As a result, the British government urged that the seven sponsoring powers (UK, US, France, Turkey, Australia, New Zealand and South Africa) of the MEC should meet in London in early March to take the first steps towards the establishment of a MEC. The British government also realized that Turkey would not join in any discussions on the MEC until she had been finally admitted to NATO; hence the British government proposed that the politico-military talks in London should begin after the NATO Council meeting in Lisbon in February. The British view was that the Council should agree that Turkey and Greece should form part of Admiral Carney's Southern Command, and should pass a resolution to this effect, to come into force automatically on their entry into NATO. From the British point of view, this would allay Turkey's fear that she would be side-tracked into the MEC before her position in NATO was firm. It should also win Turkey's agreement to start discussions on the MEC immediately after Lisbon.[75]

The State Department welcomed the new British initiative. It recognized that the establisment of the nucleus Middle East Command Organization in Cyprus was a second-best solution, compared to its establishment with the concurrence of the Egyptian government in the Suez base. The State Department also favoured the British suggestion for the inclusion of Greek and Turkish forces in Admiral Carney's Command.[76]

On 18 February, Turkey finally joined NATO and attended the Lisbon meeting of the Atlantic Council on 20–25 February as a full member. The

Turks saw this as the confirmation of their status as a European nation. They had previously made it clear that they did not regard association with the proposed MEC as a satisfactory alternative to joining SHAPE, and that nothing less than full integration into the European Command, under the same conditions as other members of the treaty, would be acceptable to them. They were therefore pleased when it was announced on 25 February that the North Atlantic Council, meeting in Lisbon, had agreed that Turkey's land and air foces would be placed under Admiral Carney's South European Command. But they still had one reserve: they were reluctant to place their land forces under the commander of an Italian general. Again matters were arranged to their satisfaction. In July 1952, a South Eastern sector of the South European Command was formed, and in September an American officer, General Wyman, established the Headquarters of this sector in Izmir.[77]

The United States government was in general agreement with British ideas regarding the importance of co-ordinated planning for the establishment of the MEC. However, from the State Department's point of view, the difficulty in the plan proposed by Britain was that it would involve only a meeting of the UK, US, France, Turkey, Australia, New Zealand and South Africa to plan for the establishment of MEC, without the presence of any Middle East state, and without provision for any Arab state or Israel to be consulted. The State Department therefore suggested that the London meeting should be described as 'preliminary', and held very quietly at a working level. In the meantime, the State Department suggested, the British government should approach the new Egyptian government, which had come to power on 28 January, with regard to the new MEC proposals. The American fear was that if Britain moved too far too fast without Egypt while there remained a reasonable prospect of securing Egyptian co-operation, the US might lessen its chances of securing a settlement with Egypt regarding the Suez Canal base. The State Department concluded that in the light of the Anglo-Egyptian negotiations, the four powers (UK, US, France and Turkey) should decide whether a planning meeting regarding MEC was desirable and, if such a meeting was agreed upon, where, when and at what level it should take place.[78]

On 11 February, Eden presented a new policy to the Cabinet, which was intended to reopen the talks with Egypt. He proposed that the MEC should be a part of an overall agreement with Egypt, which would also define the future of the Suez Canal base, and the status of British troops there. When Egypt agreed to join the MEC, talks would begin with the other powers. However, at a Cabinet meeting a week later, Churchill objected to handing the Suez base to Egypt before the MEC was set up, and said that the base should come directly under MEC control. In his view, the four powers should have talks with Egypt immediately. Eden pointed out that the Egyptians wanted bilateral talks with Britain first, not with the other powers. As a result, in March, a new approach was made to Egypt, and talks between the British and Egyptian governments continued until June without any success.[79]

Meanwhile the Americans, too, were defining their ideas. On 17 March, a National Intelligence Estimate concluded that a settlement of the Anglo-Egyptian dispute was essential to the establishment of any inclusive Middle East defence organization. Egypt would not join until its dispute with Britain was settled, and no Arab state was likely to if Egypt did not. However, a settlement of the Anglo-Egyptian dispute that would permit Egyptian participation in a Middle East defence organization would require British acceptance of at least the principle of early and complete evacuation of British troops from Egypt, and British recognition of King Farouk's title as king of the Sudan as well as of Egypt. Moreover, the National Intelligence Estimate concluded, in the long run, the Arab–Israeli dispute would have to be solved in order to establish an effective Middle East defence organization.[80]

On 16 April, a State-Defense Working Group on the MEC suggested that the MEC should be established as soon as possible, with headquarters in Cyprus; that the Supreme Allied Commander Middle East, a British national, should be appointed; that there should be some kind of authority for the direction of SACME, such as a Military Committee or a Standing Group; that SACME should devote himself to 'planning, co-ordinating and liaison'; and that liaison between SACME and the interested Arab states should be maintained by a Middle East Defence Liaison Organization. However, the working group suggested a new name instead of MEC. They proposed a 'Middle East Defence Organization' (MEDO), which, they thought, would sound less like a military command and less offensive to Arab ears. The Working Group recommended that the United States should support the establishment of a MEDO in the belief that such an organization might contribute to the political stabilization of the Middle East, and in the long run increase the capacity of the area to resist Soviet aggression, but urged that the United States's participation in the command should be limited to participation in the integrated command staff and the provision of some military aid to certain states in the Middle East. No commitment of United States forces to the defence of the Middle East should be contemplated.[81]

On 24 April, State Department officials discussed the report prepared by the State-Defense Working Group and decided to go along with the establishment of the MEDO without delay, but decided that it should be only a political entity at first. The State Department warned that to go ahead without the Arabs might be dangerous and destructive, as it might be construed by the Arabs as a combination of the West against the Middle East.[82] On the same day, at a National Security Council meeting, the State Department recommended that the United States should take more responsibility for the Middle East, in co-operation with Britain, France and Turkey through MEDO. The State Department indicated that the United States and Britain could no longer defend the Middle East in the 'old 19th century fashion', and the Middle East states had to be recognized as part of the 'community of nations'. From the State Department's point of view, MEDO was important for encouraging co-operation and its establishment was a worthwhile objective. Therefore, the United States should assist Britain to set it up.[83]

On 29 April, the British Embassy in Washington handed the State Department a memorandum proposing that the proposed Seven-Power meeting on MEC should be further postponed until the Anglo-Egyptian negotiations became clearer, and suggesting the desirability of inviting Egypt and Iraq, but none of the other Arab states, to such a meeting when held. Egypt would be invited because of its political and strategic importance. Iraq would be invited because of its friendly interest in the MEC, its strategic importance and its economic and military potential. The argument against bringing in any other Arab states, other than Egypt and Iraq, was that it would make the conference unmanageable, would confront Britain with an Arab League bloc within it, and would highlight the exclusion of Israel.[84]

The State Department shared the British view in favour of postponing the conference of the seven sponsoring powers until the outcome of the Anglo-Egyptian negotiations became clearer. However, the State Department doubted the wisdom of an exclusive invitation of Iraq and Egypt to the planning meeting, at least unless these countries alone indicated willingness to provide important base rights to MEC. Otherwise such discrimination would violate the important principle of area-wide co-operation on a basis of equality, which the State Department considered a feature fundamental to the success of the MEC concept. Although convinced of the desirability of consulting the Arab states while MEDO was still in the planning stage, the State Department was equally convinced that prior to such consultation, it was essential to co-ordinate the views of the seven sponsoring powers concerning the general character and structure of an organization acceptable to the Arab states. After this co-ordination, the State Department thought, all Arab states should be approached at the same time and on the same basis, with a view to obtaining their reactions to the proposals considered acceptable by the seven powers. In addition, when the Arab states were approached, the State Department believed that it would be desirable to inform Israel of developments and reassure the Israeli government that Israel's security and interests would be safeguarded.[85]

However, in June, the Anglo-Egyptian negotiations collapsed. Therefore, the British government decided it could no longer delay a meeting of the seven sponsoring powers, and on 18 June it gave the United States a memorandum regarding establishment of a MEDO. The British government proposed to create a 'planning, co-ordinating and liaison organization' which would eventually evolve into 'a full-fledged defence organization' and suggested changing the name from 'Middle East Command' (MEC) to 'Middle East Defence Organization' (MEDO).[86]

The idea of setting up a MEC or MEDO with or without the Arab states was pursued mainly by Britain in 1952–53 though the United States remained interested. Nevertheless, faced with the ongoing argument over the structure of MEDO and the continuing difficulties with the Arab states, the United States began to lose interest in MEDO. American support for the concept of MEDO was to be gradually withdrawn by the new Republican Administration, which came into office in January 1953. With the failure of British plans for an Egypt-centred defence organization, the new Administration was beginning to look to Turkey and Pakistan to form the core of an anti-Soviet bloc in the Middle East.

NOTES

1. CAB 129/45 CP(51)95, 30 March 1951. PREM8/1432, 'Alignment of US-UK policy in Middle East', 11 Sep. 1951. Peter L. Hahn, 'Containment and Egyptian Nationalism: The Unsuccessful Effort to Establish the Middle East Command, 1950–53', *Diplomatic History*, Vol.II, No.1 (Winter 1987), pp.23–40.
2. *FRUS*, 1950, Vol.V, pp.1–8.
3. Roger Bullen and M.E. Pelly (eds.), *Documents on British Policy Overseas, Series 2, Vol.2* (London, 1987), document 65i. George McGhee, *Envoy to the Middle World: Adventures in Diplomacy* (New York, 1983), pp.205–12. Wm. Roger Louis, *The British Empire in the Middle East, 1945–1951: Arab Nationalism, The United States, and Postwar Imperialism* (Oxford, 1984), pp.583–9.

   NSC65/3, approved by President Truman on 19 May 1950, affirmed that United States security interests required a military strengthening of Middle Eastern countries by friendly sources. Nonetheless, major responsibility in the Middle East would rest with Britain. See *FRUS*, 1950, Vol.V, pp.163–6.

   However, on 25 May, the United States agreed with Britain and France to issue a joint declaration, the so-called Tripartite Declaration, which attempted to preserve the existing armistice lines between Israel and the Arab countries, and to control the supply of arms to both sides. According to the declaration, arms would be provided to these states only on the assurance that they were required for self-defence. Although the declaration was largely ineffective to end the arms race between Israel and the Arabs, it was the first sign of Western co-operation in the Middle East. The United States, for the first time, had publicly committed itself to regular consultation with Britain over Middle Eastern issues. See Shlomo Slonim, 'Origin of the 1950 Tripartite Declaration on the Middle East', *Middle Eastern Studies*, Vol.23, No.2 (April 1987), pp.135–49. *FRUS*, 1950, Vol.III, pp.975–84. *FRUS*, 1950, Vol.V, pp.141–6.

By offering military aid to those states volunteering 'to play their part in the defense of the area as a whole', the declaration was also intended to lay the foundations of a regional collective security system. See Wm. Roger Louis and Roger Owen (eds.), *Suez 1956: The Crisis and Its consequences* (Oxford, 1989), pp.19–29.

At the beginning, the Tripartite Declaration remained influential but finally proved wholly ineffectual. Long afterwards, Dean Acheson admitted that the Declaration served no useful purpose and implied that it was ill-conceived. See Dean Acheson, *Present at the Creation: My Years in the State Department* (London, 1969), p.396.

4. David Devereux, *The Formulation of British Defence Policy towards the Middle East, 1948–1956* (London, 1990), p.46.
5. CAB 131/9 DO(50)40, 19 May 1950. Louis, *The British Empire in the Middle East, 1945–1951*, op. cit., p.583.
6. PREM8/1359, 'Copy of letter from Slim to King Farouk', 13 July 1950. Louis, op. cit., p.589.
7. Geoffrey Aronson, *From Sideshow To Center Stage: U.S. Policy Toward Egypt 1946–1956* (Boulder, CO, 1986), pp.17–22, 25. Devereux, *The Formulation of British Defence Policy towards the Middle East*, op. cit., pp.39–42.
8. Robert J. Donovan, *The Presidency of Harry S. Truman: The Tumultuous Years, 1949–1953* (New York, 1982), pp.204–5.
9. *FRUS*, 1950, Vol.V, pp.188–92. *FRUS*, 1950, Vol.I, pp.367–9.
10. Ibid.
11. Louis, op. cit., pp.588–9, 714.
12. *FRUS*, 1950, Vol.V, pp.188–192.
13. *FRUS*, 1950, Vol.III, pp.233–8, 1686–9, 1691–993. *FRUS*, 1950, Vol.V, pp.193–6, 217–38, 591–3, 610–11.
14. For Turkey's search for security after the Second World War, See E. Athanassopoulou, 'Western Defence Developments and Turkey's Search for Security in 1948', *Middle Eastern Studies*, Vol.32, No.2 (April 1996), pp.77–108.
15. The statements made by Bevin and Acheson at the time of the signature of the Atlantic Pact, and again at the conclusion of the Tripartite Foreign Ministers' meeting in London in May 1950 made it clear that both the United States and Britain were concerned for the continued independence and integrity of Turkey, Greece and Iran. Bevin, on 19 May 1950, reaffirmed 'that H.M.G. remain vitally concerned in the independence, integrity, and security of Greece, Turkey and Persia ... H.M.G. are determined to continue their policy of direct support to them and to other countries who are striving through military and economic efforts to safeguard their independence and territorial integrity'. Acheson spoke in similar terms. See Margaret Carlyle (ed.), *Documents on International Affairs, 1949–1950* (London, 1953), pp.76–9. See also FO 371/87949/RK1071/23, Minute by Wright, 26 July 1950.
16. J.C. Hurewitz, *Diplomacy in the Near and Middle East: A Documentary Record: 1914–1956, Vol.II* (Princeton, 1956), pp.226–8.
17. The May 1950 election defeat of the Republican Peoples' Party (the RPP), who had been in power since the establishment of the Republic in 1923, resulted in a change of direction in Turkey's political life. The electorate gave their votes in a large majority to the Democrat Party (the DP) as a protest against the economic difficulties they had lived under RPP rule, particularly during the war, and to bring an end to the rule of single party elite in the government. Thus began a decade of Democrat rule. In spite of the radical changes to take place in Turkey's domestic policy under DP rule, a similar change was not to occur in the country's foreign policy. The DP's election campaign was largely focused on domestic issues, proposing to change economical management by moving towards liberalization of the economy and political life. The only foreign policy matter made an issue during the election was the accession of Turkey to NATO. On coming to power, the Democrats pointed out that they would not make any radical change to Turkey's foreign policy. In fact, it was soon realized that the difference between the Democrats and their predecessors was in the execution of the policies, not in the policies themselves. Concerning Turkey's admission to NATO, the West met with increasing pressure to accept it. The outbreak of the Korean War on 25 June 1950, one month after the Democrats' victory, meant that the new government

could pursue its campaign for NATO membership with more conviction. As a result, the government decided to send 4,500 troops to Korea on 18 July 1950, hoping for an easy accession to NATO.

18. FO 371/87933/RK1011/1, Charles to McNeil, 4 January 1950. FO 371/87949/RK1071/31, Charles to Bevin, 15 Aug. 1950. FO 371/87948/RK1071/16, Minute by Rumbold, 16 June 1950. FO 371/87949/RK1071/34, Minute by Rumbold, 9 Aug. 1950. NA-RG 59–680.82/11–1552, 'Turkish Relations with the Arab States and Iran'.

    On Turkey's participation in the Middle East Command and her admission to NATO, see Ömer E. Kürkçüoğu, *Türkiye'nin Arab Ortadoğusuna Karşı Politikası, 1945–1970* (Ankara, 1972), pp.33–47. Bülent Ali Rıza, 'Turkish Participation in Middle East Defence Projects and Its Impact on Turco-Arab Relations, May 1950–June 1953' (unpublished PhD thesis, St Antony's College, Oxford, 1982).

    In early 1950, the Turkish government had in mind some kind of Eastern Mediterranean Pact, linked with the Atlantic Pact. The Turkish argument was that the security of the Middle East was a complementary part of Western Europe security. However, according to the British Ambassador to Turkey, the Turkish government's real aim in urging the formation of an Eastern Mediterranean Pact was to involve the Western Powers in more specific guarantees of Turkish security. See FO 371/95267/RK1011/1, Charles to Bevin, 8 Jan. 1951. See also Ayşegül Sever, *Soğuk Savaş Kuşatmasında Türkiye, Batı ve Orta Doğu, 1945–1958* (Istanbul, 1997), pp.60–61.
19. FO 371/87948/RK1071/11, Minute by William Strang, 31 May 1950 and 1 June 1950. FO 371/87948/RK1071/16, Minute by Rumbold, 16 June 1950. FO 371/87948/RK1071/18, Minute by Rumbold, 1 August 1950.
20. DEFE5/23 COS(50)331, 28 Aug. 1950. DEFE4/36 JP(50)138, 13 Oct. 1950. *FRUS*, 1950, Vol.III, pp.1218–20, 1284–5. McGhee, op. cit., pp.265–76. Peter L. Hahn, op. cit., pp.23–40. Melvyn P. Leffler, 'Strategy, Diplomacy, and the Cold War: The United States, Turkey, and NATO, 1945–1952', *Journal of American History 71*, March 1985, pp.807–25.
21. FO 371/95267/RK1011/1, Charles to Bevin, 8 Jan. 1951. Turkey offered the United Nations a brigade of 4,500 fully equipped troops, which arrived in Korea in Nov. 1950.
22. FO 371/87949/RK1071/34, Minute by Rumbold, 9 Aug. 1950. FO 371/87949/RK1071/42G, FO to Washington, 7 Sept. 1950.
23. Ibid.
24. DEFE4/36 JP(50)138, 13 Oct. 1950. *FRUS*, 1950, Vol.III, pp.1218–20, 1284–5. Peter L. Hahn, op. cit., pp.23–40. Melvyn P. Leffler, op. cit., pp.807–25. McGhee, op. cit., pp.265–76. According to the British Ambassador to Turkey, Noel Charles, the Turkish government was greatly disappointed when Turkey's admission was rejected, but regarded Turkey's acceptance as an 'associate member' as a first step towards admission to the Atlantic Pact itself, and it would not relax its efforts to obtain full membership of the pact. Charles commented that membership of the Atlantic Pact was desired primarily because it would carry an American guarantee with it. (FO 371/95267/RK1011/1, Charles to Bevin, 8 Jan. 1951).
25. *FRUS*, 1951, Vol.V, pp.4–6.
26. Acheson, op. cit., pp.562–563. *FRUS*, 1951, Vol.V, p.22.
27. *FRUS*, 1951, Vol.V, pp.29–36. McGhee, op. cit., pp.265–6.
28. Ibid.
29. McGhee, op. cit., pp.265–266. *FRUS*, 1951, Vol.V, pp.56–60, 114–15.
30. DEFE5/27 COS(51)43, 30 Jan. 1951. DEFE4/40 JP(51)22, 9 Feb. 1951. Devereux, op. cit., pp.48–50.
31. FO 371/95284/RK1073/31G, Minute by Cheetham, 1 March 1951. FO 371/95284, FO to Ankara, 21 Feb. 1951. FO 371/95284, Charles to FO, 26 Feb. 1951. FO 195/2672, Minute by E.M., 6 Dec. 1951.DEFE4/40 JP(51)22, 9 Feb. 1951. CAB 129/45 C.P.(51)130, 'Admission of Greece and Turkey to the North Atlantic Treaty', 17 May 1951.
32. DEFE5/29 COS(51)167, 28 March 1951. On 14 March, the National Security Council adopted NSC 47/4, which was approved by President Truman on March 17 as NSC 47/5. According to this paper, the United States would attempt to reverse recent adverse trends by endeavouring to establish the concept of regional defence co-operation in the Middle East.

To this end, NSC 47/5 concluded, the United States and Britain should obtain the military rights in the region that they considered necessary. Also, they should initiate a limited arms supply programme to the Middle Eastern countries and provide early deliveries of token quantities of equipment. See Walter S. Poole, *The History of the Joint Chiefs of Staff: The Joint Chiefs of Staff and National Policy*, Vol.4, 1950–1952 (Washington, 1980), p.335.

33. FO 371/95285/RK1073/38, Washington to FO, 3 March 1951. FO 371/95284/K1073/28, Washington to FO, 21 Feb. 1951. CAB 131/11 DO(51)57, 4 May 1951.
34. Hurewitz, op. cit., pp.226–8.
35. CAB 129/45 CP(51)95, 30 March 1951. CAB 128/19 CM24(51), 5 April 1951. McGhee, op. cit., pp.367, 377–8.
36. FO 371/96845/JE1011/2, Creswell to Eden, 26 June 1952. CAB 131/11 DO(51)57, 4 May 1951. McGhee, op. cit., p.367.

Meanwhile, Britain also faced a problem with Iran concerning the Anglo-Iranian Oil Company (AIOC). On 15 March, the Iranian government announced the nationalization of Iran's oil industry, in which Britain had a major share. The controversy over the AIOC dated back to 1947, when the Iranian Majlis had requested the Iranian government to review the Anglo-Iranian oil concession of 1933. In July 1949, a supplementary oil agreement was initialled between the Iranian government and the AIOC, providing Iran with more favourable arrangements than the 1933 agreement. However, a year later, the Oil Commission of the Majlis recommended its rejection. The Prime Minister, General Razmara, appealed to the AIOC to make the supplementary agreement more appealing by giving more concessions, which the AIOC refused. Meanwhile, in January 1951, the Arabian-American Oil Company (Aramco) announced a new deal with the Saudi Arabian government based on a fifty-fifty system of profit-sharing. This removed any credibility from the supplementary agreement. On 8 March the Oil Commission recommended the nationalization of Iran's oil industry to the Majlis, which accepted the nationalization bill on 15 March. Britain did not accept the nationalization of Iran's oil industry. Anglo-Iranian relations were overshadowed by the oil dispute, which developed into a long-drawn affair. In April, Mossadegh, the leader of the nationalist movement, became Prime Minister. The Soviets tried to take advantage, through the Communist Tudeh Party, of the tensions created by the nationalization of Iran's oil industry. On 1 May the Tudeh Party, officially outlawed, organized a mass anti-Western demonstration in Tehran, which caused great concern in the United States, where it was feared that if the Mossadegh government fell, Iran would be dragged behind the Iron Curtain. Therefore, although it proclaimed its neutrality in the conflict between Iran and Britain, the United States later tried to mediate and bring about an amicable settlement between the two countries. See McGhee, op. cit., pp.318–44, 388–404. Acheson, op. cit., pp.499–511. Louis, op. cit., pp.632–89. FO 371/91448, 'Annual Review of Iran: 1950'. FO 371/98593, 'Annual Review of Iran: 1951'. FO 371/109988, 'Annual Review of Iran: 1952'. Also, see H.W. Brands, 'The Cairo-Tehran Connection in Anglo-American Rivalry in the Middle East, 1951–1953', *The International History Review*, Vol.XI (1989), pp.434–56. Hurewitz, op. cit., pp.188–96, 305–308.

37. DEFE4/42 JP(51)88, 10 May 1951. DEFE4/43 COS(51) 84th meeting, 21 May 1951. DEFE5/31 COS(51)309, 28 May 1951. *FRUS*, 1951, Vol.V, pp.144–7.
38. CAB 128/19 CM36(51), 22 May 1951. CAB 129/45 C.P.(51)132, 'Turkey and Greece and the North Atlantic Treaty', 17 May 1951.
39. *FRUS*, 1951, Vol.V, pp.144–7. *FRUS*, 1951, Vol.III, pp.522–4.
40. DEFE4/43 COS(51)91st meeting, 4 June 1951. CAB 131/10 DO(51)15th meeting, 7 June 1951.
41. *FRUS*, 1951, Vol.III, pp.537–541. CAB 131/11 DO(51)81, 28 June 1951.
42. DEFE4/44 COS(51)100th meeting, 20 June 1951. DEFE4/44 COS(51) 103rd meeting, 25 June 1951.
43. DEFE4/44 COS(51)109th meeting, 2 July 1951. DEFE4/45 JP(51)129, 24 July 1951. DEFE4/45 JP(51)130, 24 July 1951. DEFE4/45 JP(51)131, 23 July 1951. CAB 131/10 DO(51) 18th meeting, 2 July 1951. *FRUS*, 1951, Vol.III, pp.552–4.

Indeed, in July 1951, Turkish Foreign Minister Fuat Köprülü wrote to the British Foreign Secretary, Herbert Morrison, that 'once the security of Turkey is assured by her inclusion in the Atlantic Pact, we will be ready to assume our full share and play the role which falls upon us in concerting with Great Britain, the United States and France in all adequate and effective measures taken in agreement between our four governments'. See FO 195/2667, FO to Charles, Annex D, Part II, 'Turkish assurances that they will play their part in the Middle East Defence', 4 Oct. 1951.

44. CAB 129/46 CP(51)214, 27 July 1951.
45. FO 141/1442/1077/24/51G, Stevenson to Bowker, 31 July 1951.
46. *FRUS*, 1951, Vol.V, pp.162–3, 372–5.
47. Poole, op. cit., pp.338–9.
48. DEFE4/46 PAO/P(51)54, 1 Sept. 1951.
49. Devereux, op. cit., p.57.
50. DEFE4/44 COS(51) 109th meeting, 2 July 1951. DEFE4/45 JP(51)129, 24 July 1951. DEFE4/45 JP(51)130, 24 July 1951. DEFE4/45 JP(51)131, 23 July 1951. CAB 131/10 DO(51)18th meeting, 2 July 1951. *FRUS*, 1951, Vol.III, pp.552–4.
51. Ibid. According to Acheson's recollection, the Defence Department accepted this plan because it would continue Britain's primary responsibility for defence of the Middle East; the State Department concurred because it could discern 'no practicable alternative'; Britain approved because creation of MEC would allow British forces to stay in Suez without incurring the odium of 'occupation'. See Acheson, op. cit., pp.563–4.
52. *FRUS*, 1951, Vol.III, pp.1232, 1291, 1261–3. Acheson, op. cit., pp.563–4. PREM8/1432, Washington Talks, 10–14 Sept. 1951. PREM8/1379, Ottawa Talks, 14–20 Sep. 1951. CAB 129/47 CP(51)266, 22 Oct. 1951. McGhee, op. cit., pp.272–4.
53. *FRUS*, 1951, Vol.III, pp.725–30. CAB 129/47 CP(51)266, 22 Oct. 1951. Acheson, op. cit., pp.563–4. McGhee, op. cit., pp.272–4. Leffler, op. cit., pp.807–25. PREM8/1379, Ottawa Talks, 14–20 Sept. 1951. D.J.K., 'Greece, Turkey and NATO', *The World Today*, Vol.VIII, No.4, April 1952, pp.162–9.
54. Ibid.
55. CAB 129/47 CP(51)266, 22 October 1951. *FRUS*, 1951, Vol.III, pp.580–81, 592–3. WO 216/795, Minute by Rose, 24 Oct. 1951. PREM8/1379, Ottawa Talks, 14–20 Sept. 1951. PREM 8/1379, from Ministry of Defence to Washington, 18 Oct. 1951.
56. Ibid. The main motive in Turkish politics at that time was passion for being European. It might seem absurd but at that time the Turkish government virtually committed itself to the Turkish public to obtaining recognition of Turkish Europeanism in co-operation in NATO. See Sever, op. cit., p.92.
57. FO 141/1452, Telegram from Cairo to the Foreign Office, 3 Oct. 1951.
58. CAB 130/71 Gen.382/1st meeting, 4 Oct. 1951.
59. FO 141/1452, Telegram from Alexandria to the Foreign Office, 9 Oct. 1951. PREM11/92, 'Events leading up to the Egyptian Government's abrogation of the 1936 Treaty and 1899 Condominium Agreement', Stevenson to Morrison, 16 Oct. 1951.
60. FO 141/1452, Telegram from FO to Alexandria, 9 Oct. 1951.
61. FO 141/1452, Record of meeting, 10 Oct. 1951.
62. FO 141/1452, Telegram from the Foreign Office to Alexandria, 10 Oct. 1951.
63. *FRUS*, 1951, Vol.V, pp.
64. Hurewitz, op. cit., pp.329–331. FO 371/90182/JE11910/96, Stevenson to FO, 13 Oct. 1951. FO 371/90182/JE11910/109, Stevenson to FO, 15 Oct. 1951. FO 371/90182/JE11910/126, Stevenson to Morrison, 13 Oct. 1951. CAB 129/49 C(52)32, 11 Feb. 1952.
65. Ibid., FO 371/90182/JE11910/141, 'A letter from the Egyptian Foreign Minister to the American Ambassador in Cairo', 28 Oct.1951.
66. *FRUS*, 1951, Vol.V, pp.725–30. Poole, op. cit., p.341. PREM11/91, 'Review of internal political developments in Egypt since the formation of Hilali Pasha's government', Stevenson to Eden, 26 April 1952.
67. Hurewitz, op. cit., pp.329–32. WO 216/796, 'Quadripartite Statement on MEC', 10 Nov. 1951.
68. Devereux, op. cit., pp.62–3. Meanwhile, the British position in Egypt became increasingly fragile. After Egypt's rejection of the MEC proposals and abrogation of the 1936 Treaty, anti-British riots broke out around the Suez Canal base. The working of the Suez Canal base itself

had been impeded by the withholding of facilities by the Egyptian government, the withdrawal of the Egyptian labour force employed by Britain in the Canal zone, and strikes of Egyptian technicians. Although the British government sent military reinforcements, the British position in Egypt was deteriorating. See PREM11/91, 'Review of internal political developments in Egypt since the formation of Hilali Pasha's government', Stevenson to Eden, 26 April 1952. Devereux, op. cit., p.63.

69. DEFE4/49 COS(51) 185th meeting, 14 Nov. 1951.
70. DEFE5/35 COS(51)726, 6 Dec. 1951. Devereux, op. cit., p.63.
71. *FRUS*, 1951, Vol.V, pp.258–62, 436.
72. DEFE4/51 JP(52)219, 9 Jan. 1952. DEFE4/51 COS(52)11th meeting, 22 Jan. 1952. *FRUS*, 1952–54, Vol.IX, pp.168–76. Devereux, op. cit., p.66. Acheson, op. cit., pp.565–8.
73. Ibid.
74. FO141/1467, COS(W)210, From Ministry of Defence, London to BJSM, Washington, 28 Jan. 1952. *FRUS*, 1952–54, Vol.IX, pp.178–84. Hurewitz, op. cit., pp.329–32. WO216/796, 'Quadripartite Statement on MEC, 10 Nov. 1951.
75. Ibid.
76. *FRUS*, 1952–54, Vol.IX, pp.178–84, 189–91. FO 141/1467, Copy of a telegram from Washington to Cairo, 8 Feb. 1952. FO 141/1467, Copy of a telegram from Washington to Cairo, 31 Jan.1952.
77. FO 371/107547/WK1011/1, Helm to Eden, 9 Jan. 1953. D.J.K., 'Greece, Turkey and NATO', *The World Today*, Vol.III, No.4, April 1952, pp.162–9.
78. *FRUS*, 1952–54, Vol.IX, pp.178–84, 189–91. FO 141/1467, 'Copy of a telegram from Washington to Cairo', 8 Feb. 1952. FO 141/1467, 'Copy of a telegram from Washington to Cairo', 31 Jan. 1952.

    These Anglo-American discussions had, in fact, taken place against the background of a fresh crisis in Anglo-Egyptian relations. Anti-British riots broke out in Ismailia on 19 Jan. After a sharp action by British troops in disarming the Egyptian auxiliary police, in which 53 of the latter were killed, the riots spread to Cairo. During massive rioting in Cairo on 26 Jan., 26 people (17 of them Europeans) were killed and 552 injured, and 700 buildings, many of them foreign-owned, were burned. King Farouk finally ordered the Egyptian Army to restore order, and dismissed the Nahas government. On 28 Jan., a new government was formed by Ali Maher. See Poole, op. cit., pp.343–4. Acheson, op. cit., pp.565–8. Aronson, op. cit., pp.39–43.

    The thoughts embodied in the British memorandum of January 28 had been prepared before the Maher government assumed office, and as a result, were subsequently altered. The Foreign Office, on 8 Feb., informed the State Department that the British government would not make any attempt at present to fix a date for the Seven-Powers meeting on the MEC or announce the intention to hold a meeting, in the expectation that the new Egyptian government might adopt a better attitude. The United States agreed, but warned the British government not to be too hopeful that Egypt would agree within the next couple of months to a defence arrangement along the lines of the Four Power Defence Proposals of Oct. 1951. See *FRUS*, 1952–54, Vol.IX, pp.186–94. FO 141/1467, 'Copy of a telegram from FO to Cairo', 8 Feb. 1952.

79. CAB 129/49 C(52)32, 11 Feb. 1952. CAB 128/24 CC18(52), 18 Feb. 1952.
80. *FRUS*, 1952–54, Vol.IX, pp.195–9.
81. Ibid., pp.213–18. The names MEC and MEDO were often used interchangeably by both the Foreign Office and the State Department, but MEDO gradually came to predominate.
82. Ibid., pp.195–9, 213–21, 226–8. NA-Lot 57 D 298 Box 16, Folder title: MEDO, From Berry to Matthews, 23 May 1952.
83. Devereux, op. cit., p.67. *FRUS*, 1952–54, Vol.IX, pp.222–6. On 24 April, President Truman approved NSC 129/1, which with respect to the MEC stated that the United States should continue its efforts to establish the command and should be prepared to reinforce political and psychological pressures in the Middle East by assigning United States token forces in a Middle East defence arrangement if United States willingness to take this action was seen to be the key to the establishment of such an arrangement and to the settlement of the dispute between Britain and Egypt. See *FRUS*, 1952–54, Vol.IX, pp.222–6.

84. *FRUS*, 1952–54, Vol.IX, pp.226–32, 234–6. The British had in mind particularly the interest shown by the Iraqi government, who had indicated that they would be willing to participate in a conference with the four sponsoring powers and Egypt. The arguments for inviting Iraq in as a co-founder were: (a) that Iraq alone of the Arab states had shown a keen and friendly interest in the MEC; (b) that after Egypt, Iraq was the most important Arab state in terms of size and economic potential; (c) that Iraq formed with Turkey the Northern bastion for the defence of the Middle East with Egypt as the natural base; d) that Iraq was in a position to provide the MEC with forces and facilities superior to those of any Arab state outside Egypt. However, Britain's main concern seemed to convert the British military rights in Iraq into general MEC rights. See *FRUS*, 1952–54, Vol.IX, pp.226–32, 234–6.
85. Ibid.
86. FO 141/1467, 'United Kingdom draft memorandum on the Allied Middle East Defence Organisation', 5 July 1952. DEFE11/87, 'Record of preliminary negotiations between the seven sponsoring powers for the establishment of a Middle East Defence Organization', Aug. 1952–Feb. 1953. *FRUS*, 1952–54, Vol.IX, pp.247–9.

The 'Forgotten Alliance'? Anglo-Turkish Relations and CENTO, 1959–65

CIHAT GÖKTEPE

CENTO was an important alliance in British policy towards the Middle and Near East. British policy towards Turkey and Anglo-Turkish relations cannot be considered in isolation. They were crucially affected by the revolutionary turmoil in the Middle East in 1958. The military coup in Iraq had taken the Western Powers and the members of the Baghdad Pact[1] completely by surprise, including the British Embassy in Iraq. Early on the morning of Monday 14 July, Macmillan was telephoned by Selwyn Lloyd with the news that there had been a violent revolutionary coup by dissident army units in Baghdad.[2] On the same day the Foreign Secretary, Selwyn Lloyd, also informed the Cabinet about the coup in Iraq:

> The position was obscure; but unconfirmed reports indicated that the insurgents claimed to have overthrown the monarchy and to have established a republican government; that King Feisal, after being initially detained, had been allowed to escape; the crown Prince of Iraq and the Prime Minister Nuri es-Said, had been killed; and that the British Embassy had been burnt and one of the member of its staff had lost his life. We appeared to be maintaining our position at Habbaniya, but it was uncertain how long we could continue to do.[3]

The British government had no intention of becoming involved in any move to restore the Iraqi regime. Prime Minister Macmillan informed the Cabinet on 15 July 1958, and emphasized that they were taking care to protect British citizens and properties adding,

> It would not necessarily be wise that we should become involved in an indefinite commitment to restore the regime in Iraq. Nevertheless we must take such steps as were open to us to protect British lives and property in that country. It might not be feasible to reinforce the station at Habbaniya which, though occupied by some 900 technical personal of the Royal Air Force and still minus wireless communication

> with the United Kingdom, was being closely watched by the rebel forces. But we should warn the insurgents in Baghdad that we should hold them responsible for injury or damage suffered by British lives and property.[4]

The Prime Minister's views were confirmed by the Cabinet at the same meeting. The Cabinet decided to invite the Foreign Secretary to gain further information.

The new military government in Iraq immediately established relations with China, the Soviet Union and other socialist countries, a series of acts that indicated the new government's desire to pursue foreign policies independent of Britain and the West.[5] It appears in retrospect now that the Baghdad Pact helped quicken the rise of nationalism, socialism, and radical regimes in the Middle East. It also speeded up the emergence of Nasser as a leader of the Arab World, brought about the decline of British influence in the Middle East and prepared the ground for Soviet penetration.[6]

This coup also opened a door for new regimes among the other regional members of the Baghdad Pact. In the same year, in October 1958 a military coup in Pakistan took place, as it did two years later in May 1960 in Turkey. The pro-Western Middle East leaders feared military coups and wanted support and military aid from the United States and Britain. Responding to President Chamoun's request just after the Iraqi coup, the US launched an operation on 15 July 1958 against Lebanon and intended to land American troops, without British military support.[7]

King Hussein of Jordan requested assistance immediately after the Iraqi revolution, from the British government and the American administration. The basis of this request was that Jordan was faced with an imminent attempt by the United Arab Republic to create internal disorder and to overthrow the regime, and that Jordan's territorial integrity was threatened by the movement of Syrian forces towards the northern frontier and by the infiltration of arms across it.[8] The Cabinet deliberated for a long time about what the UK response to the King's request should be. At the same time Prime Minister Macmillan had always consulted US President Eisenhower and Secretary of State Dulles. The Foreign Secretary, Selwyn Lloyd, also went to the US to discuss the situation. During the Cabinet meeting of 17 July, Macmillan summed up the position. He emphasized that the UK should intervene in Jordan, because of its political and economic interest in the region. They thought they should support the pro-Western administration in Jordan. Geographically speaking, Jordan was an important location for British interests in the Gulf and in the Middle East. They emphasized that this movement would be restricted in scope and meant to stabilize the existing regime and prevent any disaffection spreading especially from the United Arab Republic. They also considered that this movement would be legal, according to the UN Charter. They explained this situation as a parallel to the US Lebanese landing. The Prime Minister informed the Cabinet:

> Militarily this was a difficult and dangerous operation. But the Chiefs of staff believed that it was soundly planned and capable of achieving the limited objectives proposed for it ... It was difficult to see that it would serve any purpose beyond that of stabilising the existing regime in Jordan and denying this territory for a time to the United Arab Republic (UAR). The political considerations were more evenly balanced. The operation would give rise to a sharp division of opinion in this country and, in view of its limited objectives, it would be difficult to show it had been successful. On the other hand, if we failed to respond to Jordan's appeal and the country passed under the influence of the United Arab Republic, the political position of the United Kingdom Government would be gravely weakened.[9]

The Prime Minister also mentioned that they were still in contact with the American Administration, and Dulles reassured him that the US would give Britain their full support, both in public statements and at the United Nations. He was also ready, on his own authority, to promise logistical support. The regional members of the Baghdad Pact declared their support for US actions in Lebanon and the British action in Jordan. President Eisenhower responded with an oral message to all heads of regional member countries and expressed his gratitude for their support.[10]

At the time when Britain had joined the Baghdad Pact in April 1955, the old Anglo-Iraqi treaty had been abrogated and replaced by a bilateral agreement. Under this Britain was to evacuate the British bases in Iraq, leaving only the RAF staging posts and a military mission, but Britain continued to guarantee the defence of Iraq.[11] The RAF retained the bases of Habbaniya[12] and Shaiba. There were 900 British technical staff; Britain could use this base as she wished according to the bilateral agreement. This base was very important for Britain's Middle Eastern policy. After the revolution Britain also wanted to maintain this base (Habbaniya) as long as she could. According to Humphrey Trevelyan, who was British ambassador in Baghdad, in the spring of 1959 Qasim told him that he agreed to staging rights for the RAF provided that the Iraqi Air Force were in charge. He wrote about this situation to London and recommended that the remaining RAF personnel should leave Iraq, since they were doing no good by staying. Their arms were locked up, so they could not defend themselves against attack.[13]

On receiving the news about the revolution the important question of the British base at Habbaniya was also raised at the Cabinet Meeting on 15 July

1958. Duncan Sandys preferred to anticipate rather than face a potential humiliating withdrawal of British forces. The Cabinet also agreed with Trevelyan's views during the meeting of 25 March when the Defence Secretary Duncan Sandys informed the Cabinet about the new situation in Iraq.

> In the light of the announcement on the previous day that Iraq had ceased to be a member of the Baghdad Pact, the RAF personnel at Habbaniya no longer served any military purpose and should now be withdrawn. It would be preferable that we should take the initiative in this matter and should not await a demand from the Iraqi Government for the withdrawal of these units ... the Cabinet agreed that the United Kingdom Government intended to withdraw the RAF personnel from Habbaniya at the earliest practicable date.[14]

Eight months after the revolution, by the end of March 1959, the British technical mission left Iraq.[15] This decision was important because it meant that the last British troops were leaving Basra. Trevelyan emphasized that he was heartily glad that they had got them out without incident.[16] As already mentioned Selwyn Lloyd did not wish it to appear that Britain had been pushed out of Habbaniya and that Britain's policy was to be dictated to by the Iraqis. The revolutionaries in Iraq tried to improve their relations with the Soviet Union and with neutral countries. At the same time they wanted to let their relations with Britain lapse. After this Britain had to try to maintain its Middle Eastern interests with bases outside the Middle East, i.e., in Cyprus and in the Eastern Mediterranean.

The coup in Baghdad brought Macmillan's 'grand design' in the region into question. Iraq was the cornerstone of British policy in the Middle East. Iraq was a source of Britain and Europe's oil supply. Furthermore, Iraq was Britain's only Arab ally in the region and in rivalry with Nasser for Arab leadership. Britain also had tremendous investments in oil there and in nearby Kuwait. The Baghdad Pact was a means of guaranteeing British interest in the Middle East. During the life of the Baghdad Pact, relations between both Iraq and Britain and Iraq and Turkey had been good. The revolution changed this pattern. It directly weakened the Pact and consequently Anglo-Iraqi and Turkish–Iraqi relations were negatively affected.

Iraq did not officially withdraw from the Baghdad Pact until March 1959, but in reality it was no longer a participating member and this situation led to the collapse of the Baghdad Pact, after which it was reorganized as CENTO (Central Treaty Organization) on 21 August 1959. From the Iraqi revolution of 14 July 1958 until 21 August 1959, the Baghdad Pact continued without Iraq's participation in the Pact's activities.

The new regime did not issue any statement about the Iraqi withdrawal from the Pact. They were trying to pursue a moderate policy towards the blocs and Egyptian nationalism. There were three regular meetings of the Baghdad Pact Council after the Iraqi revolution. The first one was arranged in London from 27 to 29 July 1958, which had been scheduled previously as the fifth session of the Pact's Ministerial meeting. The delegations from the member countries were led by their Prime Ministers who, according to the US representative Dulles, were in a state of considerable gloom as a result of the coup in Iraq.[17] During this time the parties arranged separate meetings as well. According to these meetings, Dulles mentioned that the primary purpose of the Pact was to preserve the unity of the Northern Tier countries. He suggested that the countries of the Baghdad Pact should go on without either rejecting or embracing Iraq. Moreover, he pointed out that there would be a greater possibility of the United States becoming a formal member of the Pact if Iraq were excluded. So long as Iraq was a member the US would have to give a parallel commitment to Israel.[18] The Pact continued to exist theoretically but not in practice.

Britain, in contrast, did not wish to exclude Iraq from the Baghdad Pact in the future, but to hold the door open for eventual Iraqi participation. The general tendency of the Pact members regarding Iraq and the future of the Pact could be described as a 'wait and see' policy. At the end of the London meeting the represented countries declared their determination to maintain their collective security and, while agreeing that the Iraqi coup had been a serious setback for the Pact, which no longer existed in its original form, they decided to continue with or without Iraq.

With regard to recognizing the new regime in Iraq, there was general agreement amongst member countries that early recognition was desirable. As regards the timing of recognition, the Prime Ministers of Turkey, Pakistan and Iran said that their governments would recognize the new regime on 31 July. The United Kingdom decided to recognize the new Iraqi regime on the following day.[19] A decision in principle to move the Pact Headquarters provisionally to Ankara was taken by the Council, following the demands of the Turkish government.[20] The Secretariat would provisionally remain in London until it moved to Ankara. It was decided at the meeting of the Council of Deputies in Ankara on 28 April 1959 that the headquarters of the Baghdad Pact would remain permanently in Ankara.[21]

After the London meeting in July, the first formal and private meetings of the Council of Deputies, without Iraq, were held in Ankara in October 1958. During these meetings it was agreed to hold the sixth session of the Pact Ministerial Council in Karachi in January 1959. During this session, on 26–28 January 1959, Turkey and Iran were represented by their respective Prime Ministers who led their delegates. Pakistan was represented by its

Foreign Minister, the UK by its Defence Secretary, Duncan Sandys, and the US by L.W. Henderson who was the Deputy Under Secretary of State. The session was inaugurated by the President of Pakistan, General Mohammed Ayub Khan. The participants discussed the previous activities under the Pact framework. They emphasized in particular the importance of the reports of the Economic Committee. They focused on progress in the field of telecommunications, rail and road projects, agriculture, health and scientific co-operation. The Council decided to hold its next session at the ministerial level in Tehran six months later. Meanwhile the Council would continue to meet regularly at the Deputies level in Ankara.[22]

The British ambassador in Ankara, Sir Bernard Burrows, in his despatch to the Foreign Office in February 1959, referred to the continuing unresolved problems affecting the very core of the Baghdad Pact. Iraq remained technically a member but did not attend meetings. Burrows wanted the situation resolved so that the alliance would remain a basic factor for stability and the preservation of British interests in the region. In expressing his views to the Deputy Under Secretary of the Foreign Office, Sir Roger Stevens, he emphasized that despite the current difficulties he hoped for a continuation of the alignment:

> ...I am myself enthusiastic for the Pact and would like to see it a going concern, but I feel that we have still not resolved the ambiguities and dilemmas which surrounded it. I presume that we see value in the Pact for some of the following reasons:- (a) as a demonstration of opposition to Russia and Communism – but in some cases we believe that neutrality will serve our interests best, e.g. Afghanistan... (b) as a means of obtaining strategic advantages for ourselves in using ‘real estate’ for our own purposes and denying it to the Russians with the help of the local inhabitants... (c) tactically as providing for the better use of local forces – but in fact most of this is up to now going on bilaterally, (d) In order to demonstrate to Russians that they cannot obtain territory without fighting for it. This is perhaps the most valuable feature, but the Iranians need to be convinced that the Pact as now organised makes a significant contribution to achieving this object.[23]

He also mentioned in the same document, alternatives: to refashion the pact, or to construct a new alliance in the region against any threat from abroad. One alternative would be to make the pact more like NATO (North Atlantic Treaty Organization); this would mean, among other things, full American membership, a Supreme Command and the allocation of forces, all of which would pose great difficulties, and would make the Pact as seen by Russia more provocative. On the other hand the advantage would be that

Iran would be irretrievably committed which, as they were at that time seeing to their cost, was by no means the case. These objectives of reassurance and commitment could also be achieved if it were possible for Iran to become a member of NATO.

> This idea has now come to the surface of Zorlu's mind and he mentioned it to me in one of our recent talks. I made the obvious comments about the feeling of Canadians, Scandinavians, etc., but he was not inclined to attach too much importance to this, no doubt remembering how the similar objections to Turkish and Greek membership had gradually been overcome. Indeed, [there are] difficulties of turning the Baghdad Pact into [a defence body like] NATO, [but] it might even seem slightly easier [to get Iran into NATO]. The provocation to Russia would no doubt be about the same. ...In the light of the disadvantages into something more like NATO, it seems desirable to look at the idea of changing the Pact's character in another direction. I mention this not in any defeatist spirit, but as part of a process of exploring alternatives and also with the thought that if Iran after all signs a non-aggression pact with Russia, and Turkey and perhaps the United States consider that Iran's continued membership of the Pact in its present form, is impossible in these circumstances and we are unable to pursue them to the contrary, we may be faced at short notice with the imminent breakdown of the Pact as a whole. The question which I think should be considered, therefore is what would be the value of the Pact as an organisation for economic, technical and cultural co-operation only... In favour of this thought it may be said that the economic and technical work of the Pact is beginning to produce quite impressive results, is leading to slightly greater sense of regional community, and, on the whole proceeds fairly smoothly without arousing political difficulties except, of course the inevitable requests for much larger supplies of aid from the United States and ourselves. A further advantage would be that the Pact in this form would no longer be a bogey to uncommitted neighbours, but might on the contrary conceivably attract some of them to join in, e.g. Iraq, Jordan and Afghanistan. The element of provocation to Russia would also be removed.[24]

Burrows also explained the difficulties of changing the pact into a new form from a military direction to an economic organization:

> Politically, it might be difficult for us and some of the other members to admit that the Pact had to be changed into a new and toothless form. If we were starting with a clean slate a purely economic organisation might look more attractive, but the transition to this from the present type of Pact would inevitably be painful for the time being. Possibly

> if our thoughts went in this direction it might be best not to announce openly that we were giving up the military side of the Pact, but in practice to let this stand still or gradually wither away and to give more and more emphasis to the economic side.
>
> I fear that these reflections do not point very conclusively in any direction, but I felt bound to let you know that I continued to feel that the Pact suffered from a serious malaise, and to start various hares which you will be more competent to pursue.[25]

His views found support in the Foreign Office; W.I. Combs, the Assistant Head of the Eastern Department, recommended that the economic side of the Pact should be strengthened.

> I entirely agree that we should aim to build up the economic side of the Pact. Although the regional members still regard it primarily as a source of additional aid for projects in their individual countries, they are also beginning to value it as an organisation for economic co-operation.[26]

The economic aspect of the pact would be a means to maintain the Pact which continued to have strategic value for British interests. In his minute Combs also explained his view about the Turkish attitude to the Pact and his view about the Pact's future.

> The Turks are bound to react badly to any proposal to disband the military side of the Pact. They could presumably argue with some justification that a guarantee of Iran's territorial integrity required in any case that there should be some form of military consultation; therefore why not maintain and strengthen the present Baghdad Pact military set-up?
>
> ... A different situation would arise if the military side of the Pact collapsed. In that case I think that an effort should be made to preserve and strengthen the economic organisation of the Baghdad Pact, presumably under another name.[27]

The regional members of the Pact signed bilateral agreements with the US Administration in Ankara on 5 March 1959, for co-operation in promoting the security and defence of the members of the Baghdad Pact,[28] as envisaged in the London Declaration. The agreements were designed to strengthen the military and economic potential of Turkey, Iran and Pakistan against direct or indirect aggression. It was envisaged as the Eisenhower Doctrine which was also suited to British interests.[29] By these agreements, the United States had become no less linked to the Baghdad Pact than if they had signed the original Pact. The United States had become a member of the Pact in all but name.

On 24 March 1959, the Iraqi Prime Minister announced the withdrawal of Iraq from the Baghdad Pact. He said that the Pact was destroyed on 14 July 1958, and uprooted on 24 March 1959.[30] With the withdrawal of Iraq from the Baghdad Pact, the question of the Pact's name came up for consideration. The matter was discussed by the Council of Deputies on 2 April but no decision was reached. There were different alternatives about the new name of the Pact; Britain suggested 'Middle East Regional Organization (MERO)', 'South West Asia Regional Organization (SWARO)', and soon. The Foreign Office in particular wanted to avoid portraying the new Pact as a defence pact.

The US proposed 'Northern Tier Defence Organisation' or 'West Asia Co-operative Defence Organization'. The US State Department wanted to avoid the term 'Middle East', because it did not wish to show that the pact was directed against any Middle Eastern countries, and wanted to improve US relations with Middle Eastern countries such as Egypt. Meanwhile America's special relations with Saudi Arabia and Israel disinclined the US from allowing the Pact to become embroiled in any Middle Eastern or Arab–Israeli dispute. Eilts, the desk officer responsible for the Baghdad Pact in the State Department, thought that there might be some advantage in a name which brought out the fact that the Pact had an economic side to it as well as a military one; the US also proposed a neutral name using the initials of Turkey, Iran, Pakistan (Treaty Organization) which abbreviated to the obviously unsuitable acronym TIPTO.[31] Burrows was also of the same mind as the US diplomat, he stressed that the name of the Pact should relate to the function of the Pact and particularly to its economic functions.[32] Both sides wanted to avoid a name with geographical restrictions such as 'Middle East' or 'Northern Tier', because they wanted to emphasize that it was an organization corresponding to Western-oriented organizations. As a result of further consideration, the Council of the Baghdad Pact in Ankara resolved that the organization should in future be known as the Central Treaty Organization, abbreviated as CENTO.[33] The name Central Treaty Organization was accepted on 21 August 1959 and signified that the countries occupied a central area between the NATO and SEATO regions.[34]

The British Secretary for Defence, Duncan Sandys, paid a visit to Turkey and met with the Turkish Prime Minister Menderes and Foreign Minister Zorlu on 19 May 1959. They discussed the situation in the Middle East especially the situation in Iraq and Qasim's ability to prevent any Communist threat. Menderes explained that both the future of Iraq and Iran were absolutely vital to Turkey. Duncan Sandys responded that as

> Iran was clearly still the weak link. As regards Iraq, he agreed that there was no certainty that Qasim could maintain his position against the Communist, but there was no feasible alternative in sight.[35]

In another document which was sent by Burrows on behalf of Duncan Sandys on the same day as the document mentioned above to the Foreign Secretary and the Prime Minister, Duncan Sandys explained his view about the Turkish government,

> However they [the Turkish government] are acutely worried by the fact that there is no agreed policy about what to do if Qasim should be overthrown and replaced by a Communist regime. Looking at it from this end it seems most important to dispel the impression of Anglo-American indecision, which undoubtedly exists here in Ankara. I realise that we cannot put forward any firm proposals until we have settled a line with the Americans. Nevertheless it would greatly ease the mind of the Turks if you could send urgently a message to Menderes telling him that the British government fully recognise the grave consequences of a Communist *coup d'état* in Iraq, that we are urgently considering the line to be followed, that we are consulting with the Americans and that we hope soon to be in a position to discuss the whole problem with the Turkish government.[36]

Both Britain and Turkey were agreed on the same policy towards the Iraqi military regime and to support Qasim. At the same time they agreed to consult with the US about the whole Middle East proposal. This was especially insisted upon by Menderes. Burrows reported on his impressions of Duncan Sandys' views,

> He seemed to feel that it was up to us and the Americans to have a stronger and clearer Middle East policy with which Turkey could associate itself, rather than waiting on events which were more or less out of control.[37]

Before the transition to CENTO there were various policy discussions between the parties about Britain's position in the future of the new Pact. According to the Washington Embassy's despatch, the regional members of the Pact claimed Britain should withdraw from the Pact and assume the status of an observer.[38] This document was passed on by the Foreign Office to Ankara for the ambassador's views. The FO informed Burrows on 7 August 1959 that:

> In connection with the forthcoming Anglo-American review of the Baghdad Pact, the desk officer (Mr. Eilts) in the State Department has put to us informally and personally, that we should consider not only

> the possibility of the United States joining the Pact, but the reverse of the medal, that is that the United Kingdom should withdraw to observer status, leaving the Pact a purely regional organisation. This idea had been mentioned to Mr. Dulles by the leaders of regional delegations to the council meeting in London last year and President Ayub had reverted to it in a recent conversation in Karachi. The chief arguments in its favour was that it would make the Pact easier to sell locally and destroy the still active myth that it was a cloak for United Kingdom 'imperialism'. Mr. Eilts was not trying to press this idea, but thought it should be considered in view of the opinions which had been expressed.
>
> ... Meanwhile, please let us know by telegram in connection with papers for the review which we are now preparing whether you consider that the idea of our withdrawal (which would certainly be regarded here as the beginning of the end of the Pact) would really in your view have any attraction for the Turks, Pakistanis and Iranians. You should on no account discuss or even hint at the idea with any member of the Government to which you are accredited nor to your Pact colleagues (including your United States colleagues).[39]

The Foreign Office did not try to influence the ambassador one way or the other. The possibility of withdrawal and the collapse of the Pact appears to have been treated as an open question. Burrows responded only a day after this despatch and he emphasized that this view surprised him, and described in detail Anglo-Turkish relations at that time:

> I am extremely surprised that the Turks should ever have advocated our withdrawing to observer status. Everything they have said to me has implied satisfaction that we are members and that this consequently gives us a place in the Middle East, and they consistently expressed the hope that the United States would one day become full member with us. I have little doubt that they would feel that our withdrawal now would be disastrous, both to the Pact and the continuance of Iran in the Western Camp. I believe it would also have quite serious effect on Anglo-Turkish relations, and particularly on the habit of intimate discussion on the Middle East and other topics which has grown up between us. As regards the Pact generally I would expect, if we withdraw to observer status and the Pact survived at all, the main result would be to increase the split between the regional and non-regional members and demands for support of all kinds by the former and on the latter. It would not solve any of our present problems, but accentuate them. It would also lead to reports that we,

> like the Americans, should enter into bilateral guarantees. ...If we or the Americans finally decided that we could not face the military and political consequences of making this Pact more of a military reality, then I think it would be soon necessary to consider radical changes in its form but it is mistaken to suppose that by changing the form of the Pact we can avoid making basic military and political decisions.[40]

Burrows supported strongly the idea of the continuation of direct British membership in the new reorganization of the Pact. Burrows's views carried great weight at the FO, and Britain maintained its membership under CENTO.

The British government decided to remain in the Pact as a full member state. Following the Iraqi coup, the Americans completely lost their faith in the Pact, but yet again tried very hard not to lose the region completely to the Russians. To achieve this objective, the US reached an agreement with each single member of the Pact.[41] Meanwhile, according to American interdepartmental communications, they believed that the US should join the Pact so as to strengthen the Pact in the region. The Assistant Secretary of this department wrote a letter to Bob Murphy, who was the Under Secretary of State for Political Affairs, on 31 August 1959, as follows,

> In the past, Defense has been advised that joining the Baghdad Pact might place some limitations on our relations with the Arab States and with Afghanistan and India, and that additionally, political problems might be presented by submission of our joiner to Congress for ratification. However, in view of the changes which have taken place in the Middle East and in India and our present commitments through bilateral agreements with the present CENTO Treaty members, and particularly in view of the need [for our membership to] strengthen CENTO, this department believes that a reappraisal of the US position on joining CENTO is urgently required.[42]

Murphy replied to this letter on 11 September 1959. He explained that the State Department had concluded that because of the political risk involved, the time was not right for the United States to join CENTO, although the Department did not rule out the possibility of US adherence in the future, but Murphy agreed that the United States should make every reasonable effort to strengthen CENTO.[43] This exchange of views shows that the US was not in favour of joining the Pact but wanted the Pact to continue in order to maintain US prestige and influence in the region.

The new position of the Pact was not promising. Britain consequently wanted to diminish her role. During the transition period Burrows and the FO were agreed on improving the Pact's economic side,

> We should aim to build up the economic side of the Pact. Although the regional members still regard it primarily as a source of additional aid for projects in their individual countries, they are also, beginning to value it as an organisation for economic co-operation.[44]

On the other hand, during the seventh session (first meeting of the Pact as CENTO) of the Pact's Ministerial meeting on 7–9 October 1959 in Washington, the members emphasized in their final communiqué that the Pact was exclusively defensive.

> The Council emphasised that the Central Treaty Organisation exists exclusively for defensive purposes, that it threatens no one, and that it sincerely desires to have close and friendly relations with the other states, and particularly with the neighbour states in the region.[45]

This statement shows that the nominal situation of the Pact was defensive, most probably they did not want to give the impression that the Pact became weaker compared to its earlier version. But in reality especially the British side agreed to change the Pact's structure to purely economic direction. But they attempted this kind of modification gradually and did not explain it overtly to the public and the other states in the region. This view was mainly recommended by Burrows.

> Possibly if our thoughts went in this direction it might be best not to announce openly that we were giving up the military side of the Pact, but in practice to let this stand still or gradually wither away and to give more and more emphasis to the economic side.[46]

Britain was of the view that 'a Baghdad Pact without Iraq is not a practical possibility'. Indeed, even though the Baghdad Pact had been popular too, CENTO never came into practice as the Baghdad Pact.[47]

In these new circumstances the British FO and Ministry of Defence thought that Britain should remain in CENTO and should encourage the members to maintain CENTO alive as long as possible. On the Turkish side the Democratic Party government favoured a continuation of the Pact as CENTO. After the revolution (27 May 1960) the new government also declared support for CENTO. The wording of the Turkish government statement is in support of NATO ('that the Turkish government had faith in NATO and was bound to it') and its support for CENTO ('only that the Turkish government was bound to it') caused doubts among regional members. Both the Iranian and Pakistani ambassadors noted these differences during a restricted meeting of the CENTO Council of Deputies held on 31 May 1960. The new Turkish Foreign Minister Selim Sarper assured the ambassadors that this difference was quite accidental and that the Turkish government had exactly the same attitude towards CENTO as towards NATO.[48]

Harold Watkinson, the British Secretary for Defence, sent a minute to the Prime Minister about CENTO's military direction. He stressed that although the regional members especially Iran and Pakistan insisted on establishing a Supreme Commander of CENTO, the US and UK were resisting this. He also explained the reasons for their opposition.

> We are having trouble with the arrangements for the military direction of CENTO. The regional members have, for a variety of reasons long wanted to establish a strong command structure. The United States have resisted this, since they believe that it would lead to large and unrealistic demands for military assistance and the commitment of forces. We share their fears, but find it difficult to argue against the command structure on military grounds. Provided the United States stands fast, we have been prepared to stand fast too.
>
> What between this and causes of trouble there is a real danger that the military side of CENTO may disintegrate. We cannot give more military aid and shall refuse to do so, but something could be done to improve the military machinery, and since this will be the main issue at the next meeting of the Military Committee in January 1961, we ought to concert plans now with the United States.[49]

The British side tried for new solutions to this problem. They asked that the CENTO Military Planning Staff should be renamed CENTO Military Staff 'CMS', and a Commander should be appointed and be a United States or a British officer. These proposals were agreed by the Prime Minister as well.[50] This demand came from Pakistan and its policy was to receive more support from the CENTO members for her policy against India. This situation caused problems in British policy, because Britain was allied both to Pakistan and to India under CENTO-SEATO and the Commonwealth. A Commander of CENTO Military Staff was not appointed despite Pakistan's demand for an American officer. The United States administration was also unwilling to provide an officer[51] because it did not want to arouse a Soviet reaction against the Pact and the US. Another reason was that the US also did not want to harm its relations with India and the non-aligned states, although the military representatives supported the establishment of a command structure. Members of the State Department for Political Affairs were not in favour of a military command structure of the Pact and described it as politically 'premature'; they explained that it was in the US interest to associate with CENTO 'only a little bit at a time'.[52]

The alternative appointment of a British officer was refused by Pakistan, because of Britain's close relations with India. Pakistani policy-makers considered that a British officer's attitude could not support their policy against India. The members did not solve this problem and there was no appointment by the end of 1965.

The British ambassador in Ankara, Burrows, nevertheless put forward an optimistic appraisal about CENTO's future and in his annual review of CENTO for 1961, he stated:

> The main aims of the present regional members who are not also members of NATO, namely Iran and Pakistan, are to make CENTO as like NATO. The general aim of all three regionals including Turkey is to use CENTO as a channel for obtaining increased quantities of military and economic aid from the two non-regional members, the US and the United Kingdom. The main object of the non-regional members on the other hand is with the minimum expenditure of military equipment, economic aid and political commitment to keep the Organisation just sufficiently alive in order to provide a framework for Iran's alignment with the West.[53]

He also emphasized that Britain should support CENTO's present structure, as necessary for British policy in region.

> From our point of view it is difficult to see how the UK position in any new system could be as important as it is in CENTO today, so that, unless we want to withdraw more completely from this part of the world, we should from time to time remember that it's worth the effort we now put into CENTO, and perhaps a little more, to keep the present system going.[54]

After the revolution in Turkey (27 May 1960) the new military government wanted to maintain the Western alliances; the Soviets (Khrushchev) hoped to persuade the Turkish government to adopt a neutral policy but were unsuccessful. Turkish foreign policy remained firmly aligned to the West.[55] The CENTO war plan was against global war particularly opposing any Communist threat, but Iran and Pakistan wanted to extend this proposal to include limited war. Their intentions were to be strong against any threat from the countries on their frontiers. Pakistan was in conflict with India over Kashmir, and Iran suspected a threat from Iraq and subversion of the Arabs in the region. The British Foreign Office was reluctant to endorse CENTO's limited war planning[56] because of close relations with India in the Commonwealth and with the other Arab States in the Middle East.

The US attitude towards CENTO was more negative than Britain's. Withdrawing from CENTO Committees had already been on the agenda of the US State Department. The Foreign Office was well aware of this from the information received from Washington. The British ambassador reported,

> ...They have also clearly found it difficult to summon up the necessary support in the Administration for CENTO as an effective military organisation, and Mathew Smith, the CENTO Desk Officer, today went so far as to tell me that there had been serious risk last year of the United States withdrawing altogether from its association with the Organisation. Smith went on to say that the situation was considerably brighter now...[57]

There were also different attitudes towards CENTO from the regional members. A Foreign Office memorandum on 7 April 1964 summed up the main weakness of the Pact. They explained the attitude of the regional members. The Turkish attitude towards the Organization was summed up by the FO Eastern Department as follows:

> The Turks since the Menderes' day, have not been enthusiastic about CENTO which they regard as poor second to NATO; they are content to receive such assistance as is offered under CENTO auspices but their overriding interest is in becoming even more closely a part of Europe. On the other hand they do appreciate the role CENTO plays in defending their exposed eastern flank and in preventing the establishment of a neutralist or even pro-Russian regime in Iran. As a result they are prepared to support CENTO loyally and not to rock the boat, but cannot be relied upon to provide it with the impetus and energy it lacks. On issues which divide the United Kingdom and the United States from the other two regionals the Turks usually feel compelled to side with the latter.[58]

It can be added that Turkey benefited from the economic and military aid from non-regional countries through CENTO; this made possible the modernization of the Trabzon and Iskenderun ports on the north and south coasts of Turkey respectively, and of the Turkey-Iran railway and highway projects which were also important for Turkey. The Prime Minister Inönü inaugurated the Muş-Tatvan section of the railway project in October 1964, accompanied by the British ambassador and other representatives from the US and Iran embassies and from the CENTO secretariat. After his speech Inönü insisted on rearranging the seating so as to place himself between the British ambassador and the senior American representative for the benefit of the photographer.[59] This was an indication that both the British and Turkish side wanted to improve their relations under the CENTO framework. The British ambassador was the only ambassador who attended the ceremony.

Under CENTO, co-operation and solidarity among the local members of the Organization both in regional and international proposal developed. The politicians of the regional countries used co-operation for their internal political advantage. In dealing with the problem of CENTO, the British suggested that the best way to improve support for CENTO among its regional members as well as to improve its public image as an organization was to emphasize its national features, for the sake of mutual defence and for raising the living standards of the regional members. The Foreign Office memorandum also set out this function:

> The British aid programme was given a CENTO label and 'in theory' channelled through CENTO machinery, so as to put more flesh on CENTO's economic bones. ...Above all it gave to the three regional governments concerned a feeling of achieving something useful from CENTO's economic board.[60]

British aid to regional members was lower than US aid, in 1965 amounting to £1,000,000 and $18,000,000, respectively. US aid was given under bilateral agreements. But the UK gave its aid under the auspices of CENTO. Britain concentrated on using it more productively and to maintain her political prestige in the region through technical and economic support.

In a memorandum of 7 April 1964 *The Problems of CENTO*, the Foreign Office set out its views on the treaty organization, clearly valuing its existence despite weakness,

> (i) The continued existence of CENTO, as a deterrent to Russian expansion and subversion and as a means of maintaining the pro-Western alignment of the regional members, in particular Iran, is an important United Kingdom and Western interest.
>
> (ii) CENTO remains a weak organization in constant need of moral and material bolstering by the United Kingdom and the United States.
>
> (iii) CENTO's weakness derives mainly from its dubious credibility as a military organization and from the divergence's in aims and policies among its members.
>
> (iv) The maintenance of the military credibility of CENTO depends to a considerable extent on the United Kingdom commitment of four Canberra squadrons in Cyprus; any weakening of the commitment could be seriously damaging. A subsidiary United Kingdom contribution is the military aid at present applied to providing a radar chain in Iran.

(v) the Ministerial Council meetings provide important occasions for strengthening CENTO morale and confidence and it is vital for the United Kingdom and the United States to make the most of them from this point of view.

(vi) The economic programme is a useful adjunct to the organization's activities, improving its public image and helping to convince the regional members of its value. The United Kingdom contribution administrated by the DTC is modest but slowly increasing and it is in our interests to encourage and support such an increase.[61]

The British ambassador in Ankara, Denis Allen, agreed and emphasized in particular that the memorandum had rather neglected the importance of keeping Pakistan, as well as Iran content with the alliance. He urged that the Pact be kept going because its collapse would be a serious blow to Western policy and prestige. Moreover, Britain had to keep it alive to encourage Iran's continued alignment with the West, instead of the reverse. But in the memorandum they thought, to recognize that this was the current state of affairs was far from perfect and not of Britain's choosing, had they been free to choose themselves.[62]

In July 1964, the regional countries formed another organization without non-regional members and named it the Regional Co-operation for Development (RCD). Their dissatisfaction with CENTO had led them to form this new organization. Other motives were probably the Shah's desire to gain political domestic and international prestige from this diplomatic initiative; President Ayub's pique with the West over India; Turkey's frustration over Cyprus; a general desire on the part of all three partners to show their independence, without asserting it to the extent of resorting to CENTO; and a conviction that there might be real economic benefits to be gained from the new Organization. The indications were that RCD did not pose any threat to CENTO and that the two organizations were complementary.[63] During the early days of this new organization, the British reaction was not positive towards it believing that the new organization was set up to duplicate and consequently to weaken CENTO, especially if it encouraged the tendency for the regional governments to neglect the institution of CENTO.[64] But the terms of reference of the new Organisation showed that it did not affect CENTO. Other assurances came from the Pakistani government to the US State Department. They emphasized that the Pakistani government did not propose to take any action which would weaken CENTO.[65] The Turkish Ministry of Foreign Affairs also emphasized that the aim of the new organization was not to be viewed as in competition with CENTO but as another opportunity for strengthening their solidarity of economic and commercial ties.[66] Publicly the Foreign Office welcomed it as an expression of constructive regional solidarity.[67]

The basic weakness of CENTO was due in the first place to the divergence between the aims and policies of the non-regional members and those of the United Kingdom and the United States, and secondly to the widely differing interests of the three regional members. The UK provided the military commitment for CENTO of four Canberra squadrons in Cyprus. Any weakening of this commitment would have seriously damaged CENTO. Economically and politically, the regional and non-regional members also were critical. The regional countries expected more aid, in contrast to the non-regionals who did not wish to increase their commitments. This situation caused a weakening of the Pact both regionally and internationally. This aspect led the Eastern Department to conclude that 'CENTO remains a weak organization in constant need of moral and material bolstering by the United Kingdom and the United States'.[68]

Since 1957 Britain had supported the regional members of the Baghdad Pact and CENTO with an annual payment averaging £600,000. These payments continued until 1969. Moreover the figure changed in favour of the regionals; in 1964 it increased from £850,000 to £1 million and the aid prevailed mainly through technical support.[69] The political function of the Pact was not primary despite regular Ministerial and Deputies meetings.

The Ministerial Meetings of CENTO were held once a year in April. The member countries were usually represented by the Foreign Ministers including the Secretary of State of the United States. The meetings were held in the capitals of member states in rotation. From 1961 to 1965 these meetings were held in Ankara, London, Karachi, Washington and Tehran respectively and called from the 9th to the 13th session of the meetings. During the meetings the Ministers discussed regional and international problems and exchanged views.[70] The inaugural messages from the host countries' Presidents or Prime Ministers were read by their Foreign Ministers. A final communiqué was also issued at the end of the meetings. The problems of CENTO, such as the Supreme Command structure, limited war planning, economic and technical issues under the CENTO framework, were discussed. The Ministers also met informally before UN meetings in New York.[71] The Council of Deputies met frequently in Ankara but its discussions were confined almost entirely to CENTO's internal problems. The Turks had recently shown some inclination to discuss such questions as Cyprus and developments in Iraq and Syria.[72] Such a discussion was described as not part of the usual and routine function of the Pact, although the meeting itself was nothing unusual, rather than an important job. On the other hand it seemed quite normal and necessary to the Turkish politicians, because their expectations of the Pact were that it would strengthen

Turkey's security and would attract more political support for the country in international relations.

In 1965 CENTO celebrated its tenth anniversary. The British ambassador in Ankara, on 28 April 1965, sent a rather depressing account of public attitudes to CENTO.

> This period included CENTO's tenth year, the anniversary of which was celebrated officially, but with little public interest in the regional countries and still less elsewhere. CENTO's modest standing in the world was neither appreciably enhanced nor diminished; nor was the hostility of its opponents, though this remained largely covert.[73]

Different in tone was special message on the tenth anniversary by the Secretary General Dr A. A. Khalatbary (Iranian):

> In a word, CENTO has kept peace with the changes in the world political scene. It has become a flexible instrument, capable of dealing with the continuing efforts of those ultimate aims which are totally irreconcilable with freedom and peace in this part of the world. And on this tenth anniversary I am confident that the experience gained by CENTO is a good augury for its future.[74]

It is quite clear that the expectations of the UK and of Iran were different. The British side wanted to maintain the existing positions of the Pact and the ambassador explained that this situation about the Pact neither enhanced nor diminished it. On the other hand, Iran wanted to improve the Pact's functioning by such innovations as appointing a Supreme Commander. It should be added that Khalatbary favoured the Pact. Denis Allen's comment about Dr A. A. Khalatbary was that 'He has shown himself sufficiently tactful and competent, if not outstandingly so.'[75]

Although there were many problems in CENTO, British policy was to maintain the organization as long as possible. From the British point of view, the main expectation of the Organization was to keep Iran in the Western alignment, because Turkey and Pakistan were already bound to the Western defence and economic alliance through NATO and SEATO respectively. Iran was a key position for Britain's short- and long-term defence, economic and foreign policies both in the region and the Far East. As Michael Stewart, the Foreign Secretary in Wilson's Cabinet, pointed out:

> In the case of Turkey and Pakistan CENTO is not the only Western alliance performing this function and Turkey inevitably attaches greater importance to NATO than to CENTO. Iran, however, lacks any such second alliance and CENTO's particular importance is that it provides a framework for Iran's co-operation with the West and with

> the United Kingdom. This is needed because of the country's key position in the area blocking the Soviet Union's most direct land route to the Persian Gulf and forming a bridge between Turkey and Pakistan. It is also needed because co-operation with Iran is important to us in seeking to preserve stability in the Persian Gulf, in encouraging her government to maintain a moderate line in oil affairs [Iran is the only non-Arab Middle East member of the Organisation of Petroleum Exporting Countries (OPEC) and has played a valuable moderating role in it], and in ensuring our overflying facilities, which are now of special importance as a result of limitations placed by the Sudanese government on the Southern route to the Middle and Far East.[76]

This situation influenced the priority given to the British economic and military aid programme towards Iran rather than the other regional member. The four radar station chains were built and fully equipped in northern Iran through British economic aid commitments.[77]

Finally it can be seen that British policy to keep CENTO functioning was based on the belief that its collapse would be a serious blow to Western policy and prestige.[78] Under CENTO, the member countries sometimes supported each other. For example the Turkish Prime Minister Suat Hayri Ürgüplü sent a letter to British Prime Minister Harold Wilson and demanded that the UK use her influence on both states in order to maintain the cease-fire between India and Pakistan, adding:

> ...Mr. Prime Minister, that along with those undertakings by the governments of Turkey, Iran and the United States will certainly have a positive effect to stimulate the activities within CENTO to continue in pursuing successfully its mission.[79]

In his response Wilson explained his view about the India/Pakistan crisis, adding that he was in agreement with his Turkish counterpart and was willing to support the UN resolutions for the cease-fire and support both regional and international peace.[80]

CENTO was described in notes prepared for the ministerial meeting of CENTO in April 1965 by Britain's new Foreign Secretary, Michael Stewart, as a defensive alliance, which had built up a sense of solidarity and cohesion among its regional members and had made a magnificent contribution to the economy of the area. He added that he was glad to express to his counterparts among the member countries that Her Majesty's government would continue support for the alliance and had confidence in its future.[81] He also emphasized that the UK keep its support at about the existing level. Since CENTO members could not expect that the US would become a full member, UK support was likely to remain a critical factor. Stewart gave an assurance that Britain would continue to give CENTO full political backing and would endeavour to impart what substance they could to its political discussions. At the same time he stressed that CENTO should continue to act in close concert with the United States administration, whose greater material capacity and assistance to the regional countries in maintaining CENTO on present lines was to be encouraged.[82]

After the establishment of CENTO, Israel's attitude was not as negative as it had been in the days of the Baghdad Pact, because there was no Arab member of CENTO. Israeli politicians even improved their relations with two of the member countries of CENTO, Turkey and Iran. In January 1965, the FO and the British Embassy in Tel Aviv discussed the Israeli *rapprochement* towards CENTO's two regional countries, Iran and Turkey. John Beith, who was the British ambassador in Israel, said,

> I believe that it is perfectly true to say that the existence of countries like Turkey and Iran within the general Middle East or Near East area has proved to be on the whole helpful to Israel and that it would be unreasonable to expect Israel not to attempt to build up as good a working relationship with those two countries as she can. ...If the estrangement between Turkey and Iran and the Arab countries were reversed, it is highly improbable that Turkey and Iran could pursue the Arab governments to soften their attitude towards Israel and highly probable that Turkey and Iran would make concessions on this issue to the Arabs. That is indeed the reason why the Israelis will cantinue to try for full diplomatic relations with both Turkey and Iran. These are of far greater concern to Israel than the rather far-fetched idea that this peripheral Moslem countries might eventually act as a bridge to relations with the Arabs. For these reasons the Israel policy of making friends with Turkey and Iran, so far as possible, is not a matter of 'short term opportunist tactics' but is something that Israel, struggling for survival, cannot afford to give up. I agree with the thesis that the presence of Turkey and Iran in the area relieves the isolation of Israel.[83]

The Foreign Office agreed that Israeli politicians were very opportunist and could gain benefit from their country's relationship with Iran only so long as the present regime lasted. It was also recognized that the regime in Iran was vulnerable because of Arab propaganda and the subversive activities and religious pressure. In contrast,

> The Turkish regime is not vulnerable to the same pressure or so easy to lead by the nose: the Turks can look after themselves.[84]

Thus it becomes clear that for Britain, Turkey remained the one stable and indispensable ally in the region. It could be said that, in the early days of the Baghdad Pact, British policy was successful from its point of view. But in later years the public and the military leaders of the regional members were not willing to continue the same policy as their governments. In 1958 there were military coups in both Iraq and Pakistan, and in 1960 in Turkey. The Iraqi coup especially effected the collapse of the Pact and was also a turning point in British policy in the oil rich region. Intensification of Soviet propaganda and the vigorous opposition of Arab nationalism were further reasons for the collapse for the Pact (24 March 1959).

To summarize then. As CENTO, the Pact continued its function without Iraq. The US administration was represented by its Secretary of State during the Pact's ministerial meetings. It meant that US relations with the new organization were closer than with its predecessor because of Iraq's withdrawal.

Turkey's aim for the Pact was to contain the danger of 'International Communism' and to serve the security of 'peace loving' countries. At the same time it could improve its relations with the Middle Eastern Arab countries. It thought that Egypt, Jordan and Syria might become members of the Pact. These expectations were not fulfilled. Turkish politicians were disappointed with the collapse of the Baghdad Pact and Turkey's isolation in the Middle East. Although the revolution in Iraq on 14 July 1958 and the collapse of the Baghdad Pact led to disappointment within the British and Turkish governments with regard to their policies in the Middle East, both sides agreed that CENTO must continue.

The Turkish governments were also expected to support this new organization mainly in order to gain more American and British economic, military and technical aid; to improve Turkey's relations with Iran and Pakistan; to support the Western bloc in their policy to contain the Communist threat in the region; and internally to utilize this platform as an opportunity to gain the support of the other member countries in international issues with regard to Turkey's foreign policy on such issues as the Cyprus question.

From the British point of view, the Foreign Office considered that Britain had to maintain and continue its presence in the region against Soviet advance during the period of the Cold War and maintain British economic, political and strategic interests in this oil-rich region. They also considered that they could not tolerate any loss of British and Western prestige during their international containment policy.

Although the Baghdad Pact was mainly conceived as defensive in character, CENTO became nominally defensive but in reality a more economic and culturally based organization, especially in response to

British suggestions for this modification. The British Foreign Office emphasized that the redirection of this organization from a defence to an economic and cultural orientation would have to be done gradually and Britain had to avoid giving the impression to the regional members that they were ignoring the defence perspective of this organization. The transformation aimed to make it easier to maintain the Pact so that Britain could preserve its prestige in the region. The British governments of Macmillan, Home and Wilson were agreed on continuing to remain members as long as possible. It was necessary to maintain the overflying right from Cyprus over Turkey and Iran to protect British interests in the Gulf area. Thus both Turkey and Iran would have to remain in the Pact. Britain was also allied with Turkey in NATO, so its main expectations of CENTO was to keep Iran as a pro-Western country, in other words to prevent her becoming a neutral or pro-Soviet state.

As a result British governments pursued close relations with Turkey in order to protect Britain's Middle East and Mediterranean interests by utilizing military and economic organizations such as CENTO and NATO in that period. In terms of British and Turkish policies, the main purpose of CENTO was to keep Iran in the Western bloc, to prevent any Communist or neutralist orientation on the part of the Iranian governments. From the regional point of view, CENTO became a medium for co-operation and collaboration between the regional member countries. In this sense CENTO has been shown to be a successful alliance, rather than a 'forgotten alliance'. It would not have lasted 20 years otherwise, until 1979 when the revolution in Iran finally brought it to an end.

NOTES

I owe a great debt to Professor John A.S. Grenville and Dr W. Scott Lucas of the University of Birmingham and to Dr Bülent Gökay of Keele University for giving me encouragement in writing this article.

1. At the end of long negotiations, both the Iraqi and Turkish governments were given the support of the United Kingdom and signed a bilateral agreement on 24 Feb. 1955, named the 'Baghdad Pact'. It was signed in the city of Baghdad by the Prime Minister of Turkey, Adnan Menderes, and the Iraqi Prime Minister, Nuri Said, as well as by the two Ministers of Foreign Affairs of Iraq and Turkey. Britain became the third member of the Baghdad Pact on 25 March 1955. On the same day Britain signed another agreement with Iraq concerning the maintenance of British military and economic privileges. Pakistan joined the Baghdad Pact on 17 Sept. and Iran was the last member of the Pact when it joined on 23 Oct. 1955. Richard L. Jasse, 'The Baghdad Pact: Cold War or Colonialism?', *Middle Eastern Studies*, Vol.27, No.1 (Jan. 1991), pp.140–55.

   Feroz Ahmad, *The Turkish Experiment In Democracy 1950–1975* (London, 1977), p.394. Robins emphasized that the Turks 'were proud of their achievement in the establishing a northern tier, and of linking NATO and South-East Asia Treaty Organisation (SEATO) through the membership of Pakistan and Turkey in the same alliance'. Philip Robins, *Turkey and the Middle East* (London, 1991), p.25. For further details about the Baghdad Pact, see, Fahir Armaoğlu, '(Amerikan Belgeleri ile) Orta Dogu Komutanligi'ndan Bagdad Pakti'na 1951–1955', *Belleten*, Vol.LIX, No.227 (April 1995), pp.189–236; Nigel J. Asthon, 'The hijacking of a pact: the formation of the Baghdad pact and Anglo-American tensions in the Middle East, 1955–1958', *Review of International Studies*, Vol.19, No.2 (1993), pp.37–65; Ayşe Jalal, 'Towards the Baghdad Pact: South Asian and Middle East Defence in the Cold War, 1947–1955', *The International History Review*, Vol.XI, No.3 (Aug. 1989), pp.409–33; Elie Podeh, *The Quest For Hegemony In the Arab World, The Struggle Over the Baghdad Pact* (Leiden, 1995); Ara Sanjian, 'The Formulation of the Baghdad Pact', *Middle Eastern Studies*, Vol.33, No.2 (April 1997), pp.226–66; Ismail Soysal, 'Bagdad Pakti' (Kongre tebligi) *Belleten*, Vol.LV, No.212 (April 1991), pp.179–238; Behçet K. Yeşilbursa, 'The Baghdad Pact and the Anglo-American Defence Policies in the Middle East, 1955–1959', unpublished PhD thesis, the University of Manchester, 1996.

2. Alistair Horne, *Macmillan 1957–1986: Volume II of The Official Biography* (London, 1989), p.93.
3. CAB 128/32, C.C.55(58), 15 July 1958.
4. CAB 128/32, C.C.57(58), 15 July 1958.
5. Marion Farouk and Peter Slugett, *Iraq since 1958* (London, 1990), p.50.
6. Kemal H. Karpat, 'Turkish and Arab–Israeli Relations', in *Turkey's Foreign Policy in Transition 1950–1975* (Leiden, 1975), pp.108–34.
7. CAB 128/32, C.C. (58) 56, 15 July 1958.
8. CAB 128/32, C.C. (59) 58, 17 July 1958.
9. Ibid.
10. *Foreign Relations of the United States* (*FRUS*) 1958–1960, Near East Region; Iraq; Iran; Arabian Peninsula; Vol.XII (Washington, 1993), p.78.
11. Humphrey Trevelyan, *The Middle East in Revolution* (London, 1970), p.134.
12. Peter Mansfield (ed.), *The Middle East: A Political and Economic Survey* (Oxford, 1980), Fifth Edition, p.328.
13. Trevelyan, op. cit., pp.154–5.
14. CAB 128/33, C.C (59) 20–25 March 1959. There was a note written by a member of PRO member and mentioned that CC(59) 20th Item 2 closed for 50 years under LCI 87, 30 Oct. 1989. Because of this note we could see only half of this document.
15. Farouk and Sluggett, *Iraq since 1958* (London, 1990), p.50.
16. Trevelyan, op. cit., p.156.
17. Yeşilbursa, op. cit., p.387.
18. Ibid., p.388.
19. Ibid., p.391.
20. FO to Ankara, 29 Aug. 1958, and 30 Sept. 1958, PREM 11/3879.
21. Burrows (Ankara) to FO, 30 April 1959, PREM 11/3879, NO; 665.
22. Karachi to FO, 28 Jan. 1959, PREM 11/3879.
23. Burrows (Ankara) to FO, 4 Feb. 1959, FO 371/140685, EB 1001/4.
24. Ibid.
25. Ibid.
26. Minute by W.I. Combs (Assistant Head of Eastern Department) 6 Feb. 1959, FO 371/140685, EB 1001/5.
27. Ibid.
28. *FRUS* 1958–1960, Near East Region; Iraq; Iran; Arabian Peninsula; Vol.XII (Washington, 1993), p.212.
29. Cristopher J. Bartlett, *The Special Relationship: A Political History of Anglo-American Relations since 1945* (Harlow, 1992), p 89
30. Hamit Ersoy, 'Turkey's Involvement in Western Defence Initiatives in the Middle East in the 1950s', unpublished PhD thesis, the University of Durham, 1994, p.254.
31. Washington to FO, 26 March 1959, FO 371/140702, EB 10113/1.
32. Burrows (Ankara) to FO, 6 May 1959, FO 371/140702, EB 10113/5.
33. *The Times*, 22 Aug. 1959, *Treaties and alliances of the World, A Survey of International Treaties in Force and Communities of States* (Keesing's Publications Ltd. Keynsham, Bristol, 1968), pp.128–31

34. Harold Caccia (Washington) to FO, 9 Oct. 1959, PREM 11/3879, For further information about the change of name of the Baghdad Pact, see FO 371/140732.
35. Burrows to FO, Ankara, 21 May 1959, FO 371/140681, E 1071/6.
36. Burrows to FO and PM, Ankara, 21 May 1959, FO 371/140681, E 1071/6(A).
37. Burrows to FO, Ankara, 21 May 1959, FO 371/140681, E 1071/6.
38. Washington to FO, 30 July 1959, FO 371/140714, EB 1071/1t.
39. FO to Burrows, 7 Aug. 1959, FO 371/140714, EB 1071/1.
40. Burrows (Istanbul) to FO, 8 Aug. 1959, FO 371/140714, EB 1071/5.
41. Ersoy, 'Turkey's Involvement…', p.246.
42. Knight to Murphy (Interdepartmental Communications) Washington, 31 Aug. 1959, *FRUS*, Vol.XII, Near East Region Iraq, Iran, Arabian Peninsula, 1958–1960 (Washington, 1993), pp.235–6.
43. *FRUS*, Vol.XII, p.236.
44. Burrows (Ankara) to FO, 4 Feb. 1959, FO 371/140685, EB 1001/4.
45. H. Caccia to FO, Washington, 9 Oct. 1959, PREM 11/3879.
46. Burrows to FO, Ankara, 4 Feb. 1959, FO 371/140685, EB 1001/4.
47. Ersoy, 'Turkey's Involvement...', p.252.
48. Burrows (Ankara) to FO, 31 May 1960, FO 371/149690, EB 10344/1.
49. Defence Secretary to Prime Minister, 5 Dec. 1960, 7 Dec. 1960, PREM 11/3879.
50. Defence Secretary to Prime Minister, 5 Dec. 1960, Prime Minister to Foreign Secretary, 7 Dec. 1960, PREM 11/3879.
51. Denis Allen (Ankara) to FO (R.A. Butler), 8 Jan. 1964 (CENTO Annual Review for 1963), FO 371/175607, EB 1011/1.
52. *FRUS*, Vol.XII, 1958–1960, Near East Region, Iraq, Iran and Arabian Peninsula, Washington, 1993, p.245.
53. Burrows to FO (The Earl of Home), Ankara, 1 Feb. 1962 (Annual Review of CENTO for 1961), FO 371/164011, EB 1011/1.
54. Burrows to FO (Annual Review of Turkey for 1962), Ankara, 18 Dec. 1962, FO 371/164011, EB 1011/2.
55. A report about Soviet policy in the Middle East, Nov. 1962, FO 371/164010.
56. FO to Prime Minister, 22 April 1963, PREM 11/4922.
57. Washington to FO, 25 Feb. 1964, FO 371/175616, EB 103145/1.
58. Memorandum by Eastern Department, 'The Problems of CENTO', 7 April 1964, FO 371/175613, EB 10112/3.
59. Ankara to FO, 26 Oct. 1964, FO 371/174005.
60. Memorandum by Eastern Department, 'The Problems of CENTO', 7 April 1964, FO 371/175613, EB 10112/3.
61. Ibid.
62. Denis Allen (Ankara) to FO, 23 March 1964, FO 371/175613, EB 10112/5.
63. Denis Allen (Ankara) to FO (Mr. Stewart), 28 April 1965, FO 371/180694, EB 1011/1.
64. FO to Ankara, 24 July 1964, FO 371/175608, EB 1014/1.
65. Washington to FO, 18 July 1964, FO 371/175608, EB 1014/5.
66. CENTO Secretary General's Statement to Council of Deputies, 25 Feb. 1965, FO 371/180718, EB 1631/14.
67. Minute by W. Morris (Head of Eastern Department) 2 Feb. 1965, FO 371/180718, E1631/6.
68. Memorandum by Eastern Department, 'The Problems of CENTO', 7 April 1964, FO 371/175613, EB 10112/3.
69. Memorandum by Secretary of State for Foreign Affairs to Cabinet Defence and Overseas Policy Committee, 31 May 1965, FO 371/180700, EB 1051/12G.
70. See for the detail of the meetings agenda and final communiqués, PREM 11/3879, PREM 11/4922, FO 371/170225, EB 1016/12, FO 371/180694, EB 1011/1.
71. Record of Meeting of the Foreign Ministers of CENTO in New York on 26 Sept. 1963, PREM 11/4922, EB 1015/74.
72. Memorandum by Eastern Department, 'The Problems of CENTO', 7 April 1964, FO 371/175613, EB 10112/3.
73. Denis Allen to FO (Mr. Stewart), Ankara, 28 April 1965, FO 371/180694, EB 1011/1.

74. CENTO Press Release, Ankara, 24 Feb. 1965, FO 371/180720, EB 1961/18.
75. Denis Allen to FO (Mr. Stewart), Ankara, 28 April 1965, FO 371/180694, EB 1011/1.
76. Memorandum by Secretary of State For Foreign Affairs to Cabinet Defence and Overseas Policy Committee, 31 May 1965, FO 371/180700, EB 1051/12G.
77. Memorandum by Eastern Department, 'The Problems of CENTO', 7 April 1964, FO 371/175613, EB 10112/3.
78. Denis Allen (Ankara) to FO, 23 March 1964, FO 371/175613, EB 10112/5.
79. Turkish Prime M. (Ürgüplü) to British Prime M. (Wilson), Ankara, 13 Sept. 1965, FO 371/180702.
80. FO to Ankara, 20 Sept. 1965, FO 371/180702.
81. FO to Tehran (Speaking notes for the Ministerial meeting of CENTO) 5 April 1965, FO 371/180695.
82. Memorandum By Michael Stewart to the to the Defence and Overseas Policy Committee, 31 May 1965, FO 371/180700, EB 1051/12/G.
83. John Beith (Tel Aviv) to FO, 7 Jan. 1965, FO 371/180645, E 1016/3.
84. FO to J. Beith, 29 Jan. 1965, FO 371180645, E 1016/3.

The Evolution of Civil–Military Relations in Post-war Turkey, 1980–95

GERASSIMOS KARABELIAS

If there is one element on which all researchers of Ottoman and Turkish history seem to agree, this is the assumption that the military institution has been the most important force behind the evolution of the social, economic and political structure of the Turkish state. 'It was the military corps that named and the military prestige that sustained the leader – once a Sultan Caliph, now a President', argue Lerner and Robinson about the role of the military institution in the political development of the Ottoman and the Turkish states.[1] Hence, any attempt to define the type of civil–military relations in post-war Turkey would be incomplete without observing and understanding the role of the military during the earlier periods.

The settlement of Turkish nomadic populations in Anatolia in the eighth–ninth century AD, the formation of their first states and the expansion of their territorial borders over neighbouring lands had a profound effect on their political organization. Two broadly defined socio-political groups dominated the political life of the Ottoman state: the *askeri* or ruling class, composed of the Sultan, the higher ranks of the military and the bureaucracy and the *ulema,* and the *re'aya*, composed of the Muslim and non-Muslim population which resided inside the state and had no direct role in government.[2] The dominant role which the military institution played in the formation and preservation of the Ottoman Empire has been emphatically pointed out by Lybyer. According to him, 'the Ottoman government had been an Army before it was anything else ... in fact, Army and Government were one. War was the external purpose, Government the internal purpose, of one institution, composed of one body of men.'[3] The expansion of the Empire into three continents and its subsequent disintegration, led to an increase in the level of contest for political power among the members of the ruling group. The result of these contests had a serious effect on the foundations of the modern Turkish state.

As the Empire expanded, the attempts of the Sultans to maintain political control over the cavalry corps, the *Sipahis*,[4] led gradually to the formation of a salaried infantry corps under their direct command, the

Yeniçeri.[5] In due course, however, and with the appearance of weak Sultans, the *Yeniçeri* started to realize their corporate strength and began to play a more direct role in the political affairs of the Empire.[6] In an attempt to save the Empire from internal disintegration and restore it as well as their political position to its previous glory, some Sultans tried to create a modern, Western-educated and trained, military and civil bureaucracy.[7] Although, initially, the new military and civil bureaucratic corps succeeded in re-establishing the imperial authority to its former powerful position, the new ideas which had been circulated among its members were bound to lead to the redistribution of political power in the ruling group.

Indeed, the exposure of the high-ranking members of the military and civil bureaucracy to Western political ideas and ideals[8] in conjunction with the increasing intervention of the state in the everyday life of the Ottoman subjects and the inability of the central government to improve the financial and military strength of the Empire, led to the identification of the Sultan as the figure responsible for all the misfortunes which had befallen the Empire. In the beginning, the Western-oriented officials succeeded in limiting the absolute political power of the Sultan by forcing him to introduce, in 1876, the first constitution and establish the first Parliament in the country's political life. However, the power struggle between these two groups could not be resolved with these changes. The disastrous results which had brought upon the Empire its continuous involvement in wars with the other Balkan states and the Great Powers, the poor performance of its economy and the spreading of instability in its social structure, offered a unique chance to the military institution to increase its corporate autonomy from the Sultan and become the political leader of the movement which was fighting for the preservation of the Ottoman-Turkish state.[9]

The Greeks, the initiators of the disintegration of the Ottoman Empire, were ironically those who involuntarily contributed to the establishment of the Turkish state and the ascendance of the military institution to the highest position in its political structure. The landing of Greek forces in Izmir in 1919 and their subsequent advance into the interior of Anatolia gave an opportunity to the then discredited pro-Union officers to lead the resistance movement.[10] With the defeat of the Greeks, the Turkish military-bureaucratic class became the most powerful political group in the new state. Since the largest part of the Ottoman officer corps became the nucleus of the Turkish Armed Forces,[11] the tradition, knowledge and experiences from past domestic and external struggles had passed on to the army of the Republic. The latter showed a strong intention of making the best use of these qualities.

The desire of the architect of the Turkish Republic, Mustafa Kemal Atatürk, to create a strong state, based on Western ideas and ideals, seemed not to be an easy task. The extermination of the Armenian and the forced exodus of the Greek populations had deprived the new state of the most Western-oriented and financially powerful social groups. The only other group which revealed strong pro-Western feelings was the military. It was the members of this group to whom Atatürk entrusted the realization of his goals. As a wise statesman, he took all the necessary measures which could guarantee that the 'Army ... [was going to be] loyal to him and the Republic'.[12] Furthermore, he made certain that most political and state institutions were infiltrated with personnel who had a military background.[13] However, Atatürk was very careful about the construction of the legacy he would leave as a bequest to the officer corps. Having learned a hard lesson from the Young Turk period, he raised legal barriers to the direct involvement of active officers in the country's everyday political life.[14] With this measure, he tried to protect the military institution from the dangers which emanate from such adventures. At the same time, he made no attempt to hide his warm feelings towards the military personnel. It was the latter rather than the civilians (politicians, merchants, etc.) whom Atatürk trusted for the accomplishment of the goals he had set for the Turkish Republic.[15]

For as long as Atatürk and his successor, İsmet İnönü, were ruling the country, the officer corps appeared to have assumed a lesser yet still important role in the evolution of Turkish politics.[16] However, the rise of the Democratic Party [DP] to power in 1950 and the new economic and social policies that it introduced, seemed to upset the officer corps, especially the middle and low-ranking ones. Although the DP did not try to introduce any radical legal changes in the country's civil–military relations, its politico-economic policies caused considerable decline in the social status and the political power of the military personnel.[17] As a result, a coup was staged in the spring of 1960 and members of the DP were punished for their past behaviour.[18] Even though the high-ranking officers did not desire the return of the country to a monoparty political system or the establishment of a military regime, they were determined to avoid the occurrence of another Menderes-style political regime. Hence, they introduced a new set of rules to the political game in Turkey. The creation of a new, liberal Constitution, the formation of a second political institution, the Senate, and the establishment of the National Security Council (NSC) as an advisory body to the Council of Ministers on issues of national security, were measures which intended to reduce the political power of the Grand National Assembly (GNA) and party leaders while at the same time legalizing the intervention of the military in the country's political and economic affairs.[19]

While the military institution played a dominant role in the formation of the coalition governments in the period 1961 to 1965 as well as in the rise of the Justice Party to power from 1965 to 1971,[20] the level of unity inside the officer corps was quite low. The increasing politicization of the military and the existence of groups of officers who opposed the practices of the civilian government[21] inevitably led to another coup. The 1971 coup through a 'memorandum' was a last-minute attempt by some high-ranking officers in order to prevent a group of 'radical' officers from gaining political power and to maintain the unity and discipline of the military. During the 1971–73 period, the Turkish Armed Forces appeared in control of all political developments,[22] as well as being capable of augmenting their power in the country's political structure.[23] Hence, when the military allowed the political parties to return to power, it appeared that it had not only solved the basic organizational problems which had forced it to stage the coup in the first place,[24] but had also emerged politically stronger.

The continuous interventions of the officer corps in the political life of the country, and its attempt to create a system that would not allow the formation of a government similar to the DP one, encouraged the development of small parties and the formation of coalition governments. Indeed, the characteristic of the period 1973 to 1980 was the absence of one-party regimes. However, the fragile unity of the coalition governments, and the desire of the smaller parties to make the most of their collaboration with the larger ones, turned the attention of political elites to partisan gains rather than to the treatment of the severe socio-economic problems which the country was facing. Naturally, there was an unprecedented explosion of social violence.[25] In conjunction with the deterioration of the economy in the late 1970s, these developments had a negative effect on the opinion of the officers and of the people about their politicians. Since the civilians had been unable to curtail the institutional autonomy and the political power of the military,[26] the latter, having taken all necessary precautions[27] staged another coup in 1980. Unlike the previous times, the co-operation of the existing political leaders was not regarded as an essential element in the remodelling of the country's political and economic structure. The military leadership was in control of developments inside Turkey.

The birth of the new regime occurred on 12 September 1980 and lasted until the 6 December 1983. Invoking the power granted to them by the Internal Service Code and citing the deteriorating social, political and economic conditions that the country was facing, the leaders of the Turkish Armed Forces staged a coup, dissolved Parliament and the government, arrested all political and union leaders and installed themselves in power.[28] Thus, for the next three years, the military institution became legally the sole political ruler of Turkey.

The first issue which the coup leaders had to face was the expansion and consolidation of their power over the country's political life. This proved not to be an easy task. Although in the beginning, the military leadership entertained the idea of appointing a civilian cabinet which could carry on the day-to-day affairs of the country under its instructions, the unwillingness of the politicians to become part of such a plan led to the formation of Ulusu's cabinet on 21 September 1983.[29] Bülent Ulusu, a retired navy commander who had been closely involved in the coup preparations, was seen by Evren and his fellow commanders as a figure who could gain the respect of both the military and the people. But Ulusu was not the only military figure of his 21-man cabinet; five of his ministers were also retired military officers while the rest were non-party technocrats. In addition to the formation of Ulusu's cabinet, hundreds of retired officers were appointed to jobs previously performed by political bureaucrats, such as under-secretaries, deputy under-secretaries, and directors general of various ministries and public enterprises.[30] This measure was considered necessary for the implementation of the work of military rulers by the state administration. Furthermore, by amending the Martial Law Act, the military regime enhanced the political powers of martial law commanders and courts[31] thus increasing the control of the central government at the local level. After accomplishing its first task, the military leadership felt obliged to prepare the ground for the period which would follow its withdrawal from the political scene.

Aware of the negative effects which their lengthy stay in power could have on the military institution itself as well as on Turkey's international relations,[32] and worried that the politicians might destroy their work when in power, the leaders of the military regime were determined to lay down new rules and limitations for the conduct of political life in the country during the post-junta period. Hence the introduction of a new constitution and its 'acceptance' by the people,[33] indicated that the process of reconstructing the country's major political institutions was irreversible. The new constitution abolished the Senate, reduced the membership of the Grand National Assembly (GNA) to 400 with an increased term of five years and enlarged the political power of the President of the Republic.[34] Interestingly enough, for the first seven-year term, the new President was granted the right to veto any constitutional amendments that the government would propose (Article 175).

Of course, the military hierarchy could not hide its concern over the type of political parties and political leaders it would like to see guiding the country's post-junta political, economic and social life. Dissatisfied with the performance of the old parties and their leaders during the pre-1980 period and disillusioned with their behaviour since the September coup, the military regime decided with some delay, on 16 October 1981, legally to dissolve the existing political parties, and, in October 1982 to ban the chairmen, general secretaries and other senior office holders from any kind of relations with future political parties during the next ten years (Provisional Article 4). The generals believed that the old politicians would try to undermine their work when the country would return to parliamentary politics and decided that Turkey needed 'a clean break with the past'.[35] Thus, on 24 April 1983, the Political Parties Law was passed which imposed certain bureaucratic restrictions on the formation of new parties.[36] Furthermore, the new electoral law which was issued in June 1983 reduced the chances of small parties to send their representatives to the Parliament[37] and made the process of forming and maintaining a stable majority government easier.

Despite all these precautionary measures, the military leaders did not forget to take certain steps that would ensure the continuing presence and influence of their institution at the highest level of political decision making. For instance, Provisional Article 1 of the 1982 Constitution stated that upon its approval the leader of the military regime, General Kenan Evren, would automatically occupy the position of President of the Republic for the next seven years. Moreover, Provisional Article 2 made clear that the other five members of the junta were to form the Presidential Council for the next six years. Furthermore, Provisional Article 15 provided with immunity all members of the NSC which exercized legislative and executive power from 1980 to 1983. Most of all, the political power of the National Security Council, in which the military retained its majority representation, was enhanced. According to Constitutional Article 118, the NSC would submit to the Council of Ministers its views on taking decisions and ensuring necessary co-ordination on issues regarding the preservation of the existence and independence of the state, the integrity and indivisibility of the country and the peace and security of the society. The government was obliged 'to give priority consideration' to the decisions of the NSC. Hence, the NSC, although not responsible to the GNA, had almost become the 'highest, non-elected, decision making body of the [Turkish] state'.[38]

In 1983, the military leaders, satisfied with their accomplishments such as the suppression of social violence, the termination of political instability, the return of the national economy to the right track and the restructuring of Turkey's political institutions, felt that they were ready to allow the transition of the country to competitive politics. However, moved by their genuine distrust towards the politicians and a strong desire to protect their work, the military leaders felt obliged to control the kind of political leadership and parties that would emerge, at least, during the early post-junta period.[39] Provisional Article 4 gave the right to the NSC to review, and if it deemed appropriate, disqualify founders of political parties. If that was not enough, in July 1983 the NSC empowered itself with the right to veto the candidates the parties put up. Thus, while several political parties were formed after the announcement of a return to parliamentary politics, only three of them were permitted by the NSC to take part in the 1983 elections. The participation of the Nationalist Democracy Party and the Populist Party was expected since both had been formed with the direct encouragement of the military leadership. As for the third, the Motherland Party (MP), although it kept some distance from the military regime, it seemed to be the one that had benefited most from the policies of the junta and could, in the long run, support their implementation. The other parties, such as the Great Turkey Party, led behind the scenes by ex-Prime Minister Suleiman Demirel, the Social Democracy Party, led by Erdal İnönü, the pro-Islamic Welfare Party, and some minor ones, were seen as possible threats to the workability of the new system, and the NSC blocked their participation in the elections.[40]

In the post-junta period, civil–military relations in Turkey passed through three distinct stages: the first when Kenan Evren was the President and Turgut Özal the Prime Minister of the Turkish Republic (1983–89), the second when Özal occupied the seat of the President (1989–93), and the third, the post-Özal period (1993–95). A short but descriptive analysis of each of them is necessary for a better understanding of the role of the military in recent political life of Turkey.

The type and the diversity which characterized the social groups that supported the Motherland Party[41] did not contribute to making it the most desirable partner of the officer corps for running the country. Since its voluntary exit from the government had assisted the military institution to retain its integrity, autonomy as well as a large proportion of its political power,[42] the lifetime of the new regime depended on the division of responsibilities between the MP and the military. Hence, during the first years of the Özal administration, the military, through the constitutional powers of President Kenan Evren and the NSC, retained responsibility over all matters relating to Turkey's internal and external security, foreign affairs and higher education. The civilian cabinet became responsible, mainly, for all issues relating to the economy.[43] Although Prime Minister Özal made some attempts to extend the influence of his cabinet in various areas and the civil bureaucracy,[44] up to 1987, the military continued to dictate the evolution of events.[45]

In due course, however, a number of events forced Özal to take certain political steps that were bound to challenge the traditional role of the officer corps in Turkish politics. Such events were the climbing rate of inflation and the criticism it raised about the economic policy of his administration,[46] the increasing pressure which the pre-1980 party leaders gradually put on the government[47] with their potential return to active political life, the demilitarization attitude of the press and the intellectuals[48] and most of all, the conciliatory attitude which the major representatives of the military institution developed towards the Prime Minister. Özal tried to curtail the influence of the military on public policy. For instance, he let the people decide (through a national referendum) on the status of Provisional Article 4 which forbade the leaders of the pre-1980 parties to establish, join or have any relations with any political party until 1992,[49] lifted the restrictions on forming new political parties and ignored those which the 1982 constitution had put on the movement of parliamentary deputies from one party to another. He passed new laws which allowed, to a certain degree, public meetings and demonstrations and the right to form associations and to make collective petitions – issues that had been illegal after the 1980 coup. Also, he replaced the military liaison appointees in each ministry with civilian administrators, reduced the maximum period of detention of suspects prior to arraignment from 90 to 15 days, and allowed all but one of the trade unions to operate. Furthermore, he attempted to extend the authority of his cabinet to the area of internal security either by creating regional governorships with extraordinary political powers or by giving the Prime Minister unprecedented powers over the recruitment and personnel policies of the National Intelligence Agency (MIT).[50]

At the same time, Özal tried to interfere with matters related to military autonomy[51] and establish political authority over it. In the summer of 1987, he overruled the recommendation of the senior military command to appoint General Necdet Öztorun to the position of the Chief of the General Staff and instead put in office the candidate he seemed to prefer, General Necip Torumtay.[52] Özal decided to break old taboo subjects and brought into public discussion the issue of defence funds. A few months later, his cabinet declared that it planned to make the Chief of the General Staff report to the defence minister, a characteristic of all Western democratic governments.[53] If that was not enough, he ordered a halt to air force training exercises over the Aegean, due to an agreement he had reached with the Greek Prime Minister Andreas Papandreou, without informing first or consulting with the military chiefs.

The mild reaction of the military institution to Özal's actions,[54] his elevation to the office of the President of the Turkish Republic in 1989 and favourable international conditions appeared to give Özal the green light to continue his policy of intruding into the hitherto untouched domain of the officer corps and attempt to curtail their political power. As the holder of the office of the President and supervisor of events inside the ruling party he had founded, Özal became the undisputed political leader of Turkey during the period 1989 to 1991.[55] The developments in the Persian Gulf in 1990 and his determination to build a new foreign policy,[56] inevitably led him into a clash with at least some sections of the military institution. Özal's tendency to assign to military chiefs and his cabinet a subsidiary or advisory role in the unfolding of events, forced the Chief of the General Staff, General Torumtay, who seemed to disagree with the way the President was handling the issue of the country's security,[57] to announce his resignation before his four-year term expired. This appeared to be an extraordinary development for Turkey's civil–military relations since both domestic and foreign observers were accustomed to see the civilian rather than the military officer leave his post (voluntarily or by the use or threat to use force) when the two of them strongly disagreed on a specific subject. The fact that Torumtay's successor, General Doğan Güreş, appeared to accept the existing situation, indicated that the all-powerful President was in charge of Turkey's political life.

The formation of a Demirel–İnönü coalition government following the November 1991 elections, however, was bound to reduce drastically the intervention of the President in the affairs of the cabinet. Demirel and Özal hated each other. But the ever-present threat from the military to intervene in case there was a breakdown of government forced them to find a way to co-exist. The threat of a coup was not a fictitious one. As Hale has pointed out, despite the changes that took place in the country's civil–military relations, one cannot suggest 'that, by 1992, the civil power had yet established the full degree of control over the military which is the norm in most democratic systems'.[58] The continuous involvement of the military in large-scale campaigns in the south-eastern provinces against the Kurdistan Workers' Party (PKK) had permitted it, among other things, to retain a large part of its internal autonomy intact.[59] The military campaign in the south-east had an enormous negative effect not only on the country's economic performance but also on its relationship with the European Union and the USA, countries traditionally sensitive on the issue of violations of human rights.[60]

The sudden death of Özal in April 1993,[61] the election of Suleiman Demirel to the office of President and his replacement in the leadership of the TPP and the government by Tansu Çiller, the first female Prime Minister of Turkey, seems to have contributed to an increase in the political power of the military institution. The unfriendly relations between the Prime Minister and the President of the Republic, the continuation of military campaigns in the south-east,[62] the direct and indirect pressure that the military leadership started to exercise upon the government,[63] the rapidly unfolding events in the ex-Soviet Muslim territories and the need for the Turkish government to react to them quickly, in conjunction with the failure of the Çiller administration to cure the economy, had forced the Prime Minister to rely on the support of the military to keep herself in power.[64] As an English reporter pointed out in March 1994, 'traditionally, the armed forces have stepped in to clear such [economic] messes. But few Turks believe a new coup is in the works. The armed forces already do almost what they want.'[65] Almost a year later, retired Air Force General Sadi Erguvenç would argue that 'civil authorities [are] not in command of [the] military'.[66]

Despite the limited amount of information available to us, since the military is still regarded as a taboo subject in Turkey, there are certain elements that characterize its behaviour and assist it in retaining its institutional autonomy as well as its superiority over the politicians.

Firstly, there is the ability of the 'military class' to reproduce itself and its values and regard its members as the only legitimate guardians of the Kemalist ideology. Commenting on the Turkish military, Orhan Erkanli argues that 'in Turkey there is a military class, just as there is a workers' and peasants' class, and the officer corps constitutes the backbone of this class'.[67] Indeed, the careful process of selection of the future corps, the early age of their entrance to military schools and their indoctrination in Kemalist principles and ideals[68] aim to breed members of an educated, statist elite capable of defending both Turkey's borders and the ideas of Atatürk, as well as being concerned with the country's domestic problems.[69] The ability of the military class of Turkey to reproduce itself[70] and its values,[71] with minimum if any interference from the civilians,[72] helps us to understand how the officers can perpetuate their superiority over the politicians.

As far as the Kemalist values of secularism, republicanism, nationalism, populism, etatism and revolutionism[73] are concerned, they were supposed to be the guidelines necessary for Turkey's attainment of a political, economic and cultural level similar to that of contemporary Western states. However, although Kemalism 'clearly and convincingly told the society what its goals were and [had] furnished guidelines for achieving them ... [it] pertained primarily to the first stage – the stage of elite modernization. It clearly had very little to say about the second stage – that of bringing mass elements into active participation'.[74] The lack of specific guidelines regarding the latter stage of political transformation in Turkey and the way the people's political demands were articulated by party leaders often appeared as a threat to the political position of the so-called protectors of Kemalist principles, the officer corps.[75]

Secondly, there is the huge size of the military establishment and the preservation of a high level of unity and cohesion in the officer corps. The presence of the second largest military force in the North Atlantic Treaty Organization in Turkey has officially been justified on the grounds of the need to secure the country's borders from threats imposed by external and internal enemies.[76] Located in a highly volatile area and taking advantage of its geostrategic importance for the West, senior officers have always been in favour of maintaining a large military establishment. The huge size of the armed forces constitutes such a source of political power that party leaders cannot ignore it. Any attempt by a civilian government to reduce either the financial and social status of the officer corps or military expenditure could easily result in its overthrow.[77]

Furthermore, the size of the military organization seems to contribute to the maintenance of unity and cohesion in the officer corps, as no attempt by any group of officers to intervene in the country's political life can succeed unless it has the support of the military leadership and especially that of the Land Forces. Even though members of the Turkish military often boast about the high level of discipline and obedience to orders from the top,[78] there are certain examples that put into question the validity of those statements.[79] However, one must admit that although the officer corps passed through some difficult moments between 1980 and 1995,[80] the Turkish Armed Forces appeared capable of maintaining a high level of unity and cohesion and preventing the party leaders from becoming heavily involved in military affairs.

Thirdly, there is the growth of the independent economic power of the military. In their attempt to safeguard the officers from the vagaries of the crisis-prone Turkish economy and to increase the military's financial autonomy from the civilian administration, the Turkish Armed Forces started, from 1960 on, to create a number of militarily-controlled financial groups that gave the officer corps a large stake in Turkey's corporate economy. For instance, the Armed Forces Mutual Fund (OYAK) which was established in 1961 (Law 205) with the aim of providing social security to military personnel has become one of the largest financial conglomerates in Turkey.[81] But OYAK is not the only militarily-controlled conglomerate. Three similar foundations, the Naval, Air-Force and Land Forces Foundations 'also have shares in a variety of civilian public sector enterprises'.[82] Furthermore, the military leadership has been actively involved in the development of a domestic defence industry.[83] As Ahmad points out, with their economic activities, the Turkish Armed Forces have been so intertwined with capitalism they 'no longer can afford to be neutral or above politics'.[84] Their economic activities have assisted not only in increasing the degree of the political and financial autonomy of the officer corps from the civilian government but also in developing closer, direct ties between the military establishment and leading industrialists both in Turkey (e.g. Koç, Eczacibasi and Sabanci Holdings)[85] as well as abroad (e.g. American, German, French, Israeli and Russian military and high-tech companies).

The external factors included, first, the inability of party leaders to impose their political supremacy over the military. Commenting on the Turkish political system in 1948, Nadir Nadi argued that the source of all problems in Turkey lies in the fact that the Western political institutions which were implanted in the country in the 1920s resembled their European models only in appearance; their way of operating was 'oriental'.[86] Indeed, since Ottoman times, state dominance has been the most salient feature of the Turkish political system.[87] The fact that even today the state is referred to as a father figure, *Devlet Baba*, is an example of its influence on the country's political structure.

A result of the state tradition in the Empire's and the Republic's political structure has been the development of uneasy relations between the 'centre' and the 'periphery'.[88] The augmentation of the political power of peripheral groups with the opening of the country to multi-party politics, appeared, in the eyes of the statist-Kemalist elite, as a threat to the national unity and territorial integrity of Turkey. As Göle argues, 'the military interventions of 1960–1961, 1971–1973, and 1980–1983 can in fact be perceived as state reactions against the "unhealthy" autonomization and differentiation of economic, political and cultural groups'.[89]

The tradition which sees the statist-military elite as the one dictating the evolution of political life in Turkey, continued with some minor interruptions during the post-1983 period. Indeed, it was the statist elite, with the military as their leader, which through the Constitution of 1982 imposed on party leaders the new rules and limitations of the political process in Turkey. Especially, Article 6 deprived political parties and their leaders of the freedom to adjust the existing institutional arrangements in accordance with their own views as well as societal needs, stating clearly that 'the Turkish Nation shall exercise its sovereignty through the authorised organs as prescribed by the principles laid down in the Constitution'.[90]

With the exception of the 1987–93 period in which Turgut Özal tried and partially succeeded in imposing his political superiority over the military in foreign policy and security issues, the latter maintained control over party leaders and political development in the country.[91] The relative absence of a 'civil society' in Turkey's political structure,[92] and the rising suspicion of the centre elites towards intermediary groups and institutions, permitted the political exploitation of the masses by local notables and religious leaders through the extensive use of patron–client relations[93] and prevented the creation of strong, autonomous, corporate social institutions.[94] The politicians, influenced by the non-democratic political culture which they inherited[95] and looking at the outcome of the elections as a 'zero-sum game', appeared to give greater priority to build their image and increasing their own power[96] rather than concentrating their efforts in finding a solution to the country's major economic, political and social problems.[97] The closure of the pro-Kurdish Democracy Party (DEP) in the Summer of 1994 was a clear manifestation of the inability of politicians to stand against the military. As Hasan Yalçin argues, 'Parliament has been relegated to the status of a yes-man that approves decisions taken by the National Security Council.'[98] Only the Turkish Industrialists and Businessmen's Association (TUSIAD) appeared to be a growing political force in the country, capable, in the long run, of challenging the political supremacy of the military

A second external factor is the capability of the Turkish elite to withstand pressures from foreign powers on the conduct of its domestic political life. Although Turkey has been one of the major beneficiaries of American military assistance, most non-leftist, non-Islamic studies tend to emphasize the minimal influence the West and especially the US government exercise on the unfolding of its domestic affairs. This observation seems to contradict the view which sees foreign aid as a tool of the donor government designed to serve its political, strategic, and/or economic self-interest.[99]

As the offspring of the ruling civil–military bureaucratic class of the Ottoman Empire, the Turkish statist elite carried both the experiences and historical lessons of its predecessor.[100] The military modernization and the Westernization of political institutions which the Ottoman and the Kemalist regimes had initiated, were regarded as essential measures of self-defence against foreign intervention.[101] As İsmet İnönü had pointed out, 'our watchword in foreign policy towards any state with which we had contact was to be fully conscious of our own complete independence and our own interests'.[102] Hence, despite the benefits that Turkey received from its entrance into the Western camp during the post-war period,[103] the realization of the ruling elite's long-time dream did not mean that the country's political life became a toy in the hands of foreign powers. In contrast, the Turkish elite made certain that it maintained control over its domestic affairs.[104]

Taking advantage of the geostrategic importance of their country for the Western Alliance during the 1980–95 period,[105] the ruling elite was able to overcome the mild external pressures on Turkey's poor human rights record, the extensive use of state violence in its south-eastern provinces, and the persecution of members of the parliament who supported the Kurdish cause as well as that of journalists who championed the application of democratic principles. Surprisingly, the political leaders helped the military establishment with their actions by having very carefully refrained from encouraging foreign governments and international organizations to intervene in the domestic affairs of Turkey.[106] Irrespective of the real motives behind this type of behaviour of party leaders and civilian authorities,[107] the ruling elite appeared strong enough to withstand the mild pressures from foreign states and international organizations and preserve its autonomous political position in the country.

NOTES

1. Daniel Lerner and Richard Robinson, 'Swords and Ploughshares: the Turkish Army as a Modernizing Force', *World Policy*, Vol.13 (1960), p.19.
2. Halil Inalcik, 'The Nature of Traditional Society', in Richard Ward and Dankwart Rustow (eds.), *Political Modernization in Japan and Turkey* (Princeton, 1964), p.44.
3. Albert Lybyer, *The Government of the Ottoman Empire in the Time of the Suleiman the Magnificent* (Cambridge, MA, 1913), pp.90–1.
4. V.J. Parry, 'Elite Elements in the Ottoman Empire', in Rupert Wilkinson (ed.), *Governing Elites: Studies in their Training and Selection* (New York, 1969), p.55.
5. With the *devşirme* system, young boys were taken away from their non-Muslim families, brought to the capital and were forced to embrace Islam. The most intelligent were trained in the art of administration while the rest had to undergo military training to join the *Yeniçeri* corps. Since the *Yeniçeri* were theoretically dependent on the Sultan for their income and social status, they contributed to the augmentation of the latter's political power. Godfrey Goodwin, *The Janissaries* (London, 1994).
6. Sir Hamilton Gibb and Harold Bowen (eds.), *Islamic Society and the West* (London, 1950), Vol.I, pp.180–82 and Bernard Lewis, *The Emergence of Modern Turkey* (London: Oxford University Press, 1961), pp.23–4.
7. Kemal Karpat, 'The Transformation of the Ottoman State, 1789–1908', *International Journal of Middle East Studies*, Vol.3 (1972) and Avigdor Levy, 'The Ottoman Corps in Sultan Mahmud II New Ottoman Army', *International Journal of Middle East Studies*, Vol.1 (1971).
8. Bernard Lewis, 'The Impact of the French Revolution on Turkey', *Journal of World Politics*, Vol.1, No.1 (1953).
9. B. Lewis (1969), op. cit., Sina Akşin, *31 Mart Olayi* (Ankara, 1970); Feroz Ahmad, *The Young Turks* (Oxford, 1969); Liman Von Sanders, *Five Years in Turkey* (Annapolis, 1972); and Eric Jan Zürcher, *The Unionist Factor* (Leiden, 1984)
10. The entry of the Ottoman Empire into the First World War led not only to the loss of its Arab territories and to a financial disaster, but also, under the Armistice of Mudros, its independent political status was threatened.
11. Dankward Rustow, 'The Military: Turkey', in Ward and Rustow, op. cit., p.388.
12. George Harris, 'The Role of the Military in Turkish Politics', *Middle East Journal*, Vol.19, No.1 (1965), Part I, p.56.
13. 'Though [the RPP regime was] technically civilian,' Frey observes, 'persons conditioned by military experience, accessible to military contacts and trusted by military personnel were at the mainspring of power.' Frederick Frey, 'The Army in Turkish Politics', *Land Reborn* (1966), pp.7–8 Also, Özbudun points out that in the early years of the Republic, 'the separation of military from politics was not complete. The civilian regime depended on the support of the army for maintaining its power and implementing its reforms ... the contentment of the armed forces with the non-political roles that they had been assigned may have been due to the fact that their ex-commanders were the leaders of the new regime and they were carrying out the social revolution which the army desired'. Ergun Özbudun, *The Role of the Military in Recent Turkish Politics* (Harvard, 1966), p.8.

14. Article 148 of the Military Penal Code prohibited 'any member of the armed forces to join a political party, hold or participate in political meetings, give a political speech in public, or prepare, sign or send to the press any declaration of a political character' quoted from Frederick Frey, *The Turkish Political Elite* (Cambridge, 1965), p.61.
15. 'Whenever the Turkish nation has wanted to stride towards the heights,' Atatürk argued, 'it has always seen its army ... as the permanent leader in the forefront of this march ... In times to come, also, its heroic sons will march in the vanguard of the sublime ideals of the Turkish nation.' Quoted from William Hale, *Turkish Politics and the Military* (London, 1994), p.87.
16. Even though İnönü tried to reduce the political power of the officers with the introduction of personnel and institutional changes in it, such as the retirement of Marshal Fevzi Çakmak, long-time Chief of the Turkish Armed Forces and the making the Chief of the General Staff directly responsible to the Ministry of Defence rather than the office of the President (Hale, op. cit., pp.82–3), the presence of the military continued to be a strong one. For instance, military interests 'dictated' the building of roads, railways and the location of factories (Harris, op. cit., p.60), military commanders in the frontier provinces combined their military and civilian duties for prolonged periods of time (Rustow, op. cit., pp.549–50) and military personnel were instrumental in the spread of Kemalist ideas to the people. Clifton Fox, 'Turkish Army's Role in Nationbuilding', *Military Review*, Vol.67 (1967).
17. An officer interviewed by Karpat after the 1960 coup argued that during the DP regime, 'the prestige of the army was declining. Money seemed to have become everything. An officer no longer had status in the society. It hurt ... to see officers ... wear civilian clothes and feel proud in them.' Kemal Karpat, 'The Military and Politics in Turkey, 1960–64: a socio-cultural analysis of a revolution', *American Historical Review*, Vol.75 (1970), p.1665. Also, George Harris, 'The Causes of the 1960 Revolution in Turkey', *Middle East Journal*, Vol.24 (1970).
18. Over 20,000 members of the DP lost their political rights while three members of the administration, Prime Minister Menderes, Minister for Foreign Affairs Zorlu and Interior Minister Polatkan, were hanged. The punishment of DP founders and associates can be seen as a message from the military to future political leaders that the latter should think twice before attempting to violate the limits of political behavior that the Turkish Armed Forces have set.
19. Roger Nye, 'The Military in Turkish Politics, 1960–73', unpublished PhD thesis (Washington University, 1974).
20. Clement Dodd, *Politics and Government in Turkey* (Manchester, 1969) and Ümit Cizre-Sakall Ioðlu, *AP-Ordu İlişkileri* (Istanbul, 1993)
21. Karpat (1970), op. cit., pp.1675–6; Nye, op. cit., Chapter 6; Muhsin Batur, *Anilar ve Görüşler* (Istanbul, 1985), pp.146, 177 and 184; Celil Gürkan, *12 Mart'a Beş Kala* (Istanbul, 1986), pp.216–18 and 230–49.
22. As Turan argues, all parties formed after the coup 'required [the] acceptance [of the] military leadership. Part of the cabinet's responsibility was to translate into policy those objectives deemed desirable by the commanders, then to mobilize support for their acceptance by the legislature'. The threat of a higher degree of intervention was often employed to stop members of the GNA from obstructing the policies of military-backed coalition cabinets. İlter Turan, *Military Influence and Coalition Governments as Inputs into Ministerial Attributes, Attitudes and Job Risks: Turkey, 1961–1972* (Istanbul, 1977), p.51.
23. For instance, the declaration of martial law and its extension up to 1973 permitted the local commanders to concentrate the judicial, legislative and executive powers in their own hands. These commanders were answerable for their actions to military not to civilian authorities. Furthermore, all amendments that were passed to the 1961 Constitution had as a goal to increase the level of autonomy as well as the political power of the military institution over the civilians. Nurşen Mazici, *Türkiye'de Askeri Darbeler ve Sivil Rejime Etkileri* (Istanbul, 1989), pp.114–16.
24. Lucille Pavsner, *Turkey's Political Crisis* (New York, 1984), p.51.
25. The number of political murders increased rapidly year after year and intraethnic and

intersectarian cleavages were aroused. National Security Council, *12 September in Turkey: Before and After* (Ankara, 1982), pp.159–99.

26. Semih Vaner, 'The Army', in Irvin Schick and Erdugul Tonak (ed.), *Turkey in Transition* (London: Oxford, 1987).
27. For example, in the autumn of 1978, the military leadership established a team 'commissioned to prepare the following questions: *Is an intervention from the armed forces required at this stage? If so, what should be the basis of such an intervention?'*. Furthermore, the Chief of the General Staff, General Kenan Evren and his fellow commanders were making frequent tours of inspection throughout the country in order to make certain that the activities of the younger officers were under the control of the military leadership. Also, the military commanders, by appearing as the only group which could bring political order and stability to Turkey, had won the support of the Americans and the international financial organizations for their action. Mehmet Ali Birand, *The General's Coup in Turkey* (London, 1987), pp.25, 39, 61–2, 65.
28. Kenan Evren, *Kenan Evren'in Anilari* (Istanbul, 1990) Vol.I, pp.546–7.
29. Birand (1987), op. cit., pp.200–2.
30. *The New York Times*, 16 March 1981.
31. Martial law commanders were given 'the right to ban strikes, public meetings, demonstrations, suspend newspapers and other publications, and to dismiss local and central government staff whose employment was deemed undesirable without right of appeal. Martial law courts were given the right to try ideological offenses laid down in Sections 141 and 142 of the Penal Code and arrangements were made to speed up trials under martial law.' Hale (1994), op. cit., p.251.
32. *The Washington Post*, 29 May 1981.
33. According to the official results of the referendum that was held on 7 Nov. 1982, 91.4 per cent of the voters in a 91.3 per cent turnout approved the proposed constitution. In addition to valid objections one can have about the final outcome of any type of elections conducted under a martial law government, it is interesting to point out that the Turkish people did not have much of a choice. As the then Prime Minister Bülent Ulusu had pointed out on 14 July 1982, if the people voted 'no' in the referendum, the military would not return to the barracks but remain in power. General Kenan Evren seemed to share the same view with Ulusu. Hasan Cemal, *Tank Sesiyle Uyanmak* (Ankara, 1986), p.550. In other words, the people had to choose between a Constitution proposed by the military or the continuation of the military dictatorship.
34. With regard to his executive function, the President's powers were: appointing the Prime Minister and accepting his resignation, presiding over the meetings of the Council of Ministers whenever he deems it necessary, calling a meeting of the NSC and presiding over it, proclaiming martial law or a state of emergency in collaboration with the Council of Ministers, appointing the chairman and members of the State Supervisory Council as well as the members of the Board of Higher Education, appointing the Chief of the General Staff, and appointing university rectors. His powers pertaining to the judicial function were: appointing the members of the Constitutional Court, one-fourth of the members of the Council of State, the members of the High Military Administrative Court, the Military Court of Appeal as well as those of the Supreme Council of Judges and Prosecutors. Ergun Özbudun, 'The status of the President of the Republic under the Turkish Constitution of 1982', in Metin Heper and Ahmed Evin (eds.), *State, Democracy and the Military: Turkey in the 1980s* (Berlin, 1988), p.39.
35. Evren, op. cit., Vol.2, pp.411–16.
36. According to Articles 4,5,8 of the Political Parties Law No.2820, to gain legal existence, political parties had to have at least thirty founder members, who had to submit to the Ministry of the Interior a formal statement of the name and address of the party, the party rule book and programme, their own names and personal details and a mass of personal documentation. Furthermore, the parties ought to be attached to the principles and reforms of Atatürk and should not adopt any of the aims deemed inadmissible under Article 14 of the constitution. In other words, 'the by-laws and programs of the parties may not be in conflict with the principle of national unity and territorial integrity of the state, human

rights, national sovereignty, and the democratic and the secular character of the Republic'. Also, 'no parties advocating domination of society by a group and the establishment of a dictatorship may be founded'. Moreover, Articles 78–90 of the Political Parties Law pointed out that 'communist parties and parties oriented toward ethnic separatism, religious distinctions and racial differences' were not going to be allowed. Article 96 specified that the new parties could not use the names and symbols of the pre-1980 parties and Article 97 barred political parties from criticizing or opposing the decisions and policies pursued by the NSC. İlter Turan, 'Political Parties and the Party System in post-1983 Turkey', in Heper and Evin (eds.), op. cit., pp.69 and 74.

37. According to Articles 33 and 34 of the Law on the Election of Deputies No.2839, all parties needed to win at least 10 per cent of the national vote to qualify for parliamentary seats. In addition, the new law set a local quota which parties had to exceed to gain any seats in the constituency. Hale, op. cit., p.259 and Turan, ibid., p.71.
38. *Cumhuriyet*, 19 Jan. 1989.
39. A prominent Turkish politician talking to David Tonge of the *Financial Times* before the 1983 elections argued that 'we [the political leaders] don't need to panic. In two years at most, the generals' creations will begin to unravel'. With regard to the junta, Tonge pointed out that 'the military's hope appears to be that once new politicians are in the saddle, they will refuse to dismount for their former leaders'. *Financial Times*, 17 May 1983.
40. Hale, op. cit., p.262–5, Turan, op. cit., pp.74–5.
41. 'Özal's MP as a centre-right, moderate force has served to draw back into the mainstream supporters of those pre-1980 parties of the right (NSP, NAP) who were formerly engaged in anti-system protest. Statistical analysis indicated that MP had created a new cleavage in Turkish politics which had cut across the old cleavages of the right and perhaps extending into the centre-left'. Ustun Erguder and Richard Hofferbert, 'Restoration of Democracy in Turkey? Political Reforms and the Elections of 1983', in Linda Lane (ed.), *Elections in the Middle East: Implications of Recent Trends* (Boulder, CO, 1987), p.37.
42. Barkey, op. cit, pp.171–3, Claude Welch Jr, *No Farewell to Arms* (Boulder, CO, 1987)
43. Metin Heper, 'The Executive in the Third Turkish Republic', *Governance*, No.3 (1990), pp.299–319 and Ustun Erguder, 'The Motherland Party, 1983–89', in Metin Heper and Jacob Landau (eds.), *Political Parties and Democracy in Turkey* (London, 1991).
44. Metin Heper, 'The State and Debureaucratization: The Case of Turkey', *International Social Science Journal*, Vol.42 (1990), p.611.
45. For instance, the military returned to the barracks according to its own timetable. Despite the gradual lifting of martial law, its presence in public life remained a strong one since those indicted under martial law continued to be prosecuted in military courts and the evolution of events in the southeast region raised a lot of questions as to whether the military would completely forego its policing duties. *Cumhuriyet*, 11 Jan. 1986 and 28 April 1986; *Nokta*, 16 Aug. 1987.
46. Erguder in Heper and Landau, op. cit., p.157.
47. The democratic legitimacy of the 1983 elections was put to the test both in the 1984 local elections in which the MP gained 41.5 per cent of the vote, to be followed by the SDP with 23.4 per cent and the True Path Party (TPP) with 13.5 per cent and in the 1986 by-elections in which the MP received only 32 per cent of the votes whereas the TPP received 23.5 per cent and the Social Democrat Populist Party (SDPP) 22.8 per cent.
48. *Cumhuriyet*, 15 April 1986 and 16 January 1987, Yalçin Doğan, *Dar Sokakta Siyaset: 1980–83* (Istanbul, 1985); Türker Alkan, *12 Eylul ve Demokrasi* (Istanbul, 1986); Yavuz Donat, *Buyruklu Demokrasi, 1980–83* (Ankara, 1987).
49. The result was in favor of amending it (50.2 per cent voted 'yes' and 49.8 per cent 'no'). The outcome benefited Özal since on the one side he eliminated the accusation that his party dominance was hiding behind undemocratic restrictions imposed by the military. Also, by campaigning in favour for the 'no' vote, Özal could claim that the majority of the 49.8 per cent were MP supporters.
50. Ahmed Evin, 'Demilitarization and Civilianization of the Regime', in Metin Heper and Ahmed Evin (eds.), *Politics in the Third Turkish Republic* (Boulder, CO, 1994), pp.35–8.
51. For instance, there was no attempt to amend Article 16 of the 1982 Constitution that

pointed out that the decisions of the Supreme Military Council are outside the scope of judicial review.

52. *The Christian Science Monitor*, 8 July 1987, and Ken Mackenzie, 'Turkey: Özal vs the Generals', *Middle East International*, 11 July 1987.
53. Except for the period 1949 to 1960 in which the Ministry of Defense had the responsibility to manage the armed forces and make the appointments, all other times it was entrusted with the minor role of the orderly recruitment of soldiers and procurement of supplies. Hikmet Özdemir, *Rejim ve Aşker* (Istanbul, 1989), pp.252–63.
54. Although the appointment of General Torumtay to the position of the Chief of the General Staff shocked some senior officers and raised a number of verbal complaints (Güneş Taner, former MP cabinet minister, argued that the incident could have led to a coup, *Hürriyet*, 14 July 1995), no action was taken against Prime Minister Özal and his cabinet. Furthermore, a remark made by President Evren in April 1988 that the Armed Forces would intervene and save the country from anarchy and terrorism, even though it was interpreted as a warning against the civilian government, it was met with a hail of criticism from government and opposition forces alike. But as analysts pointed out, the time was not ripe for the military to take such action. *Financial Times*, 23 May 1988.
55. Özal 'urged the party to elect his newly appointed prime minister [Yildirim Akbulut] as party chairman at the next convention ... he [continued to pay] special attention to the management of the economy, quickly forging independent links with key ministers and bureaucrats ... [and] was fairly active in dealing with problems of law and order ... İnönü complained that the new president was abusing his office acting as "the de facto leader of the governing party".' Metin Heper, 'Consolidating Turkish Democracy', *Journal of Democracy*, Vol.3 (1992), p.111.
56. *Milliyet*, 7 Dec. 1990.
57. *Turkey Confidential* (Jan. 1991), pp.4–5.
58. Hale, op. cit., p.294.
59. According to a *Financial Times* report, the Demirel–İnönü coalition government under pressure from the military not only excluded Kurdish areas from coming under the umbrella of a proposed human rights legislation but also gave to the military a *carte blanche* in the fight against the PKK. Demirel was quoted to explain his decision on the basis that the security forces would be left with no authority if that type of legislation were implemented in a region whereas the fight against terrorism was going on. (*Financial Times*, 2 Oct. 1992). However, it was the same person, Prime Minister Suleiman Demirel, who in Dec. 1991 urged the people of Turkey 'to recognize the Kurdish reality' and had promised in his election campaign to withdraw the emergency regime from the southeastern provinces (*Milliyet*, 9 Dec. 1991).
60. *Guardian*, 24 Nov. 1994.
61. It is interesting to notice that the 'sudden' death of Özal occurred during a period when the President of the Republic had started, once more, seriously to challenge the political power of the military institution. For instance, Özal became actively involved in the Kurdish issue and proposed to end the emergency rule which 'never yielded positive results' and suggested that the Turkish government ought to make 'some kind of "goodwill gestures" to ease tensions in southeast Anatolia and create a true atmosphere of rapprochement between the people of the area and the state'. He even started contacts with the leader of the Patriotic Union of Kurdistan (PUK), Jalal Talabani, inviting him to Ankara to discuss the conditions of a ceasefire, without informing the MIT (the Turkish Central Intelligence Organization) or the country's military intelligence. (*Turkish Daily News*, 31 March 1993). Knowing that the military was against any diplomatic solution to the Kurdish issue (*Turkish Daily News*, 15 March 1993), the initiatives of President Özal, naturally, upset the majority of the officer corps (*Hürriyet*, 8 Jan. 1995). In fact, some circles started to think of 'President Özal as the mentor of Apo (Abdullah Öcalan, the PKK leader)' (*Turkish Daily News*, 1 April 1993). Also, Özal challenged the political power of the armed forces by calling for a military intervention in Armenia in the wake of the Armenian attacks against Azerbaijan, although he knew that the Turkish military leaders were reluctant to engage in such a highly risky adventure (*Turkish Daily News*, 5 March 1993, *Milliyet*, 5 April 1993).

Özal's death a few days before submitting a major proposal for 'Kurdish reforms' to NSC raised a lot of questions.

62. Whereas 'Özal had closed the doors to the military ... in the Kurdish dispute ... [using] this policy to restore "civilian" democracy in Turkey ... Demirel opened the door for the military in fear of loosing his own authority if he limited the authority of the commanders ... Çiller allowed the military to walk through the door opened by Demirel and has given "full authority" to the military'. *Turkish Daily News*, 24 March 1994. Also, *Observer*, 26 March 1995.
63. A few months after the formation of the new post-Özal government, in July of 1993, rumours of an imminent military takeover started to circulate in Ankara. The issue of military intervention was back on the agenda in February 1994 and in January 1995. It is interesting to note that even though in 1990 Demirel, while in opposition, declared that there was an urgent need for restructuring civil–military relations in Turkey starting with 'the position of the Chief of the General Staff [that] should be under the Minister of Defence' (*Milliyet*, 28 May 1990), when he became the new Prime Minister, he made certain that a bill which was presented in the Parliament ready to pass these changes, was defeated by his own party votes on 14 May 1992.
64. *Milliyet*, 26 May 1994.
65. *The Independent*, 23 March 1994.
66. *Turkish Daily News*, 14 March 1995.
67. Quoted in William Hale, 'The Turkish Army in Politics', in Andrew Finkel and Nükhet Sirman (eds.), *Turkish State, Turkish Society* (London, 1990).
68. Regardless of the social background of the cadet, Birand notes that 'once the ceremonies are over, a gigantic piece of machinery goes into action ... and transforms him [the cadet] into a totally different person'. Mehmet Ali Birand, *Shirts of Steel: An Anatomy of the Turkish Armed Forces* (London, 1991), p.26.
69. *Le Figaro*, 2 July 1997.
70. According to Brown's survey, 22.2 per cent of the military cadets were sons of officers while 22.4 per cent were sons of civil servants. 'The recruitment of the officer corps,' Brown points out, 'primarily [from] 'sons of military' and civil servants, suggests a perpetuation of kinship and personal ties to Atatürk and the Revolution he wrought'. James Brown, 'The Military and Society: The Turkish Case', *Middle Eastern Affairs*, Vol.25 (1989), pp.399 and 400.
71. 'Always bear in mind', says an instructor of the Military Academy to the cadets, 'that you are superior to everyone and everything, and that you are trained here to have superior knowledge and superior qualities ... As an officer of the Turkish Army ... you are different from your friends in civy street'. Quoted in Hale (1994), op. cit., p.321.
72. If there is a case of civilian interference in the military schools or in the officer corps, high-ranking officers quite often expel the cadets and officers involved. Those expelled are not able to take their case to court since the 1982 Constitution stipulates that decisions of the Supreme Military Council cannot be contested judicially.
73. Suna Kili, 'Kemalism in Contemporary Turkey', *International Political Science Review*, Vol.1 (1980)
74. Frederick Frey, 'Patterns of Elite Politics in Turkey', in George Lenczowski (ed.), *Political Elites in the Middle East* (Washington, 1975), p.70.
75. 'We are the army of the [Kemalist] regime. It is our duty ... to keep the state sound and the regime secure', says an officer to Birand. Another claims that 'politicians [give] priority to his [sic] own re-election ... [and] are not concerned "for the state" as much as we are'. Birand, op. cit., p.22. The former Chiefs of General Staff, Generals Kenan Evren, Necip Torumtay and Doğan Güreş, all seem to share similar views. Evren argues that it is the party leaders who tend to deviate from the Kemalist principles (Kenan Evren, *Kenan Evren'in Anilari* [Istanbul, 1990], Vol.II, p.185). He believes that the military acts the way it does towards the civilian government because it has the support of the people (ibid., p.363). Torumtay argues that Atatürk entrusted to the military the norms on which the republic rested and his perception of the military's display of professional traits and civilian's lack of them lead to the conclusion that the former should have as much

autonomy as possible from the civilian authority (Org. Necip Torumtay, *Orgeneral Torumtay'in Anilari* [Istanbul, 1994], p.36 and p.90). Also, Güreş points out that the military, the guardian of Atatürk's ideas and ideals, is directly responsible to the people from whom it derives its authority rather than from the civilian government (*Milliyet*, 19 March 1991 and 6 June 1992).

76. Ihsan Gürkan, *NATO,Turkey and the Southern Flank* (New York, 1980) (Agenda Paper No.10), pp.17–18 and NATO'S SIXTEEN NATIONS, *Defence Industry Policy of Turkey* (Ankara, Special Edition, Dec. 1989), p.10.
77. It is interesting that although the outlawed PKK offered a 'cease-fire' to the Turkish civilian governments, with the exception of Özal, no other party leader attempted to deviate from the directives of the military. İlnur Çevik, commenting on the Çiller government's decision to freeze all army discharges in a move towards a national mobilization, points out that 'we know well how decision-making mechanisms work in Turkey. Çiller is there to oblige the military and the name of the game is civilian rule'. *Turkish Daily News*, 11 Jan. 1994.
78. *Le Figaro*, 2 July 1997 and Birand, op. cit., p.41.
79. The 1960 coup is an exception to the rule, since it occurred outside the military hierarchy. However, it must be pointed out that the military leadership proved capable of gaining control of the movement soon after it took place.
80. The military junta of 1980–83 did not appear to face any threat from middle-ranking and junior officers due to the maintenance of the hierarchy within the armed forces, the climate of co-operation between the military rulers and the active commanders and the precautionary measures taken by the military hierarchy. Hale (1994), op. cit., pp.248–50.
81. OYAK derived its income from the obligatory contribution of all active and reserve officers as well as civilian employees of the Ministry of National Defence, deducting ten per cent from their monthly salary, and from its financial investments in various sectors (in the Automotive Industry with OYAK-Renault, MAİŞ (Motorlu Araçlar İmal ve Satiş) and Goodyear, in the cement industry through Çukurova Çimento, Ünye Çimento, Mardin Çimento, Bolu Çimento and YASAŞ, in the electronic industry through ASELSAN, in the service industry through OYAK Sigorta, OYAK MENKUL KİY and OYTAŞ İç ve Diş Tic., in the construction industry through OYAK Insaat A.S., OYAK-Kutlutaş konut, OYAK-Kutlutaş Paz, OYAK-Kutlutaş In. and OYAK-Kutlutaş Ist.Prf., in the food industry through Tam Gida, Tukaş, Entaş Tavuk, Pinar Et and Eti Pazarlama, in the agricultural industry through Hektas, in the petroleum industry through Türkiye Petrolleri A.O., Petro-Kimya A. O. and Seylak, in the travel industry through OYTUR and in the stock exchange industry through AXA). Serdar Şen, *Silahli Kuvvetler ve Modernizm* (Istanbul, 1996), pp.159–62.
82. Ömer Karasapan, 'Turkey's Armaments Industries', *Middle East Report*, No.144 (Jan.–Feb. 1987).
83. Some of the companies involved in the domestic defence industry are: the Military Electronic Industries Inc. (ASELSAN), the Military Battery Industry (ASPILSAN), the PETLAŞ Tire Co., the Electric Industry (IŞBIR), the Sivas Textile Industry (SIDAS), the Machinery and Chemical Industries Establishment (MKE), the Turkish Aircraft Industries (TUSAŞ), the Turkish Engine Industries (TEI), the Turkish Airspace Industries (TAI), the Turkish Electronics Industry and Trade Corporation (TESTAŞ), the TaşkÍzak and the Gölcük Shipyards, the Heavy Maintenance Factories located in Kayseri and Arifiye, Air Force complexes in Kayseri and Eskişehir and others. Ibid. pp.29–30 Although the Turkish military leadership argues that the development of the domestic defence industry 'will result in accelerated growth of the Turkish economy, creation of new employment potential, and increase of the general welfare' (*Nato's Sixteen Nations*, op. cit., p.38), Ball points out that the development of a domestic industry in developing countries 'does not provide an answer to either he problem of unemployment/underemployment or that of human-capital formation'. In addition, 'far from reducing the foreign exchange requirements of the defense sector, domestic production of arms may actually increase them, particularly in the short-to-medium term'. Nicolle Ball, *Security and Economy in the Third World* (Princeton, 1988), pp.382–5.

84. Feroz Ahmad, *The Turkish Experiment in Democracy, 1950–1975* (Boulder, CO, 1977), p.281
85. Barkey argues that due to pressure exercised by the Sabanci and Koç families on the military, in 1982, Özal was forced to resign from his position as Minister of Finance. Henry Barkey, *The State and the Industrialization Crisis in Turkey* (Boulder, CO, 1990), p.184. Also, the 1980 coup seems to have come as a relief to the industrial elite of Turkey (*Wall Street Journal*, 10 Oct. 1980) as well as the labor laws that it imposed (1982 Constitution, Articles 51–55).
86. *Cumhuriyet*, 27 July 1948.
87. Metin Heper, *The State Tradition in Turkey* (Walkington, England, 1985) and Şerif Mardin, 'Power, Civil Society and Culture in the Ottoman Empire', *Comparative Studies in Society and History*, Vol.12 (1969).
88. Şerif Mardin, 'Center-Periphery Relations: A Key to Turkish Politics', *Deadalus*, Vol.103 (1973). Mehmet Altan was pointing out in 1994 that: 'we have never managed to become a truly "democratic republic". When the republic was founded in 1923, the army shaped it according to its own model, putting the "will of the military bureaucrat" before the "popular will" ... the "First Republic" set up a state ... which told them [its citizens] how to behave, how to dress, how to think, and what to eat. These rules were drawn up according to the army's concept of "modernism". The "army modernism" has been, as in totalitarian countries, the sole "compass" for the country. The agenda determined by the "army modernism" did not include such items as how to stop being peasants, how to expand the meagre social provisions ... Those who were promoting the "official ideology, official culture and official history" sided with the state, and the nation wailed about its fate.' *Sabah*, 9 May 1994.
89. Nilufer Göle, 'Toward an Autonomization of Politics and Civil Society in Turkey', in Heper and Evin (1994), op. cit.
90. Compared to 1924 Constitution, which simply stated that the Turkish Nation would exercise its sovereignty through the Grand National Assembly, the 1982 one clearly indicated the strong desire of the statist elite to regulate the evolution of political process in Turkey.
91. Metin Heper, 'State and Society in Turkish Political Experience', İlter Turan, 'Political Parties and the Party System in post-1983 Turkey', in Heper and Evin (1988), op. cit.; Ahmed Evin, 'Demilitarization and Civilianization of the Regime' and Ergun Özbudun, 'Democratization of the Constitutional and Legal Framework', in Heper and Evin (1994), op. cit.
92. Frey (1965), op. cit., p.391.
93. Engin Akarli and Gabriel Ben-Dor (eds.), *Political Participation in Turkey* (Istanbul, 1975)
94. Commenting on the functioning of non-traditional organizations in Turkey, Bianchi argues that even 'the emergence of class-based associations among workers, employers and professionals is generally inhibited by the organization of primordial solidarities based on religion, ethnicity and localism'. Robert Bianchi, *Interest Groups and Political Development in Turkey* (Princeton, 1984).
95. Various writers have often emphasized the notion of authoritarianism in Turkish society. For instance, Tamkoç argues that Turkey's 'social as well as political structure is autocratic in character and functions from top down, each stratum exercising domineering power and influence backed by coercive sanctions over inferior ones'. Metin Tamkoç, *The Warrior Diplomats* (Salt Lake City, 1976) Özbudun points out that 'Turkish political culture attributes primacy not to the individual but to the collectivity ... most social institutions (families, schools, trade unions, communities) display authoritarian patterns in their authority relations'. Ergun Özbudun, 'Turkey: Crises, Interruptions and Re-equilibrations', in L. Diamond, J. Linz and S. Lipset (eds.), *Politics in Developing Countries* (Boulder, CO, 1990), p.201. Also, in the 19th Economists' Week which was held in Istanbul in Spring of 1994, Ismail Cem (CHP's Deputy Chairman) pointed out that the political problems that Turkey was facing had their source in the absence of democratic tradition in Turkey's history and Ercan Karakaş (SHP's Deputy) argued that Turkey needed to apply democracy at home, in the workplace, in school in associations and in political parties and bring it into being part of everyday life. *Turkish Daily News*, 23 April 1994.

96. Cengiz Çandar points out that the Grand National Assembly is composed 'of deputies without ideas or principles and whose only goal was to enter the Parliament. Deputies of this type elected from the ranks of various parties become "individualized" once they find themselves in Parliament ... These "individualized" deputies have lots of room for maneuvering against their leaders with whom they do not share any ideology or principle ... Anything can be expected of such a Parliament.' *Sabah*, 1 Dec. 1995.
97. Ergun Özbudun, 'Turkey: How Far from Consolidation', *Journal of Democracy*, Vol.7 (1996).
98. *Aydinlik*, 9 Oct. 1993. Hikmet Özdemir also argued that 'the government has no other function than to implement the policies determined by the NSC'. *Turkish Daily News*, 1 July 1994.
99. Michael Todaro, *Economic Development in the Third World* (New York, 1981), p.411.
100. Selim Deringil, 'Aspects of continuity in Turkish Foreign Policy: Abdulhamid II and Ismet İnönü', *International Journal of Turkish Studies*, Vol.4 (1987), p.40.
101. Arnold Toynbee, *Change and Habit: The Challenge of Our Time* (London, 1966), p.154 and James Piscatory, *Islam in a World of Nation-States* (Cambridge, 1986), p.52.
102. Deringil, op. cit., p.53.
103. 'Thanks to it [NATO]', Kuneralp, a retired diplomat, argues, 'not only our military strength but also our civilian potential increased. With NATO money, airfields, communication facilities, fuel pipe-lines and other things were built in our country. These were a permanent addition to our national wealth, an addition we could not have achieved alone ... We [for our part] assigned to it our whole army, we tied ourselves closely to it ... [But] the balance sheet was in Turkey's favor.' Zeki Kuneralp, *Sadece Diplomat* (Istanbul, 1981), pp.96–7. But as General Gürkan points out, Turks are 'very sensitive toward all alliances and international agreements ... the United States and NATO will be expected not to jeopardize the security of Turkey in the course of superpower rivalry'. Gürkan, op. cit., p.36.
104. For instance, it was the Turkish ruling elite, which decided to transform the regime toward a multi-party system. Ferenç Vali, *Bridge Across the Bosporus: The Foreign Policy of Turkey* (Baltimore, 1971), p.64. Also, the restructuring of the Turkish political system by the military, in the post-war period (1960, 1971, 1980), appears to have been a pure domestic affair. Gerassimos Karabelias, *O Rolos ton Enoplon Dynameon sten Politike Zoe tes Tourkias kai tes Ellados* (Athens, 1998), Chapter Four.
105. Graham Fuller, *Turkey Faces East: New Orientations Toward the Middle East and the Old Soviet Union* (Santa Monica, CA, 1992) and Ian Lesser, *Bridge or Barrier? Turkey and the West After the Cold War* (Santa Monica, CA, 1992).
106. It is interesting that Suleiman Demirel when he was still not allowed to participate in the country's political life told the journalists that 'there is no need for the West to defend democracy in Turkey ... They should not applaud or criticize us. They should just let us do things our own way. Turkey is able to solve its own problems.' *Turkish Daily News*, 24 March 1985.
107. According to an evaluation of Turkish political behaviour, 'the extreme touchiness of the general public in this country and the pronounced inferiority complex so deep-rooted in its intellectual circles, do not qualify Turkey [to serve] as a convenient vessel for imbiding the spiritual and cultural treasures of another country. An instructive, if primitive, illustration is the response of local spectators when a foreign sports team is gaining the upper hand. A setback on the sportsfield is perceived as a national calamity of enormous dimensions.' Meroz to Foreign Ministry, 17 July 1952, Israel State Archives, 2536/12/A quoted from Amikam Nachmani, *Israel, Turkey and Greece: Uneasy Relations in the Mediterranean* (London, 1987), p.58.

Determinants of Turkish Foreign Policy: Historical Framework and Traditional Inputs

MUSTAFA AYDIN

Turkey is not one of the great powers of the twentieth century. Its geopolitical location, however, has enabled it to play a potentially higher role in world politics than would have been otherwise possible. It holds the key not only to the Turkish Straits but lies along the roads from the Balkans to the Middle East and from the Caucasus to the Persian Gulf. It is a member of the biggest surviving military bloc and of most European organizations, as well as an associate member of the European Union. Its political involvement and exposed position assign it an importance hardly matched by any other medium power. Accordingly, the correct evaluation of this country's policies is of crucial importance. Furthermore, as one of the small number of non-Western societies successfully struggling to modernize both country and people, together with the aim of evolving workable parliamentary democracy, Turkey has long seemed to offer lessons and insights into an important political process.

Yet, the interest it is getting in the Western media and the amount of scholarly works on Turkey, produced especially from an international relations perspective, do not match the importance conferred upon it by other players in international politics. Given its frequently expressed strategic importance on the edge of Europe, the Middle East, and the former Soviet Union, this may seem surprising. For this very reason, however, it is difficult to place Turkey into any neat category that the area specialists and foreign policy analysts like to draw before starting their research. Not only does Turkey not appear to fit any one geographical category, but it does not fit any one cultural, political or economic category either. About 97 per cent of its land mass lies in Asia, and yet Turkey's progressive elite consider their country as part of Europe. About 98 per cent of its population is Muslim, and yet Turkey is a secular country by choice and its religious development through the years has taken a different path from that of other Islamic countries. Culturally, most of the country reflects the peculiarities of the wider Middle Eastern culture, and yet it, with an equal persistency, participates in European cultural events. It professes to have a liberal economic system, but the remnants of the planned economy still hamper the country's development. In religious, historical and geographical senses it is a Middle Eastern country, yet any development impinging upon the status quo of the Balkans and the Caucasus directly affects Turkey just as much. These conflicting facts indicate wider uncertainties about the placing and the role of the country.

A sense of confusion about Turkey seems to reign not only in external appearances, but also in the deep-rooted convictions of its people. Age-old discussions within the country between the 'eastern ideal' and the 'western ideal', about the exact nature of the country and its people, appear to be as lively today as they have ever been. This uncertain self-identity and sense of confusion are likewise common among Western statesmen, scholars, and journalists alike, where Turkey's intentions and foreign policy priorities are concerned. Particularly since the 1970s, Western political analysts and statesmen have seemed increasingly confused about Turkey's intensified *rapprochement* with Islam in both the domestic and international spheres. Although they seem to agree that the implications of a reversal in Turkey's Western-oriented, secular foreign policy could be serious for Western security interests, they do not appear yet to comprehend the extent of changes both in Turkey and its foreign policy. If one looks through recent literature about Turkey, it appears that almost everyone seems to agree that something is happening in Turkish foreign policy which has not been satisfactorily explained by Turkey specialists. But there seems to be no agreement as to what is happening and where it leads the country.[1]

One may ask why there are so many and often such conflicting arguments about Turkey and its intentions. The obvious answer is that, in the absence of in-depth studies covering exclusively different aspects of Turkish foreign policy and its fundamentals, it would be too optimistic to expect an analysis to be accepted without further critical inspection.[2] The truth is that studies of Turkey in general, and Turkish foreign policy in particular, have not yet progressed to the point where a 'standard' view of the country and its prospects has emerged. Isolated by Ottoman history, language and culture from the West, and by Republican history and political choice from the East, Turkey thus stands as a unique case, one which has not often been considered to be of great interest to scholars of international relations in general. Hence Turkish foreign policy appears to be of interest only to Turks and a narrow circle of Turkish-speaking scholars, who, under the various constraints, seem to concentrate their studies on the relatively narrow paths of practical descriptions of Turkey's relations with a number of countries such as Greece, the US and more recently the EU. As a result the very small number of general ideological and foundational analyses of Turkish foreign policy and various attempts to present Turkish reality as a coherent whole have long been outdated by the rapidly changing character of the country. Furthermore, since there is a new surge of arguments, yet again, about possible 'Turkish moves' and 'Turkey's options' after the 'final rejection of Turkey's European ideal', it is time to examine the Turkish experience to see what, in general, drives Turkish foreign policy. As the country is preparing to celebrate the 75th anniversary of its restructuring as a Republic, it may be worthwhile to take stock and try to understand the basic undercurrents of the country's foreign policy.

I must however state at the outset my firm belief in Frankel's perception that 'the foreign policy of every single state is an integral part of its peculiar system of government' and reflects its special circumstances.[3] There is among scholars, no matter what discipline they study, the temptation to generalize when evidence of apparently similar experiences and development processes is readily at hand. It is generally assumed that there are patterns in the foreign policy of nations and not just single acts. A knowledge of the pattern – the 'policy' – of an actor is expected to be useful for explaining and predicting actions.[4] But there is also danger that such generalizations may prevent us from recognizing the diversity of forms which foreign policy can actually take. Therefore, our understanding of foreign policies is likely to be much more productive if we avoid starting from the assumption that there are general forms of behaviour in international relations which could explain all the relationships between states. Instead each case needs to be located in its specific conditionalities within the international system. Rather than imposing general labels on states, we should aim to understand the development of the international system by trying to explain the varying forms which foreign policies could take in different situations and at different times. In this context, Turkey is one part of the international system, and needs to be understood as a unique part of that system, yet as a part which is in a complex set of interrelations with other parts. Although one part or another of its interrelations could be fitted into, or explained by, one of the various different international relations and foreign policy analysis approaches, almost all of them, however, fail after a certain point to explain Turkish foreign policy as a coherent whole.[5]

Nonetheless, it has been suggested that analysis cannot begin until certain choices are made.[6] Indeed, the analyst must specifically decide, either explicitly or implicitly, what foundation to base the analysis upon and at what level to set it up. Clearly, foreign policies are not made in a vacuum. Foreign policy-making bodies of any state receive inputs (demands for action, values, threats, feedback) from the outside world and respond to them. If we wish to make sense of the foreign policy process we need to look at these inputs and their interrelationship. However, what makes it difficult to use these factors (inputs and outputs) as a useful tool of analysis is their elastic character which needs to be adjusted and changed to fit a given historical and concrete situation. Therefore, it is hardly possible to specify a precise number of factors that affect foreign policy-making of all countries in the same way all the time.

Moreover, analysis of a specific policy, or a specific situation may require a different emphasis on various factors.[7] Thus, especially when studying the foreign policy formulation of a specific country in a specific time period, some thought should be diverted beforehand to the question of which factors contribute to the foreign policy-making of that country. As in today's complex society, foreign policy formulation is by no means a simple process, the factors that can determine and condition the plans and choices made by foreign policy officials are too numerous and too varied to be enumerated.[8] And the fact that foreign policy formulation is more often a response to immediate pressures from other states and to the flow of events rather than a result of long-range planning,[9] makes it all the more difficult to get to the root of the matter.

Nevertheless, experience and tradition over time – in combination with basic values and norms – create a set of relatively inflexible principles.[10] What affects the process of formation of these principles varies from state to state. Yet, while looking at the elements that shape the foreign policy of any country, one can see, with some degree of over-simplification, the interplay of two kinds of variable. One kind, which may be called *structural variables*, are continuous, and rather static. The other, which may be termed *conjunctural variables*, are dynamic and subject to change under the influence of domestic and foreign developments.[11]

The *structural factors* are not directly related to the international political medium and the daily happenings of foreign politics. They can exert a long-term influence over the determination of foreign policy goals. Geographical position, historical experiences and cultural background, together with national stereotypes and images of other nations, and long-term economic necessities would fall into the category of 'structural variables'. *Conjunctural variables*, on the other hand, are made up of a web of interrelated developments in domestic politics and international relations. Although not displaying any long-term continuity like the structural static factors, these conjunctural dynamic factors do exert temporary influence on a country's foreign policy and especially on its daily implementation. Conjunctural changes in the international system, such as the end of the Cold War, shifts in the world's present balance of power, domestic political changes, daily scarcities of economic factors and the personalities of specific decision-makers, would fall into this category. Since, in this context, in order realistically to portray any country's foreign policy, one has first of all to appraise carefully the elements and principles which shape it, this article aims to look at the structural determinants of Turkish foreign policy.

During the early years of the Ottoman Empire, its foreign policy was motivated by its military-offensive character. Subsequently, when the Empire first stagnated and then started to crumble, the main foreign policy objective was the preservation of the status quo by military and diplomatic means, of which the latter had had very little significance until that time.[12] When, finally, the Turkish nation-state emerged out of the ashes of the Empire, it was surrounded with a new international environment which was no longer identical to that which existed prior to the First World War. First of all, the breakup of the Ottoman, Russian and Austria-Hungarian Empires signalled change for the international system. The disintegration of these three empires increased the number of actors in the international system. Most of the new actors were politically unstable and economically weak compared to the victorious powers of the First World War. Furthermore, throughout the war the international system had ceased to be a 'European system' and became a global one in which Europe was no longer predominant. Moreover, the new Turkey was no longer an empire, but a nation-state. It had no desire for territorial conquest and had no power to do so even if it had desired it. It needed a new, realistically sound foreign policy which could respond to the challenges of the new international system without endangering the existence of the state. Atatürk's new directions for Turkish foreign policy were thus enormously important. His foreign policy objectives reflected a departure from the militant expansionist ideology of the Ottoman Empire. He was genuinely concerned with independence and sovereignty, thus with his motto of *peace at home, peace in the world*; he, while aiming to preserve the status quo, sought a deliberate break with the Ottoman past in virtually every aspect of life.

Nonetheless, the new Turkey could not totally dissociate itself from its Ottoman heritage. Today, the Turkish nation carries the deep impressions of the historical experiences of being reduced from a vast empire to extinction, and then having to struggle back to save the national homeland and its independence. The struggle for survival and the play of *realpolitik* in the international arena, together with an imperial past and a huge cultural heritage left strong imprints on the national philosophy of Turkey and the character of its people.

Furthermore, historical experiences cannot be separated from the present day life of a nation. Like individuals, nations react to both internal and external forces within the international political arena, on the basis of their historical impressions, prejudices and national image of themselves and other nations. Good or bad, right or wrong, historical experiences colour a nation's reaction to events and forces in the political system. They limit the foreign policy options of the political leadership and are filters for viewing international reality.[13]

Some other important foreign policy inputs of Turkey grew out of the country's geopolitical reality. As Rosenau puts it:

> The configuration of the land, its fertility and climate, and its location relative to other land masses and to waterways ... all contribute both to the psychological environment through which officials and publics define their links to the external world and the operational environment out of which their dependence on other countries fashioned.[14]

The Turkish Republic, which has inherited from the Ottoman Empire the historic role of serving as both a land bridge and a fortress connecting Europe, Asia and the Middle East, constitutes a very good example of how and to what degree geography determines a country's foreign policy. The foreign relations of Turkey, and the Ottoman Empire before it, have been in large part governed since the eighteenth century by the attempts of the Russians to gain control of the Straits, and the efforts of Britain and France (and lately the United States) to stop them.

Turkey has undergone profound changes since the 1920s. But its location and its strategic value have not changed. Even if its relative importance to other states has changed, what the Turkish decision-makers perceive about their geographical importance and threats reasoned from this particular location have not yet radically changed. And as far as the foreign policy-making of a country is concerned, the perception of decision-makers about themselves, their country and other countries, is the most important factor to take into account.[15]

Therefore, this essay shall deal with three main traditional inputs of Turkish foreign policy; namely the Ottoman experience and its long-lasting legacy; the geopolitical realities of Turkey; and the ideological foundations defined under the leadership of Atatürk.

Turkish imperial history ended with the collapse of the Ottoman Empire at the end of the First World War. The Treaty of Lausanne, signed after three years of nationalist struggle on 24 July 1923, replaced the dictated Peace Treaty of Sèvres and established the new Turkish nation-state with complete sovereignty in almost the whole territory included in today's Turkish Republic. Although it contained a few restrictions on the Straits and granted some commercial and judicial privileges, the Treaty of Lausanne was essentially the international recognition of the demands expressed in the Turkish National Pact.[16]

The Sèvres Treaty in contrast was detrimental to Turkish independence and destructive of its homeland.[17] It stipulated that Greece was to receive the remaining portion of the Empire's European territory (except the Straits Region which was under Allied occupation) as well as Izmir (Smyrna) and its hinterland in western Anatolia.[18] In addition to the abandonment by the Turks of all Arab lands, a sovereign Armenian state and an autonomous Kurdistan were eventually to be formed in eastern Anatolia. Furthermore, France, Italy and Britain were allowed to carve out 'spheres of influence' from the remaining Anatolian heartland. Capitulations, abolished during the war, were to be restored, and the Straits were to be governed by an international regime. Thus the Turks were only allowed to keep a small part of desolate central Anatolia under various restrictions. However, the Treaty of Sèvres remained still-born as the Nationalists, organized around Mustafa Kemal in Anatolia, refused to accept it and successfully fought to overturn its terms.[19]

Nonetheless, the fact that the sovereign rights and independence of the Turkish people had been disregarded by the Entente powers, and that the Turks were forced to fight to regain their independence and the territory they considered as their 'homeland' after rapidly losing an empire, was to have an important effect upon both subsequent Turkish attitudes *vis-à-vis* foreign powers and on their nation-building efforts. It should be mentioned that, though displaced by a later treaty, the Treaty of Sèvres, together with the arguments and counter-arguments about the killings of Armenians during the First World War by the Ottomans, formed a basis for subsequent Armenian claims on Turkish territory. Furthermore, perhaps more relevant to the discussion of Turkish foreign policy during the 1980s, the Treaty of Sèvres gave form and inspiration to Kurdish nationalism and today Kurdish nationalists still refer to it as an international recognition of their aspirations for an independent Kurdish homeland.[20] However, it should not be forgotten that at the time most of the Kurdish tribes sided with the Turks against the 'invading powers' as both nations' primary identification was based on religion rather than along ethnic or racial lines. It was only after the dissolution of the religious characteristics of the new state from 1924 onwards and the full-fledged development of Turkish national consciousness from the 1930s onwards that the Kurdish and Turkish interests seemed to diverge and various Kurdish uprisings, motivated by a mixture of nationalist and religious feelings, took place against the Turkish state during the 1920s and 1930s.[21]

The Turkish Republic was born out of the Ottoman Empire, but bore little resemblance to its forerunner. The new Turkey was not an empire, but a relatively small nation-state; not an autocracy or theocracy, but a parliamentary democracy; not a state founded on expansionist principles, but a nation dedicated to the existing status quo; not a multinational, multiracial, and multireligious state, but an almost 'homogeneous' society.[22] Her aims were not to create and expand an empire, but to build and perpetuate a strong, stable nation within the boundaries of its homeland. Those were not ephemeral happenings at that critical time of history but the facts created by the deliberate choices of the leaders of the new Republic.

Although at one time the Turks formed an important part of the ruling classes, they were actually one of the smaller nations within the multiethnic empire. Moreover, the Ottoman Sultans did not consider themselves Turks as such, but as Ottomans. Therefore when the Turks fought for their independence after the First World War, they did not fight only against the Entente invaders, but also against the Ottoman Sultan and the forces of the old system: a point that is usually overlooked.[23] Hence it is not surprising to see that the leaders of the new Turkish state sought to break with the Ottoman past which they identified with ignorance, corruption, backwardness and dogmas. To establish a truly new state, they had to clear away the ruins of the Empire, disown its legacy and discover new virtues based on the Turkish nation. The new Turkey had to have no connection with the old.[24] But this does not necessarily mean that the Turkish Republic did not inherit some of the fundamental features of the Ottoman Empire. A closer look at these features would help one to understand the background of Turkish foreign policy.

The new Turkey was not only established in the very heart of the old Empire's geopolitical setting, that of Asia Minor and Thrace, therefore acquiring its complications, but it also retained most of its ruling elite. Since the bureaucratic elite of the Empire in its last days was dominated by Turks, the new Turkish state found an experienced bureaucracy, rather scarce in other post-empire states. Fortunately nineteenth-century experiments with Western education had produced an educated official class. Later this elite group of administrators, under Atatürk's guidance and within the one-party authoritarian regime, formed the nucleus of Turkey's modernizing elite – the Republican People's Party – and imposed revolutionary changes from the top. Though this elite, on the one hand, secured a strong political power base for Atatürk and thus enabled him to carry out the most needed radical reforms in order to break down the traditional social and spiritual culture of Turkey and transform it into a secular and Western culture, on the other, they somewhat contradictorily supplied a material connection between the Empire and the new Turkish Republic.[25]

One of the fundamental features of Turkish foreign policy has been its Western orientation. Despite the fact that Turkey had fought against the Western powers during the First World War, after independence it opted for the Western world. This was expressed first in cultural and, after the Second World War, in political and military terms. This orientation has been deliberate and continues to be a policy choice that cannot be explained with the limited aim of 'countering an imminent threat' or such formulations as 'the economic interests of the ruling elite'. These kinds of explanation would not only be unsatisfactory, but also misleading. Instead, one should look into Turkish history which has helped to shape Turkish understanding of its environment and its governmental philosophy.

Throughout their history, the Turks have been connected to the West, first as a conquering superior and enemy, then as a component part, later as an admirer and unsuccessful imitator, and in the end as a follower and ally. Ottoman settlement after the Mongol invasion of Anatolia in the Valley of the Karasu, where they were in direct contact with the Byzantines, was the beginning of the influence which had such a profound effect on their subsequent history. They began, indeed, to face the West; before they had any status in Asia Minor, the Ottomans were already an empire based largely on south-east Europe.

> It is an important historical fact which is not often appreciated that the Ottoman Turks started their career as a people in extreme north-west of Asia Minor, facing Europe; that they founded their Empire not in Asia but across the Sea of Marmara in Thrace and the Balkans, in other words in Europe, and that they expanded eastwards into Asia Minor a century after they had already become a European power. It was, in fact, only during the course of the fifteenth century that they became an Oriental power as well as a European.[26]

Not only did Europe have an effect on the Ottoman Empire, but the Turks, from the time that they first entered the European continent, played a role in the destiny of Europe. They were not only the enemy of the European monarchs, but frequently allied themselves with one or more of the European countries against the others, and operated within the European system. It is, however, one of the ironies of history that the Ottoman Empire, whilst it had progressively become more and more alienated from Europe through the eighteenth and nineteenth centuries, was 'officially' re-admitted to the European legal system at the Paris Congress of 1856.

It is only natural that Ottoman rule over one-third of Europe for 400 years would have important effects on the Empire's outlook.[27] Its adaptation to a somewhat secular state system, especially in the conduct of foreign affairs and in the administration of the various *millets*, was part of this influence. Although serving the cause of Islam was an important element behind most of the Ottoman conquests, so long as the state was strong, the Ottoman rulers did not use the title 'caliph', the religious leader of the Muslim community. It was only after the continuous dismemberment of the Empire's non-Muslim subjects in the nineteenth century that the sultans, notably Abdülhamit II, upheld the idea of pan-Islamism in order to prevent the disintegration of the Empire's Muslim subjects. In fact, the Ottoman Empire, in time, had come to create its own peculiar understanding of Islam, somewhat 'secular' and different from that of the Arabs. Moreover, it must be remembered that there was no institutionalized religious authority independent from the state. Therefore, it was easy for the Ottoman Sultan to make peace with the infidels, whenever he considered it necessary, and to seek the necessary Western help when modernizing the empire.

Given this background, the introduction of the Western-oriented secular state in the 1920s was not in opposition to the overall experience of the Turkish people. In fact, modernization in terms of the West was started after a series of Ottoman defeats at the hands of the Western powers.[28] Most Ottoman and Turkish modernizers did agree upon one basic assumption, as put by Abdullah Cevdet, that 'there is no second civilization; civilization means European civilization, and it must be imported with both its roses and thorns'.[29] Turkey owed a great deal to the late Ottoman intellectuals, who advocated most of the reforms which were finally realized under the guidance of Atatürk in the 1920s and 30s. Atatürk's success derived from his belief in European civilization and his willingness to accept 'both its roses and its thorns', whereas earlier reformers had only tried to imitate them with limited success.[30]

Another point of historical significance is the realistic outlook of Ottoman diplomacy, which was shaped during the nineteenth century with extraordinary success. During the last hundred or so years of its life, the Ottoman Empire was weak in comparison to the Western powers and was forced to pursue its foreign policy among the tensions between its own interest and those of other powers. Nonetheless, by playing one great power against another for survival, the Ottomans were able to maintain the territorial integrity of much of the Empire for a long time. Thanks to the contemporary international system of the 'balance of powers', and the Ottomans' understanding of its main features, the Empire's decline took 300 years and its collapse came only with a world war.

As a student of this remarkable diplomacy, Atatürk would later use all the advantages of the international system, such as the differences between England, France and Italy at the end of the First World War, and the greater antagonism between the Western powers and the Soviet Union. One can also see that after the Second World War, Turkey's well-played role as a continuously threatened nation gained resulting American aid which went up to $738.9 million in the year 1986, its highest point, third after Israel and Egypt.[31]

Along with the above-mentioned constructive elements, Turkey also inherited some complications from its Ottoman past which are still visible in Turkish foreign policy construction. The foreign policy which the Ottomans pursued during their final years, that of playing the powers off against each other, made the Ottomans extraordinarily wary about their environment and suspicious of other powers' intentions. They also learned, as a result of centuries-long hostilities with their neighbours, not to trust any state, to rest on nothing but their own strength, and to be ready to fight at any given time. This is indeed reflected in the common Turkish saying: 'Water sleeps, enemy never sleeps.'

Consequently, Turkish diplomats are famous today, among other things, for being sceptical and cautious. The Foreign Ministry always takes its time in answering any given foreign statement or memorandum as if searching for the real intentions behind the lines. There is also a sense of insecurity in Turkey, a direct legacy of the Ottoman Empire, reflected even today in such statements as 'Turkey's historical position indicates that it is obliged to pursue a policy based on being strong and stable within its region...[since] it is surrounded by unfriendly neighbours.'[32]

When discussing caution and scepticism in Turkish foreign policy, one should bear in mind that the Empire had been subjected repeatedly to propaganda attacks, exploitation and outright aggression by the self-appointed protectors of its minorities. The Ottoman Empire restricted itself to minimum interference in the affairs of the subject peoples. The authority granted to the head of *millets*, or religious communities, included church administration, worship, education, tax collecting and supervision of the civil status of their co-religionists. Because the Ottoman rulers did not seek to impose Turkish on their subjects and did not force conversion on Christians and Jews, but rather used the religious leadership of these communities to administer their co-religionists, the persistence of strong non-Muslim religious identity and linguistic differences served as a natural basis for the growth of nationalism and eventual separatism by the subject peoples in the nineteenth century. These religious communities, by attracting European attention, therefore caused the continued involvement of the West in Ottoman affairs. Thus, when the central authority weakened, the *millet* system, once an excellent instrument of governing, precipitated the self-destruction of the empire. In particular Greek Orthodox and Armenian communities were used as a means of interfering in Ottoman authority throughout the nineteenth and early twentieth centuries. Hence, Turkish sensitivity about Greece's efforts on internationalizing the Orthodox Patriarchate in Istanbul, or the refusal to accept Armenian genocide claims, has to be seen against this background.

Naturally, Western Christian nations' interference in Ottoman authority on behalf of its Christian minorities caused a follow-up feeling among Turks that this difference in religion, though rarely articulated, is relevant to their international relations. This is especially true for those who usually refer to the European Union as a 'Christian Club' and air their worries about whether these Christians would accept an Islamic country among themselves.

Another bitter legacy of the late Ottoman Empire for the Turks is the memory of financial control exercized by European powers through *Duyun-u Umumiye*, Public Debt Service, on Turkish soil after the Ottoman Empire went bankrupt in 1881. Thus it was not surprising to hear from Atatürk that '... by complete independence we mean of course complete economic, financial, juridical, military, cultural independence and freedom in all matters. Being deprived of independence in any of these is equivalent to the nation and country being deprived of all its independence.'[33] Knowing that the Ottoman Empire, in its last years, had lost its independence, to a large extent because of foreign intervention, privileges granted to foreigners, and the Capitulations, the Ankara governments were thus very sensitive about infringements upon their sovereignty as well as about foreign economic entanglements. Hence, for example, Turkey was very uneasy about the suspicion that United States forces could use Turkey as a stepping stone for operations in the Middle East. In the economic sphere, this suspicion showed itself by very tight control over foreign companies operating in Turkey and strict rules governing financial problems.

Still another point of historical significance is that there is a sense of greatness, in the common Turkish mind, based on belonging to a nation which has established empires and been master of a world empire, which was only brought down by a world war. Given that in the final years the Empire was nothing more than a name, devoid of all real power, nonetheless it was still a name, a symbol to which most of the Turks responded and in which they took pride. Though the grandeur of empire and its pride are matters of the past for contemporary Turks, it is still frustrating for them to be in the position of, and regarded as, a second-rate power. This frustration, perhaps in large part, explains Turkish sensitivity to insult and criticism, related to its dependence upon the great powers, and to exclusion from important international conferences. On the other hand, centuries-old Ottoman supremacy over the Arab states and the Balkans left the Turks with a conviction of their superiority. The ordinary Turk is inclined to look down upon the Arab as a man who really cannot control his own affairs in a civilized fashion. The periodic recurrence of conflicts in the Middle East tends to confirm, in the ordinary Turkish mind, this prejudice. A vicious circle is thus established as the Arabs react to Turkish haughtiness.[34]

The long, and in its last days inefficient and unpopular, Ottoman domination over these lands created ill-will against the Turks, and modern Turkey had to face the legacy of neighbours who have bitter memories of Ottoman rule. Certainly, the imperial past has something to say about the bitterness between Turkey and Greece. The late nineteenth century witnessed rising Greek nationalism and the modern Greek state was the first nation-state in the Balkans to come out of clashes between nationalism and the Ottoman Empire. In the early twentieth century the Turkish struggle for independence reached a climax when the Greek army landed in Izmir in 1915 to attain the 'Megali Idea' (the long-lived Greek dream of reconstituting the Byzantine Empire), and at the end the Turks had to fight against the Greeks to claim their independent nation-state. The frustrated hopes of reaching the Megali Idea on the Greeks' part, and having been forced to fight against ex-subject people for its independence on the Turks' part, together with the stories about wartime atrocities on both sides, were enough reasons for the continued bitterness in the early 1920s and 1930s. Though some of the potential for conflict was eliminated between Atatürk and Venizelos by the arrangement of a compulsory population exchange in the 1920s, past bitterness provided a base for hostility when differences erupted from mid-1950s onwards.

One of the deep-rooted principles in Turkish foreign policy is that its northern neighbour presented the primary threat to the country's security. Since the seventeenth century, Russia's expansionist policies helped it to become the 'arch enemy' of the Ottomans. A succession of major defeats at Russian hands consistently confronted the Ottoman government with the realities of its declining power. Moreover, it was Tsar Nicholas I who described the Ottoman Empire as the 'sick man of Europe' when he proposed to the British in 1853 that the Ottoman Empire be partitioned.[35] The last of the 13 Russo-Turkish wars was, of course, the First World War. This course of conflict over the past four centuries, naturally generated a full measure of hostility and distrust between Turks and Russians. Even during the period of the Treaty of Friendship and Neutrality, when good neighbourly relations were enjoyed by both sides, the historical Turkish distrust of the Soviets was well evident. In 1934, during a conversation with General Douglas MacArthur, Atatürk predicted a major war in Europe around 1940 and also saw the real victors of the war as the Soviet Union:

> We Turks, as Russia's close neighbor, and the nation which has fought more wars against her than any other country, are following closely the courses of events there, and see the danger stripped of all camouflage...The Bolsheviks have now reached a point at which they constitute the greatest threat not only to Europe but to all Asia.[36]

A history of distrust, hostility and continued wars, made the Turks extraordinarily wary. Hence they did not hesitate to accept American aid when the Soviet Union placed great pressure on Turkey after the Second World War for territorial concessions and special privileges on the Straits.

Modern Turkey, thanks to its geostrategic location with borders on Europe, the Middle East, and the Soviet Union, has been able to play a role in world politics far greater than its size, population, and economic strength would indicate. Historically, Turkey is located on one of the most, if not the most, strategic and traditionally most coveted pieces of territory. It controls the historic invasion routes from the Balkans and the Caucasus mountains onto the high Anatolian plateau, which in turn commands the entire Fertile Crescent down to the oil-rich Persian Gulf and the Red Sea. Turkey is also at the crossroads of major air, land, and sea routes of modern times, joining the industrially advanced lands of Europe with the petroleum-rich lands of the Middle East. Furthermore, the country possesses the sources for most of the water irrigating lands as far as the Persian Gulf. On the other hand, during the Cold War Turkey was also on the line of conflict between the zones of two military superpowers and their respective alliances. And from the north to the south, it was in a rather sensitive part of the Mediterranean, where both superpowers tried to expand their spheres of influence and counterbalance each other.

This particular geographical position makes Turkey a Balkan, Mediterranean, and Middle Eastern country all at the same time. It also makes Turkey doubly susceptible to international developments near and far and, therefore, greatly sensitive to the changes in the international political balance as well as the regional one. Thus the peculiarities of the Anatolian peninsula are worth looking at, before anything else, since the various effects of Turkey's geographical position, which influence Turkish foreign policy, are derived from these peculiarities.

Settlement in Anatolia dates back to as early as 7500 BC. Being at the crossroads of land connections between Europe, Asia, and Africa has on the one hand increased the importance of any state established in Anatolia; but, on the other hand, being also the main channel for migrations from the east, and invasions from both the east and the west, has encouraged a sense of insecurity as well. The Anatolian peninsula is highly mountainous in the east, permitting only small gateways. Each side of Anatolia is surrounded by the sea, and against the coasts on the north and the south run parallel mountain ranges with forests and rivers, which make this area all but impermeable. As Toynbee describes, '...only towards the West does the plateau sink in long fertile river valleys to a clement, and sheltered coastline'.[37] This geographical setting has forced all states located on the Anatolian peninsula, including the Ottoman Empire and the Turkish Republic, to look to the West rather than to the East for trade and cultural exchange.

The physical features of a land may make it easy to defend or otherwise. From a military point of view, the Anatolian peninsula is a 'strategic region'.[38] The seas on both sides and the fortress-like mountainous terrain in the east are difficult to penetrate by force, and make natural boundaries for Turkey. European Turkey, on the other hand, is difficult to defend and the Straits are also vulnerable to air attacks. It is true that possession of the Straits conveys political and military advantages, and raises Turkey from the position of a purely local power to one having crucial international influence. Simultaneously, however, the Straits pose one of Turkey's major security concerns by attracting potential aggressors. The fact that Turkey deployed its most powerful First Army to protect the Straits and the area surrounding them shows the full realization of this phenomenon by Turkey.

Another important factor in Turkish security thinking is that the Aegean islands, if under the control of an enemy power, would deny Turkey the use of its two principal harbours, Istanbul and Izmir, and could prevent access to the Straits. In this case, navigation would be safe from the eastern Mediterranean so long as the island of Cyprus, which could bloc the area, was controlled by a friendly government. Hence, the scenario that Enosis (union of Cyprus with Greece) would cut Turkey off from the open sea encouraged Turkey's resistance to such designs since the 1950s. It is the very same fear that is behind the Turkish declaration of *casus belli* against the Greek claims about 12-mile territorial waters in the Aegean, thus putting all open-sea exits from the Aegean within its territorial seas.[39]

Another important reason for Turkey's geographical insecurity is the fact that it is surrounded by many neighbours with different characteristics, regimes, ideologies, and aims; and that the relations between them and Turkey would not always be peaceful, and especially in the Middle East, may occasionally take the form of armed clashes. A country's borders may be a source of strength or of weakness depending on their length, the number and intentions of the neighbours, and the relative power available to the affected parties. In the early days of the Republic, Turkey had borders with seven states, including four with major powers: Greece, Bulgaria, the

Soviet Union, Iran, Great Britain (mandate in Iraq and possession of Cyprus), France (mandate in Syria), and Italy (possession of the Dodecanese Islands). Although the Soviet Union and Iran posed no threat at that moment, their predecessors, the Russian and Persian Empires respectively, had deadly quarrels with the Ottoman Empire. Bulgaria, though an ally during the First World War, had fought against the Ottoman Empire in order to gain its independence and the memories of the Balkan Wars, during which the Bulgarians had advanced as far as the fortresses of Istanbul, had not been forgotten by Turks.

In the interwar period, though it enjoyed good neighbourly relations in general, Turkey had problems with Britain (concerning Mosul), with France (concerning Hatay or Alexandretta), and with Italy because of the latter's open imperialistic tendencies towards the eastern Mediterranean after the 1930s. After the Second World War, Turkey's borders dropped to six, leaving Greece, Bulgaria, the Soviet Union, Iran, Iraq and Syria as neighbours, and the Republic of Cyprus joined them in 1960. This composition of neighbours left no need for further explanation and Turkey's sense of insecurity proves what Most and Starr argue that '...a nation that borders on a large number of other nations faces a particularly high risk that it may be threatened or attacked by at least some of its neighbors...and confronts its neighbours with uncertainty because it must protect and defend itself against many potential opponents'.[40]

To counterbalance potential opponents and to reduce its sense of insecurity, Turkey sought alliances with regional states and outside powers. Between 1920 and 1955 Turkey entered into a number of pacts and alliances, as well as signing friendship declarations with all its neighbours and bilateral security treaties with the United States. This sense of insecurity went too far as it entered the Balkan Pact (1953) and Alliance (1954) and the Baghdad Pact (1955), all of which became meaningless, as far as Turkey's security was concerned, after its adherence to NATO in 1952.

Another geographical influence on Turkish foreign policy derives from the facts that Turkey effectively controls the only seaway linking the Black Sea with the Mediterranean; that the Soviet Union was a major Black Sea power as well as being a superpower; and that Turkey also shared a common border with the Soviet Union. As already mentioned, by possessing internationally important waterways, Turkey has been able to exercise much more influence on world politics than would otherwise have been possible. As summed up by Váli, '...an Anatolian state that did not control the bridge toward Europe would only be another country of the Middle East; united with this historic region however, it is bound to play more eminent role either offensively or defensively'.[41] This intercontinental position has proved an element of strength as well as of weakness. For five centuries,

Istanbul provided a home base for the Ottomans 'from which they were able to exercise control in all directions, in the Balkans and central Europe, the Black Sea region, the Aegean and Mediterranean, Mesopotamia and Arabia, Syria and North Africa'.[42] The Straits have also supplied a resource for the Ottoman Empire and its successor, the Turkish Republic, that could not be duplicated in manpower as a means to influence the actions of the Russian Empire, and later the Soviet Union.[43]

On the other hand, however, controlling these vital waterways brought the Ottoman Empire into perennial conflict with the Russians, beginning in the seventeenth century when Peter the Great began his drive to the south. It has always been vitally important for Russia to have its outlet to the Mediterranean unimpeded, independent of its neighbours' goodwill. But it has been equally important for Western powers not to let Russia gain control over this important passage. So much so that Napoleon is said to have placed such importance on the Turkish Straits that he declared his willingness 'to abandon mastery over half the world rather than yield Russia those narrow Straits'.[44] Indeed, during the nineteenth century, the struggle for control of the Ottoman Empire in general, and of the Straits in particular, was the major part of the assertions of European diplomacy. And in the latter half of the nineteenth century the 'Eastern Question', in essence the fate of the Ottoman Empire, became the major factor in the global balance of power. Consequently, the Ottomans, 'even though militarily weak, economically bankrupt and politically anomalous', were still able to subsist for another century 'on the conflict of interests between Russia, on the one hand, and Austro-Hungary, France, Britain, on the other'.[45]

While the question of the Turkish Straits and the historic hostility between the Russians and the Turks has been at the heart of Turkish–Soviet relations for many years, having a superpower neighbour also had its effects on Turkish foreign policy. During the first two decades of the Republic, relations with the Soviet Union which supplied political and material support to Turkey, were good and were strengthened by the Treaty of Neutrality and Non-Aggression of 1925. This era of mutual understanding came to an end on 19 March 1945, with the Soviet Union's unilateral denunciation of the 1925 Treaty and demands for a new treaty 'in accord with the new situation'.[46] It further demanded territorial concessions from Turkey and bases on the Bosphorus. These Soviet demands strongly influenced Turkish foreign policy attitudes and reinforced its Western orientation. Since Turkey was only able to refuse these demands with the United States' backing, the Turkish Government sought a formal alliance with the USA, and the link with the Western defence system was formalized with Turkey's accession to NATO on 18 February 1952.

Although, after Stalin's death, the Soviet Government officially declared that its policy towards Turkey had been wrong and that the Soviet Union did not have any territorial claims on Turkey,[47] the time had already been passed for the Soviet Union to revise its relations with Turkey, since the historic Turkish distrust of the Russians reappeared on the horizon. The belief that the Soviet Union posed a primary threat to Turkey's security dominated relations between the two countries during the Cold War. It was only after the blow of Johnson's letter that Turkey showed an interest in Soviet efforts to normalize relations. It took nearly a decade for it to accept the fact that détente between the Soviet and the Western Blocs had been started in the 1960s, and a further decade to improve its relations with the Soviet Union. Nevertheless, having a common border with the Soviet Union was still cause for concern and remained a contributing factor to Turkey's extremely cautious foreign policy and its continued membership of NATO.[48]

Another complication for Turkey's political and security thinking is the fact that Turkey is a Middle Eastern country as well as a Balkan and Mediterranean one. The strategic importance of the region does not need further elaboration. The single fact that the Middle East owns most of the known oil resources makes the region one of the most important in the strategic thinking of all parties concerned. Turkey, like most of the Western countries, is dependent on Middle Eastern oil. Not only is the functioning of the Turkish economy dependent on continuous flows of Middle Eastern petroleum, its military has become increasingly reliant on massive fuel needs, which are normally larger in times of war than under peacetime conditions.[49] Therefore, Turkey's growing political and diplomatic concern in the region has been, in part, a result of the intensifying economic ties which were forced upon it by its dependence on Middle Eastern oil.

The significance of geography on Turkey's destiny has never been more clearly demonstrated than by the fact of its losing the oil-rich Arab lands, which left it with the need to import oil. This increased its financial dependence on the West and contributed to periodic economic crises, which in turn caused social and political instability within the country. Although the consecutive governments in Ankara continuously declared that Turkey had no territorial demands on any country, the memories of losing these territories with their extensive resources is still fresh in the ordinary Turkish mind. This can explain, in part, Turkish sensitivity about developments concerning the Aegean seabed. Not to give up possibly oil-rich areas once again is one of the reasons behind Turkish arguments that the eastern portion of the Aegean seabed is an extension of the Anatolian continental shelf and, therefore, Turkey should have jurisdiction for purposes of exploration and exploitation of seabed and subsoil resources.[50] The fear of losing another potentially oil-rich area (though any prospect of finding substantial oil resources in the Aegean is fairly remote)[51] is so strong in

Turkey that it will not, in the near future, waive its claims to the Aegean seabed, even at the risk of a military conflagration with Greece while the dispute remains unresolved.

Apart from oil, there are other reasons why the Middle East possesses a great place in Turkish security thinking. The region has been continuously unstable since the First World War and the breakdown of the Ottoman Empire. Turkish foreign policy in the Middle East, while depending on the status quo, requires stability, and any destabilizing development in the region would create security problems for it. Thus the general insecurity of the region has attracted a great deal of concern from Turkey. It is enough to point out that four Arab–Israeli wars, the unending Palestinian problem, the Lebanese civil war and foreign interventions, the Suez crisis, the Iranian revolution, the Iran–Iraq war and the latest Gulf War, have all occurred within the immediate reach and security zone of Turkey. Such developments, and the ever-increasing possibility of superpower involvement, have inevitably created great concern in Turkey over its immediate security. Beside cultural aspirations and ideological, economic, and political factors, the stability of Europe in comparison to the Middle East since the Second World War has also encouraged Turkey to remain in the Western camp. A secure place within the multinational fora, which have created stable political, social, and economic conditions in Europe has always had a considerable attraction for Turkey, a country which is placed in one of the most unstable and insecure regions of the world.

Although experiences and memories of the Ottoman past, together with its geostrategic location, served as a foundation for and influenced the subsequent foreign relations of Turkey, it is Atatürk's theory and practice of foreign policy which has been the most important factor in shaping Turkish foreign policy. He not only completely controlled Turkish foreign policy in his lifetime, but he also put forward an ideological framework by which the pursuit of Turkish foreign policy could be achieved. Although the original Kemalist goals of national foreign policy underwent various mutations, especially under the relatively free democratic system of the 1961 Constitution, practically all Turkish governments, regardless of their standpoints, put his 'indisputable dogma' into their programmes and could not implement policies that ran counter to Kemalist principles. His influence over the Turkish people, in general, and Turkish foreign policy in particular, has been so deep and so fundamental that there are at times intimations, and often open warnings, that anything other than his principles would be disloyal to him and to the country in general.

In particular, Turkey's foreign policy has been influenced by the following goals and principles laid down by Atatürk: establishment and preservation of a national state with complete independence conditioned by modern Turkish nationalism; promotion of Turkey to the level of contemporary civilization by means of Kemalist principles; and attachment to realistic and peaceful means in foreign policy actions.

Atatürk's foreign policy views, like his political views in general, represented a break with the past. He aimed at a renunciation of three strains which had been important during Ottoman times: the imperial-Ottomanism, pan-Islamism, and pan-Turanism. Incidentally, policies which could break these strains coincided with the three of his political principles; Republicanism, Secularism and Nationalism respectively.

Atatürk's foreign policy was clearly an extension of his domestic policies. He recognized the vital relationship between the internal organization of the new Republic and its foreign policy.[52] He also realized that a peaceful foreign policy was needed in order to achieve his far-reaching reforms inside Turkey. Once he said, 'What particularly interests foreign policy and upon which it is founded is the internal organization of the state. It is necessary that foreign policy should agree with the internal organization.'[53] Therefore it is not surprising to see that in his famous motto – 'peace at home, peace in the world' – while he was connecting internal stability with international peace and order, he put the home front first.

Atatürk did not want to see the Turkish nation as a foreign or hostile community set apart from the nations of the world and did not want the nation to belong to a group holding such views. He wanted Turkey to be part of the civilized world. However, in order to achieve this, a change was necessary, not only in the system of government, but also 'in the mental disposition of the Turkish people'.[54] His political reforms were directed to this aim, namely, to change the centuries long backwardness and ignorance of the Turkish people, and to accustom them to the modern way of life. The ideological guidance which was necessary to achieve this end was to be derived from his political principles, which were formalized at the 1931 Congress of the Republican People's Party and written into the constitution in 1937.[55] They were symbolized by the emblem of the RPP: 'six arrows'. Each of them actually represents one of the key words of Kemalist ideology: Nationalism, Secularism, Republicanism, Populism, Etatism, and Revolutionism. These six key words did not encompass all aspects of the Kemalist ideology but they did, in a concise manner, represent its pillars and many of them had foreign policy implications.

As the foundation of Kemalist ideology, Republicanism comprises the notions of popular sovereignty, freedom and equality before the law. It was against the totalitarian tendencies and the notion of the Empire, which was revisionist and imperialist. While accepting the existing status quo as a main foundation of the new state, Atatürk said that '...the state should pursue an exclusively national policy...I mean...to work within our national boundaries for the real happiness and welfare of the nation and the country...'.[56] Republicanism was not only a change in the governmental system, but also a turning point in the political philosophy of the Turks. The new Turkish Republic was a nation-state founded by the Turkish nation, by its own accord. Throughout history all Turkish states had been dynastic. Therefore, the extra stress on republicanism was necessary to help accustom the Turkish people to the idea that the change in regime after the War of Independence was non-reversible. From this point of view, republicanism constituted a doctrinal barrier against those who still hoped for a return to the Sultanate and the Caliphate.

Secularism was a necessary component of modernization, covering not only the political and governmental but the whole social and cultural life.[57] From a foreign policy viewpoint, it has a much more general meaning than one which refers more narrowly to a specific process of separating religion from state.[58] Indeed, the main struggle of Kemalist secularists was not over the question of separating the spiritual and temporal, but over the difference between democracy and theocracy. A theocratic Islamic state, as a way of government, was obliged to see Christian powers as infidels, and according to Islamic belief the state of warfare never ended between believers and infidels. By choosing a democratic system of government and dismissing the idea of an Islam-protector nation, the new Turkish state ended centuries of hostility and established the basis for peaceful relations with Western Christian countries. Another reflection of secularism in terms of Turkish foreign policy can be seen in its rejection of the idea of pan-Islamism. To unite different Muslim nations under one common name, to give these different elements equal rights, and found a mighty state, was seen as a brilliant and attractive political solution for the Empire's problems in its last years. But it was a misleading one. The new state would not be world-conquering or Islam-protecting any more. Such claims could endanger the existence of the state.

> There is nothing in history to show how policy of pan-Islamism could have succeeded or how it could have found a basis for its realization on this earth. History does not afford examples as regards the result of the ambition to organize a state which should be governed by the idea of world supremacy and include the whole humanity without distinction of race. For us there can be no question of the lust of conquest...[59]

Since the Islamic Ottoman Empire could not try its Christian subjects with Sharia (Islamic law), it allowed them to be tried before Christian courts, which in turn resulted in foreign interventions and caused the Ottoman Empire to become involved in conflicts with the Western powers over the supremacy of the *millets*. Hence it seemed that the Islamic religious establishment of the Empire had played a major role in accelerating and enhancing the Empire's decline and decay. Consequently, Mustafa Kemal was determined not to allow the same thing happen to the new Turkish state.[60] In other words he could not give a reason to the Western powers to intervene in Turkish affairs.

Nationalism, as a source of Turkish existence, stood for a Turkish-nation state in place of Ottomanist or pan-Turanist ambitions, and was bound up with the national borders, which were first laid down by the National Pact of 1920 and later legalized by the Lausanne Treaty of 1923. Nationalism, a movement which was rediscovered by the Empire's Christian subjects in the early nineteenth century, and was therefore partly responsible for its disintegration, had come in touch with the Turkish population only in the early twentieth century. When the Entente powers started to partition the Empire's heartland, it became clear that they were taking advantage of the lack of a unified nationalist movement. It was obvious to Mustafa Kemal that the main requirement for the independence of a nation was the effort towards a common goal and public awareness of the nation's historical consciousness. The creation of nationalism on the European model was essential for a successful struggle towards independence *vis-à-vis* the supremacy of the Imperialist European powers.[61] Therefore, the idea of a Turkish nation in Turkey was the basic innovation in the early days of the Kemalist revolution.

Mustafa Kemal's declaration in the Amasya circular of 21–22 June 1919 that 'only the will and the determination of the nation can save the independence of the nation', became the main principle of the National Independence Struggle.[62] This principle invited every individual of the nation to share a common obligation and responsibility. Atatürk had realized the necessity of basing his movement on the reality of 'nationhood'. But it was no easy task to accustom a people who had been attached to a religion and a dynasty, to the new meaning of Turkey. Even the expression 'Turkey' was neither used nor known by the people. The concept of nationalism, and the establishment of a national state, which had begun in the West centuries before and had slowly spread and become the very property of the people, was unfamiliar to the Turks. Therefore, with the War of Independence and the realization of the reforms following it, non-national political and social values had to be replaced by the values of the Turkish people.

He also realized that any nationalist claims must be supported by a very strict definition of national identity. He was opposed to the expending of the country's energy on a quest for virtually unobtainable goals. 'We know our limitations. We are not worldly-minded'.[63] Directing the country in the path of adventurism could very well result in the loss of what had already been achieved. Therefore, he rejected the utopian ideas of pan-Islamism and pan-Turkism and did not build Turkish nationalism on religion or race.[64] He defined nation as 'a political and social body formed by citizens bound together by the unity of language, culture and ideas'.[65] Hence Turkish nationalism, like that of Europe, was based on common citizenship, and did not extend its aims beyond the national borders.[66]

Basing Turkish nationalism on a common citizenship instead of 'ethnicity' was a realistic option for the population of Turkey consisted, and still does, of 'individuals from many different ethnic backgrounds but, according to the Turkish Constitution, all citizens of Turkey are Turks'.[67] This official, legalistic, approach to Turkish 'national homogeneity' allowed the early Turkish leaders, in accordance with the principle of populism, to be representative of all the peoples of Turkey irrespective of their class, religion, or ethnic origin. *People* was officially defined as 'all individuals who, without demanding any privileges, accept absolute equality before the law'.[68] In this context, the nation was regarded as resulting from 'historical and sociological conditions',[69] different from *race* which 'is a biological occurrence', and from *umma* 'which is a group of people believing in universal religion'.[70] The role of nationalism then, was to 'form a bond between the people's collective memories of the past and adherence to the goals of the future'.[71]

From this point of view, various ethnic groups within the Turkish state were accepted as 'building blocks of the nation' which 'joined together to create the national culture'. In connection with this, the demands of ethnic groups for national status, 'regardless of the social anxiety causing the demand', were considered contradictory to 'the spirit and law of history' and thus 'unrealistic and wrong'.[72] As a result, when faced with different ethnic claims emerging within the 'unified Turkish nation', the Kemalist regime chose to dismiss them as plots of 'enemy agents', an attitude continued until the 1990s:

> In today's Turkish national, political and social community we have patriots and citizens who have been subjected to propaganda about the Kurdish, Circassian, and even Laz and Bosnian nations. But these misnomers, which are a result of despotic ages long past, had no influence on the individuals of this nation, except for a few enemy agents and brainless reactionaries, and have left our people in grief and sorrow. Because the individuals of this nation, as members of the integrated, unified Turkish Community, have a common past, history, morality and law.[73]

In the process, however, what started as an attempt to create a homogeneous Turkish nation through constitutionalism using public consensus, turned into an attempt to force various elements within the Turkish state into a homogenous society through demographic homogenization.[74] This, on the one hand, contradicted the original claims of the Kemalist ideology, and on the other hand, alienated the masses who felt ethnically distinct from the Sunni-Turkish speaking majority.[75] When coupled with the persistent denial of the Turkish ruling elite of the latter's existence, especially since the mid-1970s onwards when the latter groups started to express and demand their cultural distinctiveness through organizational structures, the 'ethnicity' issue came to determine the ideological boundaries of Turkish national identity, and also constrained its constitutional evolution. This aspect of Turkish nation-building is especially relevant to our discussion of Turkish foreign policy during the 1980s as it essentially interacts with the Kurdish issue which became an element of both Turkey's domestic and external policies during this period.[76]

Turkish national liberation should also be distinguished from the anti-imperialist movements of the post-1945 period during which the African and Asian peoples who struggled for their independence came into conflict with the colonial powers in so far as political, economic and social ideas were concerned. Nationalism in Turkey, however, was an anti-imperialistic programme for independence, on the one hand, but it was also, paradoxically, a programme for cultural and political Westernization. Atatürk himself often reiterated that his struggle was directed against Western imperialism rather than against the West itself. Turkey fought the West, but by fighting with the West, entered into the Western sphere and Western system of society.

Other Kemalist principles, which were interlocked, also had somewhat indirect effects on the foreign policy of the new state. Populism, by referring to the equality of citizens and by denying the existence of classes within Turkish society, would expect to avoid creating class conflicts and, therefore, would maintain internal peace and stability, a concept, according to Kemalist ideology, that international peace and order should be based on. Statism was a programme of economic development and a way 'to attain a rank worthy of...new Turkey'.[77] All these principles were protected by nationalism against foreign aggression, and kept alive by the revolutionary dynamic process of the transformation of the Turkish state and society towards the modern Western ideal.[78] The revolution meant a transformation in outlook, the adoption of a Western way of life, a fight against ignorance and superstition, the import of new techniques, economic development, and, in particular, a constant change in people's minds. In this sense, Kemalist revolutionism was more like an evolutionary ideal, different from the intentions of other revolutionary states. Its main aim was to protect the results of the Turkish reforms from counter-revolutions, not to export its ideas and influences outside the boundaries of Turkey as many contemporary revolutionary movements did. Like Turkish nationalism, the revolution was an internal not an external phenomenon.

Such ideas as these Kemalist principles led Turkey to develop good neighbourly relations and join in with international collaborations for collective security and peace. Moreover, Turkey's Western orientation in foreign policy was a natural adjunct to Atatürk's overall embracing of the West and rejection of the East, as he said at the end of the War of Independence that 'there are many nations, but there is only one civilization. For the advancement of a nation, it must be a part of this one civilization...We wish to modernize our country. All of our efforts are directed toward the establishment of a modern, therefore Western, government.' [79] As can be seen, Atatürk identified 'modernization' with 'Westernization' and used them synonymously.

In the Atatürk period Turkey's Western-directed foreign policy was carried out in conjunction with the establishment of cultural ties with the West. The victories won against the Western states during the National Struggle gave a psychological boost to the Turkish nationalist movement and thus, as stated above, enabled swift Westernization to take place. Turkey's special feature of never having been a colonized country, and therefore not displaying any post-colonial resentments, unlike other Third World countries which gained independence after the Second World War, was also an important factor affecting Turkey's attitude towards the West. But above all, the influence of Mustafa Kemal, who even during the period of the National Struggle favoured a Western style of thinking, was of great importance in this orientation.

At the beginning of the National Struggle, Mustafa Kemal's major goal was the liberation of the country from foreign occupation and the establishment, within national boundaries, of a Turkish national state which would be master of its own fate. In its foreign policy behaviour, the government of the Grand National Assembly favoured the application of the basic principles arrived at during the peace deliberations following the First World War. Since every nation was to be permitted to form a state of its own, it was felt that Turkey also should be allowed to enjoy this right of establishing an independent country. In fact, the Grand National Assembly was the result of one of the newest national movements in 1920, similar to the European national independence movements in the course of the last century. This Turkish belief, too, attracted Turkey to the West's democratic ideals.

After the War of Independence, the main concern of Atatürk's foreign policy was complete independence. Because of foreign interventions, privileges granted to foreigners, and the Capitulations, the Ottoman Empire in its last years had to a large extent lost its independence. Following its defeat in the First World War, the last Turkish state was in the position of being completely erased from the map. This was the reason for Mustafa Kemal's initiation of the War of Independence and it was stated in the following terms in the 6th Article of the National Pact:[80]

> In order to render possible our national and economic development and to succeed in achieving orderly administration, like all states we must possess absolute independence and freedom in the achievement of our development. For this reason we are opposed to all limitations on our political, juridical or financial development. In the settling of our assessed debts there shall be no change in this matter...

Thus, 'by complete independence', he said to H. Franklin-Bouillon, representative of France, on 9 June 1921, 'we mean of course, complete economic, financial, juridical, military, cultural independence and freedom in all matters. Being deprived of independence in any of these is equivalent to the nation and country being deprived of all its independence.'[81]

Furthermore, he in no way accepted the idea of a 'mandate' or a 'protectorate'. But this principle was not against alliances or the political and military agreements made with other countries. Article 7 of the Sivas Congress Resolution reads that '...we shall gladly accept technical, industrial and economic aid from any state which will show respect for the ideals of nationalism and will not pursue the aim of seizing our country...'[82] Therefore, 'complete independence' does not mean that a state cannot enter into military and political co-operation with other states for the purpose of balancing its own power with that of potential aggressors, as long as these allies are respectful of the country's right to existence. Atatürk himself played the leading role in the establishment of the Balkan Pact in 1934 and the Sadabad Pact in 1937, and accepted economic aid from the Soviet Union.

One of the key elements of Atatürk's foreign policy was that the new Republic would seek to preserve the national territory encompassed by the armistice line of 1918, and would renounce any other territorial claims. In the Treaty of Lausanne the borders determined by the National Pact were, for the most part, realized. With Turkey's territorial situation and new borders satisfactorily settled by the Treaty of Lausanne, there was no more reason for military adventurism on Turkey's part. This was one of the overall principles of Mustafa Kemal's foreign policy.

As a state which was defeated in the First World War, the position of Turkey with regard to the situation existing in Europe after the war is noteworthy. If Turkey had acted emotionally it would have been natural for it to join the bloc of nations opposed to the status quo. But Atatürk, who had taken the responsibility of determining the direction of Turkish foreign policy, avoided leading the country down the general path of adventurism. Thus, although Turkey attempted to maintain good relations with all states, it nonetheless established closer ties with non-belligerent states in their opposition to those states which were attempting to destroy the international peace.[83] In contrast to a good number of other contemporary states, Turkey showed great willingness to solve its major problems by legal means. During the inter-war period, it would have been possible to resolve some of Turkey's problems left behind by Lausanne (such as those of the Straits and the Sanjak of Alexandretta) by force or *fait accompli* without waiting patiently for an opportunity to solve them peacefully, but Atatürk rejected such adventures.[84]

Further, he regarded humanity as one body, and each nation as one of its parts. Accordingly, the prosperity and happiness of the nations of the world could not be divided.

> Pain in the finger-tip of the body causes all the other members to suffer...If there is an illness in some part of the world or other...it must concern us exactly as if it were among us. It is this idea that saves nations from selfishness. Whether selfishness is personal or national, it must always be regarded as bad.[85]

After stressing the definite need of peace for all the civilized world, he indicated also the measures which he thought necessary for the continuation of world peace:

> If a lasting peace is desired, international measures must be taken to better the conditions of communities. The prosperity...of mankind must replace hunger and oppression. The world must educate its citizens in a way that will remove them far away from envy, greed and vindictiveness...[86]

As a soldier, he knew the horror of war and promised in 1920 'to refuse absolutely to waste the nation's time and resources in the pursuit of dreams of domination'.[87] It has been observed by Most and Singer that 'success may embolden a nation's leaders' notion of confidence and optimism and thereby stimulate their entry into subsequent conflicts'.[88] The Turkish case, however, has proved otherwise; the victory over the Entente powers decreased the likelihood of subsequent conflicts. As Edward Weisband concluded, of all the 'great socio-political revolutions in the history of the modern state...the Kemalist Revolution in Turkey represents the only one that has produced an ideology of peace'.[89]

This line of foreign policy also shows, on the part of Turkish leaders, the full realization of the country's limitations. As Lenczowski puts it, '...perhaps the greatest merit of Kemal [Atatürk] and, his followers was their sober realization of limitation and their moderate, realistic foreign policy. There was nothing romantic or adventurous in Kemal's foreign policy'.[90] In fact, his foreign policy had to be free from adventurism in order to give him time to initiate the socio-economic reforms necessary for the modernization and reconstruction of the Republic. Once he said:

> The government of the Turkish Grand National Assembly is national and material in its labors. It is realist...We are not swindlers who, in pursuit of great dreams, seem to do what we can not do...This is the whole trouble. Instead of pursuing ideas which we can not accomplish and increasing enemy pressure against ourselves, let us return our natural, our legal limits. Let us know our limits...[91]

Bearing in mind these principles, Turkey, during the interwar period, was able to establish a long-enduring peace with the Western powers by renouncing its claims on Mosul and Western Thrace, which would cause problems. Atatürk's realism further showed itself in Turkish–Soviet relations. Although he was against the ideals of communism, he signed the Turco-Soviet Friendship Pact of 1921. This co-operation was the natural outcome of the conditions prevailing at the time, and the product of Atatürk's realistic foreign policy.[92] According to him states had no eternal enemies, and no eternal allies. They do however have national goals. A state which recognizes these goals and can help to achieve them could be a friend. At any particular time, it was not ideology, but national and international realities which determined his foreign policy towards any particular state.

For a correct evaluation of Turkish foreign policy, it is important to distinguish between the fundamental goals of Turkish national foreign policy and its long or short-term objectives. Although the short-term policies for the realization of the national goals have undergone considerable changes through the years, the fundamental goals of national policy, as determined under Atatürk, have not radically altered until recently.

Atatürk attempted to replace the traditional beliefs of the Turkish people with 'national' values in order to transform the old imperial society into the modern nation-state.[93] Since then its foreign policy, too, has been appraised in terms of national interest. Because the evaluation of the national interest is more often than not a controversial issue, Turkish decision-makers have based their individual decisions on Atatürk's 'dogma' and terminology, thereby guaranteeing, at least, the support of the ordinary Turk and often the Kemalist military and civilian elite. As long as Atatürk's 'dogma' remained unquestioned, foreign policy could be based on his ideological framework. The national goals, put forward by Atatürk, together with the effects of imperial history and the geostrategic location, are the traditional inputs which have long governed Turkish foreign policy.

Since the traditional inputs are not only confined to the past, historical legacies that continue to contribute to Turkish foreign policy may thus be summarized:

(i) Turkey's important and sensitive geostrategic position has meant that national security concerns have always been paramount in foreign policy considerations. A critical element in these concerns has been Turkey's proximity to and traditional distrust of the former Soviet Union. Moreover, the fact that Turkey has borders with the Balkans and the Middle East, areas of traditional conflict, makes Turkey very sensitive to changes in both the international and regional political balance.

(ii) Turkey's security thinking is also coloured by the historical experiences of foreign intervention and economic dependency. As a result, the foreign relations of Turkey, since Atatürk's time, have been dominated by concerns for genuine independence and sovereignty. Although the Soviet threat after the Second World War persuaded Turkey to move away from Atatürk's uncommitted posture to seek politico-military alliances, it is still sensitive to any real or implied infringements on its sovereignty.

(iii) Turkey's location at the intersection of the 'West' and the 'East' (the USSR and the Arab and Islamic World) also resulted in an identity crisis, both national and international. The tendency of the Kemalist ruling class to look towards the West for inspiration has not alienated the cultural and religious affiliation to the Arab-Islamic world by the general public.

As Turkey moves toward the twenty-first century, the question of religion and secularism on the one hand, and the related issues of ethnicity, nationhood and the territorial state on the other, are coming to the fore. Although the old certainties of the ruling class' self-image as belonging to a modern, European-oriented, secular Turkey, which has been based almost exclusively on the territory of Anatolia, is coming under increasing challenges both from the left and the religious right, the legacy of the Turkish state and nationalism, embodied in a ruling class or elite with a strong commitment to Kemalist principles, still greatly affects Turkey's internal and external policies. In this context, despite the emergence of a seemingly homogeneous Turkish-speaking, traditionally Sunni-Muslim society within Turkey's borders, the obvious failure of the Kemalist attempt at homogenizing Turkey, based on a majority language and Western ideals, continues to haunt both the Turkish identity and the Turkish state, as the ruling elite still refuses to acknowledge the ethnic and structural pluralism of Turkish society 'which should be understood as essential to the formation of a modern multiethnic democracy'.[94]

(iv) Turkey's self-desire to become an economically developed country has not changed since the early days of the Republic. Apparently, its economic development is not only a social need but also a source of strengthened power for the nation. Moreover, economic development, in the eyes of the Kemalist elite, is one of the prerequisites of a European identity. The Turks' ambition for development and modernization is not confined to technological equality with the industrially advanced Western countries. They wish to be recognized as Europeans and to be assimilated into European civilization, which had been acknowledged as superior by Atatürk.

(v) Another important factor through which Turkey's foreign policy should be seen is the legality of its actions in the international arena. In Turkey it is honourable to comply with international commitments.[95] Any intimation to the contrary, such as the US intimation about its NATO commitments during the Cyprus crisis of 1964, usually causes widespread surprise and astonishment as well as disappointment in Turkey. Although its inflexible policies, which have often resulted from an all too legalistic approach toward international questions, would delay and sometimes prevent possible solutions, Turkey still insists on abiding by rigid legality. This could be, as Váli argues,[96] a direct result of the memories of the last years of the Ottoman Empire when the only way to preserve its existence and independence was the reliance on international agreements. It may also be argued that this attitude is simply a continuation of a tradition established and carefully followed by Atatürk in the early days of the Turkish republic.

(vi) Another factor which should be kept in mind when evaluating Turkish foreign policy is Turkey's desire to improve its image among the international community. Although Turkish politicians and diplomats usually argue otherwise, contemporary Turkey cares for 'international public opinion' and responds to pressures from the international arena. Given the fact that one of the most insistent national foreign policy goals of Turkey is to become a member of the European community of nations, it is not surprising to see that even the military junta of 12 September 1980, both before and after the intervention, was sensitive to perceptions abroad.[97]

In conclusion, it should be emphasized that structural factors, as discussed above, have played a stabilizing role in, and ensured the continuation of, Turkish foreign policy. Therefore the characterization of Turkish foreign policy as having a high degree of rationality and sobriety[98] has much to do with the heritage of the Ottoman Empire, which was forced to pursue its foreign policy amid tensions between its own interest and those of other powers.[99] At the same time, it is also in accordance with the demands placed upon Turkey by its geopolitical situation: the fact that Turkey lies on the boundaries of Europe, the Middle East and the Soviet Union necessitated, in the past and more recently, a balanced, multi-sided foreign policy.

NOTES

1. For different, and sometimes contradictory, explanations of what is happening in Turkish foreign policy see D. Barchard, 'Turkey and Europe', *Turkish Review Quarterly Digest*, Vol.3, No.17 (1989); W. Weiker, 'Turkey, the Middle East and Islam', *Middle East Review*, Special Issue on Turkey, Vol.17, No.3 (1985); K. Mackenzie, 'Turkey Racked by March of Islam', *Observer*, 18 Jan. 1987; D. Rustow, 'Turkey's Liberal Revolution', *Middle East Review*, Vol.17, No.3 (1985); F. Ahmad, 'Islamic Reassertation in Turkey', *Third World Quarterly*, Vol.10, No.2 (1988); O. Tunander, 'A New Ottoman Empire? The Choice for Turkey: Euro-Asian Center vs. National Fortress', *Security Dialogue*, Vol.26, No.4 (1995); A. Mango, 'Turkey in Winter', *Middle Eastern Studies*, Vol.31, No.3 (July, 1995); S. Hunter, *Turkey at the Crossroads: Islamic Past or European Future?*, CEPS Paper No.63 (Brussels, 1995).
2. When I am talking about in-depth study of Turkish foreign policy, I have Ferenc Váli's *Bridge Across the Bosporus* (Baltimore, London, 1971) in mind.
3. J. Frankel, *The Making of Foreign Policy; An Analysis of Decision-Making* (London, 1963), p.1.
4. K. Goldman, *Change and Stability In Foreign Policy; The Problems and Possibilities of Détente* (New York, 1988), p.3.
5. For examples and a more general discussion of this issue see M. Aydın, 'Foreign Policy Formation and The Interaction Between Domestic and International Environments: A Study of Change In Turkish Foreign Policy, 1980–1991', PhD thesis, Lancaster University, 1994, pp.8–32.
6. B. White, 'Analysing Foreign Policy: Problems and Approaches' in M. Clarke and B. White (eds.), *Understanding Foreign Policy: The Foreign Policy Systems Approach* (Aldershot, 1989), p.9.
7. F. Gros, *Foreign Policy Analysis* (New York, 1954), p.97.
8. J.N. Rosenau, 'The Study of Foreign Policy' in J.N. Rosenau, K.W. Thompson and G. Boyd (eds.), *World Politics: An Introduction* (New York, 1971), p.17.
9. K.R. Legg and J.F. Morrison, *Politics and International System; An Introduction* (New York, 1971), p.134.
10. Ibid., p.141.
11. This line of categorization of the sources brings to mind Rosenau's time continuum, in which he puts the sources that tend to change slowly at one end, and the sources that tend to undergo rapid change at the other end. His categorization also includes the systemic aggregation which includes systemic, societal, governmental, and idiosyncratic sources. See J.N. Rosenau, op. cit., and *The Scientific Study of Foreign Policy* (New York, 1971).
12. For a detailed study of early foreign relations of the Ottoman Empire and the system of the 'foreign office' see Lord Kinross, *The Ottoman Centuries: The Rise and Fall of the Turkish Empire* (London, 1977); and S.J. Shaw and E.K. Shaw, *History of the Ottoman Empire and Modern Turkey* (London, 1977).
13. Legg and Morrison, op. cit., p.110.
14. Rosenau, *Study of Foreign Policy*, pp.19–20.
15. See R.C. Snyder, H.W. Bruck and B. Sapin, 'The Decision-Making Approach to the Study of International Politics' in J.N. Rosenau (ed.), *International Politics and Foreign Policy: A Reader In Search and Theory* (New York, 1961), pp.189–90.
16. The only exception was Hatay, the district around İskenderun (Alexandretta), which

remained in Syria as an autonomous region for the time being, and later in 1939 rejoined Turkey by majority vote of its parliament. For the text of the Lausanne Peace Treaty see J.C. Hurewitz, *Diplomacy in the Near and Middle East: A Documentary Record, 1535–1956* (Princeton, 1956), Vol.II, pp.119–27. For text of the National Pact see M.K. Atatürk, *Nutuk*, 3 Volumes (Ankara, 1981), Vol.3, Doc. No.41. Hereafter referred as '*Nutuk*'. Also reprinted in Hurewitz, ibid., pp.74–5.

17. For the text of the Treaty of Sèvres see Hurewitz, ibid., pp.81–9. For the Entente plans to partition the territories of the Ottoman Empire see H.N. Howard, *The Partition of Turkey: A Diplomatic History* (New York, 1966); R.S. Sonyel, *Turkish Diplomacy, 1918–1923: M. Kemal and the Turkish National Movement* (London, 1975), pp.1–13; A.F. Toynbee and K.P. Kirkwood, *The Modern World: A Survey of Historical Forces, Volume VI: Turkey* (London, 1926), pp.61–8 and 136–42.
18. With an indigenous clause, the right to use and govern the area were given to Greece, but not the sovereignty. However, there was a possibility of transfer of sovereignty by majority vote in a plebiscite that was to be held after five years of Greek administration.
19. For detailed study of Turkish nationalists struggle for independence and its external relations see M. Gönlübol *et al.*, *Olaylarla Türk Diş Politikası* (Turkish Foreign Policy With Facts), 6th ed. (Ankara, 1987) pp.3–48; Sonyel, op. cit.; E.R. Vere-Hodge, 'Turkish Foreign Policy, 1918–1948', PhD thesis, Imprimerie Franco-Suisse, Ambilly-Annemasse, 1950, pp.23–50; and *Nutuk*.
20. P. Robins, 'The Overlord State: Turkish Policy and the Kurdish Issue', *International Affairs*, Vol.69, No.4 (1993), p.659; and R. Sim, 'Kurdistan: The Search For Recognition', *Conflict Studies*, No.124 (1980), p.4. The Treaty itself, although it did not define the exact territory of proposed autonomous Kurdistan, stipulated that after one year it might ask the League of Nations for a conformation of its status as an independent state. Conformation of this status was to be based on the evaluation of mandatory power(s).
21. Sim, op cit., pp.17–18; G.L. Lewis, *Turkey* (London, 1955), pp.84–8; For contemporary discussion of how the Kemalist Turkey dealt with the Kurdish issue see Toynbee and Kirkwood, op.cit., pp.259–74.
22. Homogeneity is used here in a very broad sense as the Lausanne Treaty presumed and also in a sense that would have been used by early Kemalists whose understanding of 'Turkish nation' was constitutional rather than ethnic-based and included Muslim minorities, such as Kurds, but excluded Christians and Muslim Arabs, left behind in Anatolia by the dying Ottoman Empire. Also bear in mind the distinction made by Salomone between *homogeneous* and *homogenous*. According to this interpretation, a homogeneous society is the one which aims at creating a uniform public consensus through differential incorporation. Homogenous society, on the other hand, necessitates a uniform culture obtainable through homogenization. For a further discussion see S.D. Salomone, 'The Dialectics of Turkish National Identity: Ethnic Boundary Maintenance and State Ideology – Part Two', *East European Quarterly*, Vol.23, No.2 (1989). However, within this broad 'homogeneity' there exist various ethnic groups and sub-groups in Turkey as detailed by P.A. Andrews (ed.), *Ethnic Groups In the Republic of Turkey* (Wiesbaden, 1989).
23. In early 1920, Sheikh-ul-Islam issued a '*fetva*' encouraging the killings of rebels as a religious duty. Accordingly, a court martial in Istanbul condemned Mustafa Kemal and other nationalist leaders to death, *in absentia*. And irregular troops, the 'Army of the Caliphate', were organized to fight the nationalists. For more detailed analysis of the early nationalist struggle against 'internal opposition' see *Nutuk*, Vol.I; Doğu Ergil, *Social History of the Turkish National Struggle, 1919–22: The Unfinished Revolution* (Lahore, Pakistan, 1977), pp.10–95.
24. *Nutuk*, Vol.1, p.59.
25. F.W. Frey, *The Turkish Political Elite* (Cambridge, 1965); L. Leslie and P.L. Noralov, *Managers of Modernisation; Organisations and Elites in Turkey, 1950–1969* (Cambridge, 1971).
26. M.P. Prise, *A History of Turkey; From Empire to Republic* (London, 1961), p.44.
27. For analysis of the impact of the West in Ottoman Empire see Toynbee/Kirkwood, op. cit., pp.31–61.

28. For modernization attempts in the Ottoman Empire see B. Lewis, *The Emergence of Modern Turkey* (London, New York: Oxford University Press, 1961); R.E. Ward and D.A. Rustow, *Political Modernisation in Japan and Turkey* (Princeton, 1964).
29. Abdullah Cevdet (1869–1932) was one of the co-founders of the Society of Union and Progress, and a political writer. Quotation taken from *Içtihad*, 89 (Istanbul, 1909) by B. Lewis, op. cit., p.236.
30. For example, one of the intellectual founders of Turkish nationalism, Ziya Gökalp, made distinction between Western civilization and culture, agreeing to imitate the first as a way towards modernization of Turkish people, but refusing the second because of their distinct culture. Mustafa Kemal, on the other hand, openly rejected this interpretation. See B. Oran, *Az Gelişmiş Ülke Milliyetçiliği* [Underdeveloped Country Nationalism] (Ankara, 1997), 3rd ed., pp.28–9.
31. E. Laipson, *Greece and Turkey: US Foreign Assistance Facts*, Library of Congress, CRS Report, No.IB86065, Washington, DC, 13 Feb. 1990.
32. Statement by Kenan Evren, 7th President of Turkey, *Newspot*, 7 Sept. 1984.
33. To H. Franklin-Bouillon, representative of France, on 9 June 1921; see *Nutuk*, Vol.1, pp.135–8. For Entente attempts at the Lausanne to keep Capitulations intact and Turkish resentment see Toynbee and Kirkwood, op. cit., pp.136–42.
34. P. Robins, 'Turkey and the Eastern Arab World', in Gerd Nonneman (ed.), *The Middle East and Europe*, 2nd ed. (London, 1993), pp.189–90; R. Robinson, *The First Turkish Republic* (Cambridge, MA, 1963), p.170.
35. Quoted in Shaw and Shaw, op. cit., p.483. For excellent history and bibliography of the Russo-Ottoman rivalry see also B. Lewis, op. cit.
36. Cited in Lord Kinross, *Atatürk: A Biography of Mustafa Kemal, Father of Modern Turkey* (London, 1990), p.464.
37. A.J. Toynbee, *Nationality and the War* (London, 1915), p.412.
38. Váli, op. cit., p.46.
39. Under present arrangements, about 35 per cent of the Aegean is designated as Greek territorial sea and about 9 per cent as Turkish territorial sea. An arrangement employing the twelve mile limit would result in a disposition where Greece's share of total Aegean Sea space would increase to 64 per cent; Turkey's would remain at less than 9 per cent, with the remaining area being designated as international waters. Figures taken from A. Wilson, *The Aegean Dispute*, Adelphi Papers, No.155 (1980), pp.36–7.
40. B.A. Most and H.I. Starr, 'Diffusion, Reinforcement, Geopolitics and the Spread of War', *The American Political Science Review*, Vol.74, No.4, p.935. In the early 1990s, the break-up of the former Soviet Union added yet more neighbours – Georgia, Armenia, Azerbaijan due to Nachivan, Russia and Ukraine – and thus created more uncertainties for Turkey.
41. Váli, op. cit., p.44.
42. Ibid.
43. Legg and Morrison, op. cit., p.101.
44. Váli, op. cit., p.ix.
45. N. Eren, *Turkey Today and Tomorrow; An Experiment in Westernization* (London, 1963), p.227.
46. N. Eren, *Turkey, NATO and Europe; A Deteriorating Relationship?* (Paris, 1980), p.16.
47. For N.S. Khrushchev's letter, dated June 28, 1960, to General Cemal Gürsel, prime minister of Turkey, see F. Váli, *Turkish Straits and NATO* (Stanford, Calif., 1972), pp.302–5.
48. H. Ülman and O. Sander, 'Türk Dış Politikasına Yön Veren Etkenler-II' [Factors Influencing Turkish Foreign Policy-II], *SBF Dergisi*, Vol.27, No.1 (1972), pp.1–24.
49. A. Karaosmanoğlu, 'Turkey's Security and the Middle East', *Foreign Affairs*, Vol.62 (1983), p.99.
50. T. A. Couloumbis, *The US, Greece, Turkey; The Troubled Triangle* (New York, 1987), p.118. Also see Wilson, op. cit., pp.4–10 and13–15.
51. Wilson, op. cit., pp.4 and 30.
52. Váli, *Bridge Across the Bosporus*, p.55.
53. *Nutuk*, Vol.2, p.218.
54. Váli, *Bridge Across the Bosporus*, p.55.

55. The 1982 Constitution (as well as 1961 Constitution) presented a modified version of Kemalist principles, declaring in Article 2: 'The Republic of Turkey is a democratic, secular and social state governed by the rule of law; bearing in mind the concepts of public peace, national solidarity and justice; respecting human rights; loyal to the nationalism of Atatürk, and based on the fundamental tenets set forth in the Preamble'.

    The preamble gave renewed credit to the Kemalist achievements and ideology by expressing 'absolute loyalty to...the direction of concept of nationalism as outlined by Atatürk...[and] the reforms and principles introduced by him'. It also expressed 'desire for, and belief in *peace at home, peace in the world*', and its determination not to protect any 'thoughts or opinions contrary to Turkish National interests...the nationalism, principles, reform and modernism of Atatürk, and that as required by the principle of secularism'.
56. *Nutuk*, Vol.2, p.229.
57. N. Berkes, *The Development of Secularism in Turkey* (Montreal, 1964), pp.479–503.
58. Ibid., p.6.
59. *Nutuk*, op. cit.
60. T. Feyzioğlu, 'Secularism: Cornerstone of Turkish Revolution', in T. Feyzioğlu (ed.), *Atatürk's Way*, Cultural Publication of Otomarsan (Istanbul, 1982), p.208. For Nationalist resentment and objections at the Lausanne Peace Conference to the abuse of the *millet* system by Western powers see Toynbee and Kirkwood, op. cit., pp.143–8.
61. O. Sander, 'Turkish Foreign Policy; Forces of Continuity and of Change' in A. Evin (ed.), *Modern Turkey; Continuity and Change* (Opladen, 1984), p.119.
62. *Nutuk*, Vol.1, pp.21–4.
63. M. K. Atatürk, *Söylev ve Demeçler* [Speeches and Statements], 5 Volumes (Ankara: TTK Basımevi, 1985), Vol.2, p.54: '*Speeches*' from now on.
64. A. Akşin, *Atatürk'ün Dış Politika İlkeleri ve Diplomasisi* [Foreign Policy Principles and Diplomacy of Atatürk] (Istanbul, 1964), p.52.
65. A. A. İnan, *Medeni Bilgiler ve M. K. Atatürk'ün Elyazıları* [Civic Lessons and Manuscripts of M. K. Atatürk] (Ankara, 1969), p.18.
66. Sander, *Turkish Foreign Policy*, p.119.
67. Salamone, op. cit., p.226 quoted from the US Department of State, *Turkey, Post Report: The Host Country*, Jan. 1986, p.1.
68. From the People's Party Status of 1923, quoted in F. Armaoğlu, *CHP Tarihi* [History of the RPP] (Ankara, 1971), Vol.I, p.38.
69. H. Eroğlu, 'Atatürk's Conception of Nation and Nationalism' in Feyzioğlu, op. cit., pp,149–50.
70. As described by T. Z. Tunaya, *Siyasi Müesseler ve Anayasa Hukuku* [Political Institutions and Constitutional Law] (Istanbul, 1966), p.66.
71. From a speech delivered at the Fourth National Convention of the RPP by its Chairman and ideologue, Recep Peker, on 9 May 1935. Cited in Armaoğlu, op.cit., p.46.
72. M. S. Arsal, *Milliyet Duygusunun Sosyolojik Esasları* [Sociological Principles of Nationalistic Sentiment] (Istanbul, 1963), p.103.
73. Quoted from M. Kemal by İnan, op. cit., p.23.
74. For further discussion see Salamone, op. cit. Also refer to note 22 of this paper.
75. The term that Mustafa Kemal used during the War of Independence to refer to the people who lived then in Anatolia was 'Nation of Turkey' (Türkiye Milleti), which was replaced after the war by 'Turkish Nation' (Türk Milleti). See B. Oran, *Atatürk Milliyetçiliği; Resmi İdeoloji Dışı Bir İnceleme* [Kemalist Nationalism; A Non-Official Interpretation] (Ankara, 1993), p.208.
76. Robins, *Overlord State*, p.658.
77. Since '...we live in an economic era...the new Turkish state will not be a world conquering state. The new Turkish state will be an economic state.' *Speeches*, Vol.1, p.215.
78. Kinross, *Atatürk*, p.457.
79. *Speeches*, Vol.3, pp.67–8.
80. *Nutuk*, Vol.3, Doc. No.41.
81. *Nutuk*, Vol.1, pp.135–8.
82. Cited in Akşin, op. cit., p.8.

83. Gönlübol, op. cit., p.8.
84. İ. İnönü, 'Negotiations and National Interest', in *Perspectives on Peace, 1919–1960* (London, 1960), pp.137–8.
85. *Speeches*, Vol.3, p.69.
86. Ibid., p.70.
87. A. Mango, *Turkey*, New Nations and Peoples Series (London, 1968), p.31.
88. Most and Singer, op. cit., p.934.
89. E. Weiseband, *Turkish Foreign Policy, 1943–1945* (Princeton, 1973), p.7.
90. G. Lenczowski, *The Middle East in World Affairs* (Ithaca, NY, 1980), p.121.
91. *Speeches*, Vol.3, p.81.
92. For the Turkish–Soviet co-operation during the War of Independence see Howard, op. cit., especially pp.262–4; S.A. Bilge, *Güç Komşuluk; Türkiye-Sovyetler Birliği İlişkileri, 1920–1964* [Difficult Neighbourhood; Relations Between Turkey and the Soviet Union] (Ankara, 1992), pp.16–79; K. Gürün, *Türk-Sovyet İlişkileri, 1920–1953* [Turkish–Soviet Relations] (Ankara, 1991), pp.1–103; Ergil, op. cit., pp.99–103 and 141–52.
93. Eroğlu, op. cit., p.161.
94. Salamone, op. cit., Vol.II, p.226.
95. 'There is a pervasive sense among Turkey's foreign policy makers that international commitments extend beyond changes in party, government and even constitutional regime, and that international treaties are to be scrupulously observed.' D.A. Rustow, *Turkey: America's Forgotten Ally* (New York, 1989), p.85.
96. Váli, *Bridge Across the Bosporus*, p.71.
97. M.A. Birand, *The Generals' Coup in Turkey; An Inside Story of 12 September 1980* (London, 1987), p.33.
98. U. Steinbach, 'Basic Orientations of Turkish Foreign Policy', *Vierteljahresberichte Probleme der Entwicklungsländer*, Vol.86 (1984), p.381.
99. H. Ülman, 'Türk Dış Politikasına Yön Veren Etkenler-I' [Factors Influencing Turkish Foreign Policy-I], *SBF Dergisi*, Vol.23, No.3 (1968), pp.241–3.

What is the Matter with Citizenship? A Turkish Debate

AHMET İÇDUYGU, YILMAZ ÇOLAK
and NALAN SOYARIK

Fundamental to the establishment of the Turkish Republic was the development of a new concept of citizenship in the national polity that would go hand in hand with the nation-building process. Mustafa Kemal, the founder of the Republic, perceived citizenship as the very core of the legitimacy of the Republic.[1] Accordingly, he himself actively participated in designing a compulsory course of civic education that was to be taught in the schools of Turkey. In those early days of the Republic, civic education in the country began with the course entitled *Malumat-ı Vataniyye* (Information about the Motherland) which was included in school curricula in 1924. In 1927, it was replaced by *Yurt Bilgisi* (again the same meaning, Information about the Motherland), and finally from 1985 on, it was offered with the title of *Vatandaşlık Bilgileri* (Information about Citizenship).[2] In other words, from the very start in Turkey, citizenship was officially taken to be one of the key elements of successful nation-building.

Despite the fact that from the very beginning, citizenship had a deep underlying significance for the construction of the new Turkish society and state, social science literature seldom explicitly discussed the concept of citizenship in Turkey beyond its ideological implications regarding nationalist heritage. In addition to these implications, Turks often thought of their citizenship as serving goals and practices of a universal kind reflected in Western political and philosophical tradition: defining the rights, obligations and identity of individuals in the country, citizenship concerns the relations that individual members of the state have among each other and with the governing body. Now, however, this comfortable scenario is challenged on two fronts. At the present time, Turkey finds itself reacting to the naturalization policies and practices of migrant-receiving states, in which thousands of its emigrant citizens are in search of access to citizenship and citizenship rights in those states, and consequently 'dual citizenship' has become an issue of increasing concern. On the other hand, it has to deal with the question of how the free expression of ethnic

(Kurdish), religious (Islamic) and sectarian (Alevi) revivalism is possible under the unitary principles of the Turkish state and citizenship, and accordingly 'constitutional citizenship' is repeatedly pronounced. In these circumstances Turkish citizens have been forced to ask whether they have a distinct 'citizenship' identity of their own which is challenged by the forces of migration, ethnicity, and religion challenge. The new citizenship debate in Turkey is essentially centred on these three forces.

The purpose of this article is to consider the extent to which issues of 'constitutional citizenship' and 'dual citizenship' are integral parts of the current citizenship debate in Turkey. Of course, one can claim that these two issues are so utterly dissimilar in nature that it is obviously ambitious to attempt to discuss them both in the same brief article. But we stress the need for an evaluation of these issues together as they come into play on the citizenship debate in Turkey today. To this end the essay explains some of the difficulties inherent in both the content of these two terms and their implications for the concept of citizenship itself. Next, an outline of approaches to citizenship from the beginning of the Republic to the present day is offered to provide perspective on the current debate concerning the level of citizenship practices that Turkish citizens enjoy. An indication of the extent of the citizenship debate in Turkey is drawn from the most recent public and scholarly discussions in the country. This latter issue is then explored in the light of recent developments in relevant social issues, such as international migration and ethnic and religious revivalism, and a discussion of the politics of mobility and ethnicity is opened up. A conclusion points the way to future directions in these areas.

The concept of citizenship has received renewed interest in the last ten years, since globalization has become a popular issue. This recent interest is as multifaceted as it is immense. Various political events and trends throughout the world are seen as being responsible for the increasing global importance of the concept of citizenship: for instance, the resurgence of nationalist movements in Eastern Europe; the stresses created by an increasingly multicultural and multiracial population in Western Europe; the refugee problem which has created a new crisis of stateless persons in the contemporary political system, and so forth.[3] What all these developments imply is that the conventional concept of the nation-state has been profoundly challenged by global events and trends, and consequently, citizenship as an issue has become prominent.

Studies which link citizenship to the rise and stability of nation-states perceive the former as an outcome of modernity, and consider it as a transition from status to contract.[4] Thus, in its simplest formulation, citizenship corresponds to the contract-like status of membership in a nation-state. But this membership has different aspects. For instance, Hammar delineates four interrelated meanings of citizenship; namely *legal*, *political*, *social and cultural*, and *psychological*.[5] The legal dimension is formal membership in a state, based on specific rules and connotes a number of rights and duties. The political dimension specifies the position of the individual in the polity as citizen, and thus forms the basis of the state. In the cultural and social sense it signifies the membership of a nation. And finally, psychologically it provides an expression of individual identification. From Hammar's perspective, it is obvious that more than a legal status, citizenship is seen as an identity expressing an individual's membership in a definitive politico-cultural community.

Similarly, Brubaker's analysis, referring to an ideal-typical model, provides an analytical study of the membership status of citizenship. Brubaker, who also defines citizenship as membership of the nation-state, draws his argument from the contention that each nation-state attempts to have a certain population as its own which can be identified as something more than individuals in order that a cohesive and homogeneous nation can be constructed. By regarding the nation-state both as an idea and an ideal, Brubaker delineates six membership norms for the ideal-typical model. According to this model, this membership should be *egalitarian*, *sacred*, *nation-based*, *democratic*, *unique*, and *consequential*.[6] The distinguishing feature of Brubaker's approach arises from the fact that he conducts a comparative analysis which attempts to elaborate the link between different conceptions of nationhood and citizenship by focusing on nation-state formations in France and Germany. More specifically, Brubaker bases the expansive conception of citizenship in the French context which he depicts as stemming from the principle of *jus soli*, on the contention that nationhood in the French vocabulary was state-centred and assimilationist. Distinguishing the German case as *Volk*-centred and differentialist, he finds the identifying features of German citizenship to be based on *jus sanguinis*. In this respect, Brubaker notes that by drawing upon a specific ethno-cultural dimension, Germany failed to integrate the egalitarian, democratic, nationalist and statist aspects of citizenship which had been realized in France. Such a remark leads him to conclude that the evolution of citizenship in Germany displayed a diversified path among formal state membership, participatory citizenship and ethno-cultural nation membership.[7] What is clear meanwhile is that both the French and German models of citizenship were deeply affected by the concept of 'nation', even though its meaning was different from one to another.

The relationship between the concept of citizenship, defined as the legally acknowledged membership of a state, and the concept of nationhood, defined as the socially acknowledged belonging to a nation, is the core context in which the various membership status of individuals and citizenship rights are questioned. Having defined state as a legal and political organization, with the power to require obedience and loyalty from its citizens, and nation as a community of people, whose members are bound together by a sense of solidarity, a common culture, a national consciousness, it is possible to argue that 'while state is a legal and political concept, nation is a cultural one'.[8] With such a distinction made, it is also possible to argue that the notion of a homogeneous nation-state, which is based on the ideal of 'one nation in one state', is more a fiction than a reality. Working contrary to the theoretical construction of an ideal nation-state, emergence of the competing forms of national, regional, ethnic, or religious identities makes an important contribution to the increasing heterogeneity of populations in the nation-states. The implied assumption is that there are fundamental challenges to governance where the society appears increasingly fragmented into a multitude of groups, each having its own distinct identity and issuing social and political demands based on their identity.[9]

Considering the question of *pluralism*, the core issue of citizenship today is the cultural fragmentation in modern nation-states. Members of these states have different and competing cultural identities which often undermine the *shared identity* signified by their citizenship. As elaborated by Marshall,[10] citizenship can be taken as a shared identity that would integrate previously ignored groups within the society and provide a source of unity. When Marshall gave an historical account of the development of citizenship in Britain through the evolution of civil, political and social elements, he indeed saw the citizenship as a tool not only to integrate the people to the common culture, but also to construct this 'common possession and heritage'. It has become clear, however, that many citizens with their distinct identities today have serious difficulties in becoming a part of the common culture in their nation-states, despite possessing the common rights of citizenship.[11] In other words, the conventional notion of citizenship fails to deal with the 'problems that are associated with equality in the context of difference'.[12] Behind this failure, it is believed that there is the notion of universality which results in both an abstract notion of citizen-individual identity and a general notion of common citizenship identity. Both of these identities, citizen-individual identity and common citizenship identity, imply that all individuals are given *the same* formal and legal rights regardless of gender, race, ethnicity, religion or class. From this conventional perspective, citizenship is an issue of viewing people as individuals with equal rights under the law. Consequently, in our contemporary world, it is seen that neither of these notions of citizenship can take account of identity differences and accommodate the special unmet needs of distinct identity groups. The conventional notion of citizenship is unable to respond to the requirements of the principle of pluralism. Keyman puts the case with the following statement: '...the unitary conceptions of modern self (as a political class identity or a citizen identity or a national identity) can no longer play their unifying function; nor are they capable of dissolving difference into sameness'.[13]

What is required then is a new form of citizenship, a membership status in a modern democratic state which neither necessitates a homogeneous socio-political community nor subordinates various identity groups, but rather recognizes the diversity of identities, even values them, and incorporates them into the larger community, or common culture. It is within this context that an increasing number of scholars emphasize the need of modelling some new types of citizenship in our modern democracies. The models currently being debated include, among others, the concepts of multicultural citizenship,[14] differentiated citizenship,[15] constitutional citizenship,[16] and dual,[17] or multiple, citizenship. Considering their relevance to our discussion of the Turkish case, two of these specific types of citizenship, multiple citizenship (generally known as dual citizenship) and constitutional citizenship, are elaborated here in some detail.

What is generally known as dual citizenship, or rarely as multiple citizenship, signifies that one person holds the membership, i.e. citizenship status, of more than one state, as a consequence of international migration. Given the importance of citizenship as a key to participation in a socio-political community, and as a symbol of commitment to the future of this community, international migration is a challenge to both the theory and the practice of governance in migrant-sending and migrant-receiving countries. Indeed, the status of millions of migrants around the world is often socially and politically anomalous. International migration leads to the emergence of large groups of foreign citizens who, for all intents and purposes, are permanent residents but cannot fully benefit from their citizenship rights. Although one can acknowledge the difficulties in coping with the diversity of established policies, practice and outlook with regard to immigration and admission to citizenship in various nation-states, the liberalization of naturalization and dual (multiple) citizenship rights seem to be practical solutions.[18] The notion of dual, multiple, citizenship suggests that citizenship is formal legal membership of a state, implying loyalty to the state rather than the nation, and it is important for both symbolic and practical reasons with the emphasis on the latter. Of course, the content of dual citizenship within the boundaries of the 'theory of citizenship' is at the centre of a significant debate. Although the full details of this debate are not in the scope of our study, some aspects of the debate on dual, multiple citizenship will be elaborated in more detail by referring to the Turkish case.

Although the concept of *constitutional identity*, or *constitutional citizenship*, remains largely undefined, we might take it 'to refer to that aspect of our collective and individual self-conception which we owe to our shared constitutional heritage'.[19] Constitutional citizenship, which often comes to the fore in relation to the possibility of a European identity transcending the identity of nation-states in the European Union,[20] implies a supra-national identity guaranteed by the constitution to function as a common identity denominator for the diversity and integrity of the different forms of life coexisting in a multicultural environment. The original idea of constitutional identity, constitutional citizenship, or constitutional patriotism suggests that democratic citizenship in our modern states does not need to be rooted in the national identity of a people. However, it does require that citizens, without divorcing themselves from their diversity of different cultural forms of life, should be socialized into a common political culture. If 'a constitution can be thought of as an historical project that each generation of citizens continues to pursue',[21] then the concept of constitutional citizenship can be seen as a driving force for the dynamic project of creating a new common identity. This collective identity provides a socio-political setting for the manner in which a common politico-cultural self-understanding would emerge by differentiation from the cultural orientations of different national, ethnic, and religious identities. On the other hand, if the constitution expresses formal consensus among various identities,[22] the concept of constitutional citizenship would contribute to the question of how to deal with a diversity of identities so that identity and otherness would complement rather than exclude one another. Accordingly, on the basis of constitutional citizenship every person would 'receive equal protection and equal respect in their integrity as irreplaceable individuals, as members of ethnic or cultural groups, and as citizens, that is, as members of the political community'.[23] It is believed that by recognizing and including the diversity and otherness in one common identity, constitutional identity would contribute to the integrative function of citizenship. It is also believed that the demand for both representational rights and multicultural rights coming from various identities is a demand for inclusion, not for exclusion.[24]

In order to understand and grasp the parameters and nature of the official concept of citizenship in Turkey (in the development of which the state played the determinant role), this section will attempt to portray the process by which it was constructed. The development of Republican citizenship is divided into three basic time periods: first, the Single Party period (1923–50); second, the period from 1950 to 1980; and third, the 1980 military intervention and its aftermath.

The laws and regulations aiming at institutionalizing the status of citizenship in the Turkish Republic had close links with Ottoman modernization. Attempts at modernization in the Ottoman Empire gained impetus by the proclamation of *Gülhane Hatt-ı Hümayunu*, which initiated a reformation period called *Tanzimat*. *Tanzimat* was based on the secularization of religious laws and implementation of new administrative, educational and financial policies for reorganizing the state structure in conformity with European models. For the first time in Ottoman history a legislative act was put into practice, dependent on the principle of securing the life, honour and property of all subjects regardless of their religion. It also brought about limitations on the Sultan's power to the advantage of the bureaucracy.[25] By the Tanzimat reform movement and the 1876 constitution, generally speaking, the subjects living in the Empire were taken as individuals making a society, not simply as the being parts of different religious-ethnic communities.[26] The first legal regulation on the issues of Ottoman citizenship was dated 23 January 1869 Tabiiyet-i Osmaniyeye dair Nizamname.[27] The Regulation was based on descent, only those born to Ottoman parents were regarded as Ottoman citizens; however, territorial understanding was exercized in a limited manner for those born in the territory of the Empire after they reached maturity.

The first attempt to search for a Turkish identity for the citizens of the Empire in light of the modern nationalist ideals appeared with the government of the Committee of Union and Progress, from 1908 to 1918. The Young Turks introduced a new understanding that 'the nation was the source of all authority',[28] and so they made the first attempt to transform the Empire into a model of a homogeneous state based on the premise of one state, one nation. Citizenship in the Turkish Republic was described in Article 88 of Teşkilat-ı Esasiye Kanunu, 1924, meaning that without regard for their religious or ethnic origins, people living in Turkey were to be considered Turks regarding citizenship. Legal regulation, dated 23 May 1928, and numbered 1312, the Türk Vatandaşlığı Kanunu (Turkish Citizenship Law), was also descent based, but territorial understanding is exercised as complementary. The law in use today, dated 11 February 1964 and numbered 403, is also based on descent, and territorial understanding is exercised as complementary in order to avoid statelessness among the foreigners in the country.[29]

The process of 'citizenization'[30] and the conceptualization of citizenship in the early Republican period, or the Single Party period, is the most significant in providing background information for understanding the current debates on citizenship in Turkey. During that era, the creation of a new Turk or Turkish citizen who had to be, first of all, 'civilized' and 'patriotic'[31] was the most significant civilizing mission of the Kemalist reformist elite. The Kemalist attempt at transforming subjects into citizens came into being with the rising concern of the political authority for describing who were Turks and who were not, or who the Turks were going to be.[32] In that ruling, the modernizing elite tried to establish a strong link between citizenship and nationality or national identity. This was regarded in most cases as inevitable in the exercise of citizenship, and, according to their cultural objectives, in defining the profiles of *civilized* and *patriotic* citizens of the Republic. It is in this respect that they appeared to take into consideration the idea that creating a shared sense of national culture and identity was a fundamental precondition for forming and strengthening citizenship. That was the main task of the Kemalist nation-building project that required, in its defining of the national and cultural identity of citizens, the total elimination of Ottoman and Islamic heritage, which was considered responsible for the backwardness of the state and society. By striving to eliminate the hegemony of traditional institutions and values over the state structure and society, the Republican elite aimed at building a 'completely secular state'[33] and a secular socio-cultural structure. That is why the Turkish reform movement stimulated by the nationalist ideology of the Kemalist modernizing state was a sort of cultural revolution or, in the words of Mardin, a 'revolution of values'.[34] Thanks to its preexistence as a strong, centralized state[35] that helped to facilitate the process of cultural and linguistic integration, the Republican state projected a particular form of a vision of socio-cultural life, a good life which each Turkish citizen should adopt. This new life would represent a common good and national interest,[36] but not a particular and individualistic one that was dangerous for national unity.

In forging a new identity, the Turkish state used its powers and agencies to accomplish its social and cultural engineering. It strove to eliminate all previously designated symbols, attitudes and manners, replacing them with its own new myths and symbols. Atatürk defined the 'new' Turk thus: 'We must be civilized men from every point of view; our ideas, our reasoning will be civilized from head to toe.'[37] For him, the nation to which new Turks belonged was composed of citizens tied together by a common language, culture and collective consciousness and ideals, being a political and social cntity.[38] This definition contains no reference to religion – Islam – or tradition. In short, the Kemalists sought to establish a common cultural content, in large measure newly formulated and of course *secular*, to be used in forging the new Turkish citizens' identity, and for manifesting their position as members of both the state and the organic whole (the nation).

The conceptualization of citizenship, as it was argued, came hand in hand with constructing a unique, unchangeable and historic Turkish identity that would be made possible only by newly fabricating and imposing a new monolithic culture, while ignoring ethnic and sub-cultural identities. That led to the designation of traditional/Islamic and local cultural symbols to the periphery of the public sphere, and even to the dictation and regulation of everyday life of the new Turks. The Republican civilizing elite, therefore, tried its best to 'penetrate into the life style, manners, behavior and daily customs of the people, and to change the self-conception of Turks'.[39] Each Turkish citizen, equipped with well-defined modes of behaviour, had to be faithful to the his/her own state which, as a representative of collective personality of the nation and citizens, preached the advantages and goodness of being a Turk, a Turkish citizen. In other words, the Republican concept of citizenship was perceived not only as equipping its citizens with the rights and responsibilities of the public sphere, but as forming a totally new man by preaching even the rearrangement of private life, or the very life-style of the people.

While people with different ethnic and cultural origins were to be called Turks, the notion of citizenship was not defined simply in ethnic terms. That is, Turkish nationality was not regarded as the product of biology or blood ties. The new and artificially constructed or 'manufactured' Turkish culture was, therefore, open to non-Turkish Muslim groups, who were accepted as members of the nation and state so long as they were willing to integrate or assimilate culturally and linguistically into Turkish culture. This is the logic of cultural assimilation, not ethnic or racist. The migration of Muslim groups (Bosnians, Albanians, Macedonians) from both the Balkans and the Caucasus was accepted, and those groups were easily naturalized; however, the migrations of the Gagavuz Turks, a small Turkish group with a Christian origin, were hardly accepted.[40] In a similar way, non-Muslim groups (Greeks, Armenians and Jews) were called Turk only in respect of citizenship but not of nationality; in terms of defining nationality they were seen as outsiders whether or not of Turkish origin, for they were not Muslim.[41] This shows that in determining the nature of Turkish nationality, in an implicit manner, religion appeared as a significant element together with ethnicity.

Herein lies the paradox of the official definition of Turkish identity and citizenship. While seeming to reject their Ottoman and Islamic heritage, the new regime (Republic) still continued to respect the common historical heritage with those non-Turkish groups mentioned above. Those groups were placed within the Muslim *millet* in the Ottoman Empire, and, it might be argued, there is a reflection of that *millet* system in the Turkish Republic in its recognition of the groups that previously were parts of the Muslim *millet* as Turks. In a similar way, the non-Muslim groups remaining in Turkey were regarded as Turkish citizens as a continuation of their community status in the Ottoman Empire. But there were debates on the status of the non-Muslim communities and the problem of their citizenship during the 1920s. The debate was around equality and the assimilation of the non-Muslim population.[42] On the other hand, it was exclusionary in the sense that the outsiders with non-Muslim origins were hardly accepted as citizens.

Consequently, until the 1950s, the concept of (national) citizenship that was closely bound up with the Kemalist secular notion of Turkishness was culturally, as well as politically, formulated on the basis of homogeneous, generalized and unique secular national culture. It was in this process that the construction of political and social citizenship was realized from above or, in the words of Bryan Turner, 'citizenship rights from above'.[43]

With the transition to a multi-party system the actual defining of the notion and content of the 'official' definition of Turkish identity became a chief objective of the political debate. As a result of such debate certain policies of the state were influenced, and to some extent began to be slowly transformed. The Democrats who put a strong emphasis on Islam and traditional, local values[44] propagated a peculiar understanding of Turkish nationalism that was more or less coupled with Islam, but that was refuted, at least in terms of their discourses, by the Kemalists in determining the boundaries and nature of the 'enlightened', 'civilized' and 'patriotic' citizen. In spite of these attempts and their later implications, until 1980, religion – Islam – did not exist as one of the officially determined, constitutive elements which were the defining features of Turkish citizens. However, with the social, political and economic changes, religion began to gain importance sociologically speaking, and consequently its impact on politics has been increasing since 1950. Following the 1960 military intervention, the 1961 constitution attempted to provide a venue wherein some civil/societal elements might express themselves. Although, in this sense, it seemed to extend the scope of citizenship, the participation of citizens was actually gained primarily by subscribing to the obligations of the state such as military service, voting and the paying of taxes.[45] It was seen as significant only in its relation to the ballot box.

The third period in the process of citizenization in Turkey started with the 1980 military intervention and continued in its aftermath. The 1982 constitution might be regarded as a brilliant perversion of the original Kemalist discourse in the sense that it placed more emphasis on 'Turkish historical and moral values';[46] and so Islam was recognized by the state elite with regard to its importance in, at least, maintaining Turkish identity and unity, and as a crucial antidote to communism and other factional and divisive movements. In addition, it was used to address the failure of the Kemalist progressive ideals to 'propagate social ethics' and to provide common cultural feelings and values that were 'equivalent for the widely used Islamic idiom'.[47] This was, one may argue, one result of the process of the domestication of the Kemalist modernizing state.[48] In the last two decades, the assessment of citizenship has been based on not much more than limited political participation (such as voting) and some other duties to the state, from which citizens' rights have been excluded. In spite of these features of the status of citizenship in Turkey, one may not ignore the fact that, in parallel with the development of some civil societal elements facilitated by the changes in the socio-economic structure, we are witnessing a continuously rising debate on citizenship.

The notion of citizenship in Turkey was conceptualized in large measure in terms of a monolithic, unique culture and identity that was the most fundamental product of the process of nation-building; in other words, in a sense, it implies the sense of belonging directly to a (national) community based on loyalty to the state. From the beginning, the formation of citizenship has been realized by emphasizing the significance of manufactured symbols. Notably, during the single party period especially, there were attempts by the regime to prescribe precisely how citizens should speak, dress, behave in public and (even) in private life, and so on. This is why citizenship in Turkey is a cultural status more than a social or political one. This sort of conceptualized citizenship has been challenged by two main trends: first, increasing international migration since 1960, and second, the new increasingly vocal and powerful religious, ethnic and sectarian movements, especially since the 1980s, namely the Kurdish, Islamic and Alevi movements. These movements have played a crucial role in expanding the claims to rights and entitlements to new areas, and in the light of that expansion and diversity of claims, they have posed questions of membership at the cultural, political and social level. The discussion of 'constitutional citizenship' and the implementation of 'dual citizenship' are the result of the controversy over the official citizenship concept that is closely bound with the 'idealized' Kemalist discourse.

As already stressed, there have been two separate social issues that contributed to the debate on the citizenship concept in Turkey since the early 1980s. The first one is associated with international migration and the citizenship position of Turkish emigrants living abroad. The other is related to the citizenship rights of some competing politico-cultural groups such as Kurds, Islamists, and Alevis. While the former has been dealt with in terms of the concept of 'dual citizenship', the latter has brought into focus the notion of 'constitutional citizenship'. It is obvious that these two concepts are very different from each other. Nevertheless, common ground exists in that both groups challenge and attempt to redefine the existing concept of citizenship, in order to create more responsive policies that will address their needs more specifically.

The first major challenge to the established notion of citizenship in Turkey was a consequence of international migration. Since the early 1960s, millions of Turkish citizens in search of work and a better life, and sometimes of political freedom, have left their homes and been admitted as legal residents of Western countries.[49] Many Turkish immigrants have lived in these states for several decades, paid taxes and been affected by political decisions, but they never gained full political rights, since they do not, or cannot, become citizens of the country in which they now live. In fact, before 1981, it was extremely rare to see Turkish emigrants anywhere in the world who had gained citizenship in their host country. Even if it had been the case, it was not possible for Turkish emigrants to assume citizenship status of another country without surrendering their original Turkish citizenship. In short, before 1981 Turkish citizens could not hold multiple (dual) citizenship. In April 1981 Turkish regulations were changed, allowing dual citizenship for the first time.[50] The effect of this has now become apparent in the numbers of Turkish emigrants gaining citizenship status in the countries where they now reside. For instance, official statistics indicate that there were 126,000 Turkish citizens granted German citizenship in 1996, and by 1998 another 125,000 Turks were expected to became naturalized, bringing the total number of naturalized Turkish citizens in Germany to a quarter million.[51]

It is obvious that, as often happens in most migrant-sending states, Turkey today prefers the blood principle of citizenship. Based on national practical interests, the country wishes to keep close contacts with its citizens abroad, and therefore tends to encourage emigrants to retain their citizenship and transfer it to their children. Of course, concerning the naturalization policies and practices in the migrant-receiving countries, no one can expect that the Turkish state would have any sympathy towards the process in which several hundred thousands of its citizens abroad will be definitely lost. Acknowledging the reality of the permanent presence of its emigrants abroad, and considering the ongoing process of access to citizenship rights in the receiving states, the Turkish state today tends to stress the importance of legal regulations which permit the emigrants to qualify for naturalization without giving up their original citizenship.[52] Accordingly, from the viewpoint of the state in Turkey, dual citizenship is increasingly seen as an important and practical tool for the integration process of its emigrants in the receiving societies.[53]

It seems that dual citizenship provides an opportunity for the Turkish state to overcome several negative consequences of the permanent settlement of its citizens abroad, while at the same time offering some practical solutions to the naturalization difficulties experienced by the migrant-receiving states and emigrants themselves. Since the renunciation of native citizenship is often considered as an enormous psychological and practical barrier to naturalization, it is widely shown that acceptance of dual nationality by the receiving and sending states will increase the inclination of immigrants to naturalize.[54] Although a basic consensus is achieved regarding the main advantage of dual citizenship, which is to facilitate an easy and quick solution to the anomalous status of immigrants in the migratory process, the inconveniences of dual citizenship have received much more attention than have the positive aspects. For instance, it is argued that dual citizenship will create some complicated situations which cannot be squared with egalitarian democratic norms, such as dual military obligations, dual loyalties, and dual political rights. However, as is pointed out by many proponents of dual citizenship, it is apparent that these inconveniences can be limited by means of bilateral and international agreements. The content of dual citizenship in itself reveals that the process of acquiring the citizenship of another country without giving up the original citizenship involves consequences for governments of both the sending and receiving states as well as for the international migrants. For instance, emphasizing the idea that 'everyone should be a citizen of one country and no one should be a citizen of more than one',[55] many Turkish emigrants living abroad have worried about the application and consequences of dual citizenship. From this perspective, and closely related to the debates concerning citizenship in Turkey, are the emigrants' perceptions and attitudes concerning their own position in the processes of access to citizenship and citizenship rights. What it means to Turkish emigrants to take out citizenship in a host country, why some of them change their membership status while others do not change: these are the questions that require some solid answers.

Some research findings[56] give us an opportunity to comment on the question of what kinds of meanings, costs and benefits are involved in Turkish emigrants' naturalization decisions. These findings show that when the emigrants were asked why they had become citizens of the receiving states or intended to do so, mostly pragmatic considerations were given as important factors affecting their decisions. For instance, apart from only a few who mentioned the advantages of travelling with the passport of the receiving state, many said that becoming a citizen in receiving states gave them a chance to live both in Turkey and in host countries without having visa and residence permit problems. Having citizenship rights and the right to seek permanent positions in public and government services, many emigrants believed that job opportunities would be more abundant not only for themselves but, also most important, for their children. For some, the reasons for becoming a citizen covered some normative and moral motivations together with pragmatic considerations. For instance, they felt that it was a proper step which should be taken after their decision to become permanent residents in the host countries, or they indicated that they would be able to use various rights of citizenship, such as voting, in the country where they live. Meanwhile, emigrants often pointed out that the legal change in Turkey in 1981, allowing dual citizenship for the first time, was a stimulus for their decision.

While those who had become citizens of the receiving states or were intending to do so often emphasized that pragmatic considerations played an important role in their decisions, a large proportion of those who indicated that they did not have any intention of becoming citizens in these receiving states, also gave pragmatic reasons to explain their attitudes. Some believed that they would not get any benefit from naturalization in the host countries; others felt that they might lose some of their rights in Turkey, such as owning property there.[57] In this context, some complained that dual citizenship regulations in Turkey were unclear and mentioned the rumour about confiscation of properties in the homeland by the Turkish government if they took another citizenship. Some of the emigrants said that they were not willing to become citizens, because they intended to go back home to Turkey for good. For others, the main reason for refusing the rights of citizenship was based on a basic psychological and moral consideration: they said that becoming citizens in these countries was inappropriate because they considered themselves Turkish rather than German, Australian or Swedish.

While Turkey was losing its comfortable certainties regarding the citizenship institution, owing mainly to its participation in the world-wide emigration system, another force made its way to the agenda of the citizenship debate: the persistence of ethnic and religious identities and their struggle for recognition as distinct groups; to be more specific, it was the identity crisis of the Kurds, Islamist and Alevis. It is within this context that the issue of constitutional citizenship began to occupy a place in the various spheres of the Turkish public, government and state. The main idea behind the concept of constitutional citizenship is the fabrication and promotion of a new socio-political identity for everyone in the country, and that identity's relation to citizenship. For instance, after becoming president in 1994, Süleyman Demirel announced the idea of constitutional citizenship several times,[58] that is the creation of a new 'super identity' for all the members of society, which appears increasingly fragmented into various identity groups who are issuing political demands based on their identities. Similarly, Prime Minister Tansu Çiller in December 1994 contributed to the debate with the statement of 'what a happiness to the one who says I am a citizen of Turkey', which was actually a converted version of the famous statement of Mustafa Kemal Atatürk, 'what a happiness to the one who says I am a Turk'.[59] It is interesting that the issue of constitutional citizenship has been a kind of item on the official agenda which suddenly appears and then again suddenly disappears. Meanwhile, however, the public[60] and academicians[61] show considerable interest in the issue.

The premises of the debate within the context of constitutional citizenship impart criticism toward the legacy of the construction of citizenship in early modern Turkey.[62] As elaborated in some detail above, in the early period of the Turkish Republic the core argument was to create a new nation, and consequently a new form of membership to this nation, which was meant to be modern, civilized, non-religious and egalitarian with regard to the hitherto hierarchical social structure that were divided across lines of religious, ethnic and national memberships. The ideas of Westernization, nationalism and secularism were considered crucial ideological and practical tools for accomplishing the sense of unity and cultural consensus that is regarded as essential in forming a new citizenship concept in the multicultural population inherited from the Ottoman past. However, it was paradoxical to construct a citizenship concept by accommodating the idea of nationalism based on Turkishness, and at the same time securing the loyalty of non-Turkish populations in the country. Even if we were reminded that the notion of Turkishness was often used with the statement of 'anyone who is bound to the Turkish state by citizenship is Turk', it was extremely difficult to deal with a national type of citizenship in a multiethnic, multinational and multireligious environment. It was also paradoxical to treat religion as glue for a cohesive nation and a bridge between society and state on the one hand and to promote secularism in the country on the other. One of the main consequences of these paradoxical elements since the establishment of the Republic is that the country has been Turkified, and some sectors of the society Islamicized. As another consequence, the recent decades have witnessed identity revivals of the Kurds, Islamists, and Alevis.

Although the most frequently declared aims of the Kurdish movement range from cultural and political rights to federalism and separate statehood, the basic problem seems to be Turkey's failure to recognize Kurds as a distinct ethnic group.[63] For the Islamists, the main problem has been the exclusion of the Islamic ethos from public discourse and the inclusion of an alien secular nationalism into the larger society.[64] The Alevi community demands accommodation of their religious identity within mainstream institutions such as the Directorate of Religious Affairs, and they wish to establish their own religious institutions. The common point of these demands is a search for a socio-political setting free from alienation and anonymity where these distinct identities can enjoy their social, cultural and political rights. What is implied is that the anomalous picture of the membership status of these distinct identities in Turkey contradicts the very abstract assumption, which is basic to democracy, that people who have their legal residence on the territory of the state are also its members and therefore shall meet all obligations and enjoy full civil, political and social rights in this state. In short, the current positions of Kurds, Islamists, and Alevis create a context in which a new citizenship based on constitutional rights rather than on nationality emerges as a political imperative from the basic principles of democratic citizenship.

Almost every state (country) in the world has its own citizens with various identities. For the most part these are defined in ethnic terms, or in terms of clear identifiable or socially defined attributes. Indeed, the notion of constitutional citizenship comes into the picture at this point. The dynamics and characteristics of the recent constitutional citizenship debate in Turkey are complex and varied. Although for each different actor involved in this debate, its meaning, scope and practice have unique aspects of their own, there is a framework common to the whole debate. To summarize, one can show four basic points which shape this framework. The first is that the struggle of the ethnic and religious identities for recognition as distinct groups has had a very significant impact on the notion of nation-state in Turkey. Second, there is a need to recognize the reality and implications of that identity-based diversity. Third, there is a greater awareness about the need for a series of policy initiatives, which will help the state better to manage the consequences of identity-based diversity in the interests of the state, citizens, and society as a whole. Fourth, there is recognition of the importance of the citizenship institution in solving the identity-based conflicts.

The identity-based conflicts in Turkey have been haunting the political rationality of the Turkish state. It is within this context that the state and public in the country seem to be attracted by the notion of constitutional citizenship as representing something more than a formal legal status of membership. Proponents of constitutional citizenship want to show that this type of citizenship has continuing relevance in securing the loyalty of distinct identity groups in the country who are open to the growing 'divisive' sentiments in society. Opponents of constitutional citizenship, on the other hand, seeing it as a danger to the nation, argue that recognition of ethnic and religious identities will not bring a sense of unity to the nation, and claim that contrary to what is expected, they will always have certain serious difficulties in meeting the basic measure of becoming a member of the nation, which is to be bound by a sense of solidarity, a common culture and a national consciousness.

If it is true that 'the development of the concept of membership in a national polity went hand in hand with the nation-states in the West',[65] then the situation in Turkey today, as has been the case in many other countries, would tell us that there has been a major transformation in recent decades: as pointed out by Silverman,[66] 'the link between the nation and the state has become visibly dislocated and the gap is likely to grow even more... the dislocation of these elements today, the breakdown in blood and soil definitions of community and the reformulation of the notion of citizenship are all factors in the contemporary crisis of the nation-state'. Although one can acknowledge the difficulties in coping with the diversity of already established policies and the practice and outlook with regard to citizenship issues in various nation-states, the concept of constitutional citizenship seems to be a practical solution. If constitutional citizenship is defined as a formal legal status of the membership of a state, and if this definition implies loyalty to state rather than nation, it will be possible, if not easy, to see that in a country like Turkey where identity-based conflicts endanger the sense of unity, citizenship rights based on constitutional arrangements are important for both symbolic and practical reasons; however, its practical significance is much more important than its symbolic significance.

The Kemalist Revolution began carefully to construct the modern concept of citizenship in Turkey 75 years ago, and there were not many occasions in which the new concept of citizenship was challenged. However, there have been two issues since the early 1980s that have made it a major topic of debate: emigration of Turkish citizens, and as one of its consequences, dual citizenship; and revival of various ethnic and religious identities and their association with the concept of constitutional citizenship. The common denominator of these issues is that they are directly related to the concept of citizenship which is an essential basis in defining the rights, obligations, and identities of individuals in modern societies. It is in these issues, we believe, that we faced the great problems and challenges which confronted Turkey in the 1980s and 1990s. These problems have occurred as previously excluded peripheral identities began to question the fabricated and imposed monolithic citizenship identity which was the product of the early Republican project of social engineering. Briefly, the formal conventional framework of citizenship today can neither accommodate the past 75 years of socio-political change nor articulate the new model of pluralism.

The principal conclusion drawn from this study is that although the pace in the recognition process for some new citizenship arrangements in Turkey was quite slow, the Turkish state has eventually become receptive to the case of its emigrants by facilitating them with dual citizenship; but while the state has been dealing with the identity-based conflicts in the country it has had considerable adaptation difficulties and has been confused by the notion of constitutional citizenship. This is of course, something we expect. Some critics have suggested that dual citizenship will create dual loyalties and rights that will encourage emigrants to use their new citizenship rights and benefits, and to ignore their implicit responsibilities to their sending state. However, it is thought that, overall, the acceptance of dual citizenship does not seriously harm these states. On the other hand, however, the notion of constitutional citizenship, which recognizes the multicultural diversity of society, is often seen as a divisive socio-political project for the identity and integrity of the Turkish state. This worry is understandable when the real picture of sociopolitical climate in Turkey is taken into consideration: for instance, Kurdish ethnic nationalism often threatens the unity of the country and creates a potential for violence and war; and religious revivalism makes the situation potentially even more explosive.

However, it seems reasonable to conclude that if citizenship is considered important mostly as a matter of *functionalism* rather than that of *normativism*, the task of formulating a new concept of citizenship is not an impossible one. As argued in this study, when access to citizenship rights in an immigration context is considered mainly as a matter of pragmatic choice rather than normative and moral commitment, the notion of dual citizenship becomes a desirable and rational choice for the involved actors. Similarly, if functionalism directs the actors of the politics of citizenship, we believe constitutional citizenship or any other similar formulation would offer promising solutions to the dilemma of pluralism.

We think that Turkey will be more stable and more prosperous only on the condition that it produces new ideas and formulates satisfying answers to the question of 'knowing how to deal with diversity'. Indeed, dual citizenship might be considered as a way of coping with diversity, so that emigrants' identities, demands and practical needs may be satisfied, at least in part, within the framework of a flexible citizenship arrangement. Similarly, within the concept of constitutional citizenship, a new and more complex formula starts imposing itself, the basis of which would combine unity and diversity in a pragmatic way, even if doing so is not easy. In short, what is needed is rethinking of the politics of citizenship.

NOTES

1. A. Afet İnan, *Medeni Bilgiler ve M. Kemal Atatürk'ün El Yazıları* [Civic Information and the Manuscripts of Atatürk] (Ankara, 1988, 2nd. edition).
2. Füsun Üstel, 'Cumhuriyet'ten Bu Yana Yurttaş Profili' [Profile of the Citizen since the Republic], *Yeni Yüzyıl*, 24 April 1995.
3. See Will Kymlicka and Wayne Norman, 'Return of the Citizen: A Survey of Recent Work on Citizenship Theory', *Ethics* 104 (Jan. 1994), pp.352–81; Bryan Turner, 'Contemporary Problems in the Theory of Citizenship, in B. Turner (ed.), *Citizenship and Social Theory* (London, 1993), p.1.
4. Turner, 'Contemporary Problems in the Theory of Citizenship', p.5.
5. Tomas Hammar, 'State, Nation and Dual Citizenship', in William Rogers Brubaker (ed.), *Immigration and the Politics of Citizenship in Europe and North America* (Lanham, New York, London: The German Marshall Fund of the US, University Press of America Inc., 1989), pp.81–96.
6. Brubaker, 'Immigration, Citizenship, and the Nation-State in France and Germany: A Comparative Historical Analysis', *International Sociology*, Vol.5, No.4 (1990), pp.380–1. According to this model, membership should be *egalitarian*, that is, there should be a status of full membership and no other. Secondly, it should be *sacred*, that is, citizens should make sacrifices or sacred acts for the state. Thirdly, membership should be *nation-based*, that is, the political community should overlap with the cultural community of shared language and character, which is acquired either by birth or through assimilation. Fourthly, membership should be *democratic*, that is, members should participate in the ruling process. Fifthly, membership should be *unique*; people should belong to only one state. Finally, membership should be socially *consequential*, that is, it should be expressed in a community of well-being.
7. William Rogers Brubaker, 'Introduction' in Brubaker (ed.), *Immigration and the Politics of Citizenship in Europe and North America*, pp.1–27; *Citizenship and Nationhood in France and Germany* (Cambridge, MA, 1992).
8. Shu-Yun Ma, 'Nationalism: State Building or State Destroying?', *The Political Science Journal*, Vol.29, No.3 (1992), p.294.
9. David Miller, 'Book Review of *Dimensions of Radical Democracy: Pluralism, Citizenship, Community* by Chantal Mouffe', *American Political Science Review*, Vol.87, No.4 (1993), p.1003.
10. T. H. Marshall, *Class, Citizenship and Social Development* (Garden City, NY, 1965).
11. See Kymlicka and Norman, 'Return of the Citizen: A Survey of Recent Work on Citizenship Theory'.
12. Anne Phillips, *Democracy and Difference* (Oxford, 1993), p.2.
13. Fuat Keyman, 'On the Relation Between Global Modernity and Nationalism: The Crisis of Hegemony and the Rise of (Islamic) Identity in Turkey', *New Perspectives on Turkey*, Vol.13 (Fall 1995), p.94.
14. Will Kymlicka, *Multicultural Citizenship: a Liberal Theory of Minority Rights* (Oxford, 1995).
15. See Kymlicka and Norman, 'Return of the Citizen: A Survey of Recent Work on Citizenship Theory', pp.352–81.
16. Jürgen Habermas, 'Citizenship and National Identity' (1990), in J. Habermas (ed.) *Between Facts and Norms* (Cambridge, MA, 1996).
17. Tomas Hammar, 'Citizenship: Membership of a Nation and of a State', *International Migration*, Vol.24, No.4 (1986), pp.735–46; *Democracy and the Nation-State* (Aldershot, 1990), pp.191–219; Mark J. Miller, 'Dual Citizenship: A European Norm?', *International Migration Review*, Vol.23, No.4 (1989), pp.945–50.
18. Ibid.
19. Robin West, 'Toward a First Amendment Jurisprudence of Respect: A Comment on George Fletcher's Constitutional Identity', in Michel Rosenfeld (ed.), *Constitutionalism, Identity, Difference and Legitimacy* (Durham, NC, 1994).
20. For a general discussion on the national and supra-national identity question in the European

Union, see John Rex, 'National Identity in the Democratic Multi-Cultural State', *Sociological Research Online*, Vol.1, No.2 (1996); for a specific discussion on the constitutional citizenship in the European Union context, see Habermas, 'Citizenship and National Identity'.

21. Jürgen Habermas, 'Struggles for Recognition in the Democratic Constitutional State', in Amy Gutmann (ed.), *Multiculturalism: Examining the Politics of Recognition* (Princeton, 1994), p.107.
22. Habermas, 'Citizenship and National Identity', p.496.
23. Ibid.
24. Kymlicka and Norman, 'Return of the Citizen: A Survey of Recent Work on Citizenship Theory', p.373.
25. Halil İnalcık, 'The Nature of Traditional Society: Turkey', in Robert E. Ward and Dankwart A. Rustow (eds.), *Political Modernization in Japan and Turkey* (Princeton, 1964), p.56; Ali Kazancıgil, 'The Ottoman Turkish State and Kemalizm', in A. Kazancıgil and E. Özbudun (eds.), *Atatürk: Founder of a Modern State* (London, 1981), p.38; and Şerif Mardin, 'Religion and Secularism in Turkey', in ibid., p.196.
26. For further details on the 1876 Constitution, see Şeref Gözübüyük and Suna Kili, *Türk Anayasa Metinleri* [Turkish Constitutional Texts] (Ankara, 1957), pp.21–55.
27. For the extended analysis of the historical development of legal status of citizens in Turkey, see Ergin Nomer, *Vatandaşlık Hukuku* [Citizenship Law] (Istanbul, 1993, 9th ed.).
28. Metin Heper, 'The State, Religion and Pluralism: The Turkish Case in Comparative Perspective', *British Journal of Middle East Studies*, 13 (1991).
29. Ergin Nomer, *Vatandaşlık Hukuku* [Citizenship Law].
30. Robert Nisbet, *The Making of Modern Society* (Great Britain, 1986), p.131.
31. Füsun Üstel, 'Cumhuriyet'ten Bu Yana Yurttaş Profili' [Profile of the Citizen since the Republic].
32. Identity', M*iddle Eastern Studies*, Vol.32, No.2 (1996), p.177.
33. Metin Heper, 'The State, Religion and Pluralism: The Turkish Case in Comparative Perspective', p.47.
34. Şerif Mardin, 'Ideology and Religion in the Turkish Transformation', *International Journal of Middle Eastern Studies*, Vol.2 (1971), p.209.
35. For further details and discussion on the strong state tradition in Turkey, see Metin Heper, *State Tradition in Turkey* (Walkington, 1985).
36. For a discussion and the views of Mahmut Esat Bozkurt (Minister of Justice in the İnönü government in the late 1920s) on the relationship between common good and life-style, see Mustafa Baydar, *Atatürk ve Devrimlerimiz* [Atatürk and Our Reforms] (Istanbul, 1973), pp.208–10.
37. Cited in Yılmaz Altuğ, 'Atatürk and the Building of a Modern State', *Turkish Review Quarterly Digest*, Vol.5, No.12 (1991), p.34.
38. For Atatürk's views and explanations on nation, culture and citizenship, see Afet İnan, *Medeni Bilgiler ve Mustafa Kemal Atatürk'ün El Yazıları* [Civil Information and the Manuscripts of Atatürk].
39. Nilüfer Göle, 'Authoritarian Secularism and Islamist Politics: The Case of Turkey', in Richard Norton (ed.) *Civil Society in the Middle East* (Leiden, 1995), p.21.
40. Selçuk Akşin Somel, 'Osmanlı'dan Cumhuriyet'e Türk Kimliği' [Turkish Identity from the Ottoman to the Republic], in Nuri Bilgin (ed.), *Cumhuriyet, Demokrasi ve Kimlik* [Republic, Democracy and Identity] (Istanbul, 1997), p.81.
41. 'One may', writes B. Lewis, 'speak of Christian Arabs, but a Christian Turk is an absurdity and a contradiction in terms. Even after thirty years of the secular Republic, a non-Muslim in Turkey may be called a Turkish citizen, but never a Turk.' Bernard Lewis, 'Turkey: Westernisation', in G. E. von Grunebaum (ed.), *Unity and Variety in Muslim Civilization* (Chicago, 1955), p.326.
42. There were, for example, volunteers for integration in the Jewish community; some of them regarded Jews as Turks from the Judaic religion while Tekinalp, a converted Jew, delineated the testament for Turkification. For the discussion of the status of Jews in Turkey see Avner Levi, *Türkiye Cumhuriyeti'nde Yahudiler* [Jews in the Republic of Turkey] (Istanbul, 1993).

43. In this connection, Turner argues, the citizen is seen as 'a mere subject rather than an active bearer of effective claims against society via the state'. B.S. Turner, 'Outline of a Theory of Citizenship', in Chantal Mouffe (ed.), *Dimensions of Radical Democracy* (London, 1992), p.46.
44. Şerif Mardin, 'Center-Periphery Relations: A Key to Turkish Politics?', *Daedalus*, 102 (1973), p.169.
45. Füsun Üstel, 'Yurttaşlık Bilgisi Kitapları ve Yurttaş Profili' [Schoolbooks on Citizenship and Profile of the Citizen], *Yeni Yüzyıl*, 25 April 1995.
46. Metin Heper, *State Tradition in Turkey*, p.146.
47. Şerif Mardin, 'Islam in Mass Society: Harmony versus Polarization', in Metin Heper and Ahmet Evin (eds.), *The Politics in the Third Turkish Republic* (Boulder, CO, 1994), pp.163–4.
48. Chris Hann describes the process Turkey entered into with the transition to a multi-party system as the domestication of the modernizing state, that is, the state began taking into consideration the pressure and demands from below, and partially rearranging its policies in accordance with these demands: Chris Hann, 'Subverting Strong States: The Dialectics of Social Engineering in Hungary and Turkey', *Daedalus*, Vol.126, No.2 (1995).
49. For a voluminous annotated bibliography of the studies on Turkish migration to Western European countries see N. Abadan-Unat and N. Kemiksiz, *Türk Dış Göçü: 1960–1984* [Turkish External Migration: 1960–1984] (Ankara, 1986). For a recent study of the Turkish emigration to Europe, see also Ahmet İçduygu. 'Migration from Turkey to Western Europe: Recent Trends and Prospects', paper presented to the Mediterranean Conference on Population, Migration and Development, Palma de Mallorca, 15–17 Oct. 1996.
50. Some articles of the Turkish Citizenship Law, originally dated 22 Feb. 1964 and numbered 403, were changed on 13 Feb. 1981, with the Law No.2383.
51. See Volkan Bozkaya, 'Life Situation, Identity and Integration of Turks in the Federal Republic of Germany', paper presented at the 3rd National Population Conference, Hacettepe University, 2–5 Dec., Ankara; in relation to the effect of the 1981 regulations, which caused an increasing trend in the number of Turkish immigrants taking out citizenship of the receiving states after 1981, see Ahmet İçduygu, 'Citizenship at the Crossroads: Immigration and the Nation-State', in Eleonore Kofman and Gillian Youngs (eds.), *Globalisation, Theory and Practice* (London, 1996), pp.154–60, and also see Ahmet İçduygu, 'Becoming a New Citizen in an Immigration Country: Turks in Australia and Sweden', *International Migration*, Vol.34, No.1 (1996), pp.257–74.
52. As an example of the increasing Turkish official interest to the dual citizenship issue, see K. Akın, 'Yurttaşlık Nasıl Korunur' [How to Protect the Citizenship], *Yeni Birlik*, Vol.11, No.11, 1988 (an interview with the Deputy Director of the Office of Population and Citizenship, Ministry of Interior).
53. For instance, the dual citizenship debate was intensified when in May 1993 five Turkish women and children were killed in an arson attack in Solingen, Germany. After the incident, Turkish officials often argued that Turkey wanted easier naturalization and dual citizenship for the Turkish nationals in Europe, which is seen as a tool to discourage violence towards Turks abroad.
54. See Brubaker, 'Introduction', pp.115–16, and Miller, 'Dual Citizenship: A European Norm?', p.948.
55. See, for instance, for a related debate, *Report on Political Participation* (Strasbourg, 1991).
56. See Ahmet İçduygu, 'Citizenship at the Crossroads: Immigration and the Nation-State', and Ahmet İçduygu, 'Becoming a New Citizen in an Immigration country: Turks in Australia and Sweden'.
57. New regulations had to be done in June 1995 about the protection of the rights and possessions of Turkish citizens in the case of their citizenship position change. See, *Türk Vatandaşlığı Kanununda Değişiklik Yapılmasına İlişkin Kanun* [Law on the Change in the Turkish Citizenship Law], Law No.4112, Date: 7.6.1995, *Official Gazette*.
58. See for instance, Ertuğrul Özkök, 'Demirel Anayasal Vatandaşlığa Dönüyor' [Demirel, Turning to the Constitutional Citizenship], *Hürriyet*, 3 Dec. 1996.
59. See, G. Zeynep Çetinkaya, 'Ne Mutlu'ya Kimlik Aranıyor' [Identity wanted to what a happiness], *Pazar Postası*, 7 Jan. 1995.

60. See, for instance, Ertuğrul Özkök, 'Demirel Anayasal Vatandaşlığa Dönüyor'. See G. Zeynep Çetinkaya, 'Ne Mutlu'ya Kimlik Aranıyor'.
61. See Ahmet İçduygu, 'Çokkültürlülük' [Multiculturalism], *Türkiye Günlüğü* (March–April 1995); Füsun Üstel, 'Anayasal Vatandaşlık, Hangi Anayasaya Vatandaşlık?' [Constitutional Citizenship, Citizenship to What Constitution?], *Radikal*, 17 Dec. 1996; Nur Vergin, 'Anayasal Vatandaşlık Ne Demektir?' [What Does Constitutional Citizenship Mean?], *Milliyet*, 26 Dec. 1996.
62. Although there is no direct reference to the concept of constitutional citizenship, the following two articles provide a historical background in which the debate was intensified: the first one is Ergun Özbudun, 'Milli Mücadele ve Cumhuriyet'in Resmi Belgelerinde Yurttaşlık ve Kimlik Sorunu' [National Struggle and the Problem of Citizenship and Identity in the Official Documents of the Republic], in Nuri Bilgin (ed.), *Cumhuriyet, Demokrasi ve Kimlik* (Istanbul, 1997), pp.63–70; and the second one is Selçuk Akşin Somel, 'Osmanlı'dan Cumhurıyet'e Türk Kimliği' [Turkish Identity from the Ottoman to the Republic]; Ömer Faruk Gençkaya, 'Revival of the Periphery: Need for Consensus or Threat to National Integrity in Turkey', *Journal of Behavioral and Social Sciences*, Vol.1 (1997), pp.75–90.
63. See, Nimet Beriker-Atiyas, 'The Kurdish Conflict in Turkey: Issues, Parties and Prospects', *Security Dialogue*, Vol.28, No.4 (1997), pp.439–52.
64. See, Hakan Yavuz, 'Turkey's Imagined Enemies: Kurds and Islamists', *The World Today* (April 1996), pp.99–101.
65. Ayşe Kadıoğlu, 'Citizenship, Immigration and Racism in a Unified Germany with Special reference to the Turkish Guestworkers', *Journal of Economics and Administrative Studies*, Vol.6, Nos.1–2 (1992), p.200,
66. M. Silverman, *Deconstructing the Nation* (London, 1992), p.35.

Turkey: Return to Stability?

SVANTE E. CORNELL

Since the mid-1990s, Turkish domestic politics have all too often been plagued by a chaotic atmosphere. The most direct origin of this is to be found in the December 1995 parliamentary elections, which did not lead to any obvious governing coalition; quite to the contrary, a number of alternatives were possible, of which the majority were eventually attempted. As is by now well known, the largest party in the parliament became the pro-Islamist Welfare party (Refah Partisi, RP) which however received a mere 21 per cent of the votes, far from a majority. This one-fifth of the ballot, with the Turkish electoral system favouring large parties and the parties that do well in the Anatolian countryside, actually gave the RP 158 out of 550 seats in the new parliament, or almost a third of the seats.[1] By contrast, neither of the two parties of the democratic right which had dominated the last decade's Turkish politics managed to achieve a leading position – actually neither of them managed to supersede the other. Former Prime Minister Tansu Çiller's True Path Party (DYP, Doğru Yol Partisi) received a larger number of seats in the parliament than Mesut Yılmaz' Motherland Party (ANAP, Anavatan Partisi), but the ANAP had a higher number of ballots cast for it than had DYP.[2] Hence both parties could still claim to represent the majority of the democratic right, something which further complicated their uneasy coexistence. This was particularly troubling for the political scene as before the elections speculations had been under way regarding a merger of the two parties under whichever would win the elections. It should be noted, nevertheless, that both parties received around 20 per cent of the votes each. Hence while the RP may have become the largest party in parliament, it is incorrect to speak of a 'triumph' of Islamism in the elections.[3] The major political faction was still by far the democratic right, as it has been during virtually the whole history of the Turkish republic. Together the two democratic right parties received the support of over 40 per cent of the electorate, which would be well enough for a stable majority in the Turkish electoral system.[4]

In the aftermath of the elections, as possible government coalitions were discussed, the major tendency both in the media and among large parts of the population was to advocate a coalition between the two parties of the democratic right. There was a near consensus that this was the most logical outcome of the elections and the most obvious coalition scenario. The reasoning was not without a point, for a number of reasons. The main reason, of course, was that even experts had difficulty explaining the distinction between the party programmes of the DYP and the ANAP. Mr Yılmaz recently called the two parties 'branches of the same tree'.[5]

The problem that prevented these parties from entering into coalition with each other, typically for the Turkish system, was the power struggle between the leaders of the two parties. A coalition, but especially a merger, would result in one of them having to step down for the other, something that each of them knows would mean an end to his or her political career. This power struggle in fact developed into a deep personal enmity between Mrs Çiller and Mr Yılmaz that has been clear especially during electoral campaigns. On the left of the political scene, the fragmentation is equally deep.[6] The social democrat parties were three in number for a short period in the early 1990s but two of them reunited in February 1995 to take down the number to two. All this has taken place in a political climate which favours big parties disproportionately, and where a 10 per cent threshold to parliament is applied.

The background to this singular political fragmentation lies in the consequences of the military coup of 1980. With the coup, all active political parties were shut down and their leaders were forced to stay out of politics for a number of years. When three years later multi-party democracy was reinstated, two military-created parties, one centre-left and one centre-right, were thought to compete for the vote. But capitalizing on public discontent with this 'guided democracy', Turgut Özal managed to get approval for his Motherland Party's participation in the election – and won a landslide victory.[7] As his party developed in the direction of the democratic right, there were now two democratic right and one democratic left party. Later, the former political leaders were permitted to return to the political scene, and immediately tried to assert control over what they felt was their logical successor party. As this led to conflicts with the new leadership, which had no interest in stepping down for the old generation, further fragmentation occurred, especially as the parties banned in 1980 were allowed to be reinstated in 1992. In a sense, thus, the fragmentation of the Turkish political scene can be seen as a malaise dating back to the 1980 military intervention.[8]

This form of intrigues and contradictions came to dominate politics, leading to a further distancing between the politicians and the population, something which was to affect deeply especially the popularity of the centre-left. As a result the early 1990s witnessed a steady rise in public discontent with politicians in general, which only accentuated with the numerous corruption scandals that struck almost all parties, except Welfare and veteran Bülent Ecevit's Democratic Left Party (Demokratik Sol Partisi, DSP). The centrist parties – which historically have commanded about 80 per cent of the electorate – proved incapable of tackling their problem. As Nicole and Hugh Pope put it, the centrist parties failed to 'catch the mood of the population', and 'continued irresponsibly down the path of self-destruction, devoting more energy to their attempts to topple their rivals rather than to the needs of the nation'.[9]

The time was ripe for the rise of populist and extremist parties. Even more than in the past, however, the extreme-left was unable to gain support except among university students, for two reasons. The first was an external factor – the perception of Communism as a failed ideology after the dissolution of the Soviet Union. A second factor was internal – a perceived close linkage between the rebellious Kurdish PKK and Marxism-Leninism, which further discredited socialism in the eyes of the public. The two political orientations which were to benefit were on the one hand the pan-Turkic nationalists of the Nationalist Movement Party (Milliyetçi Hareket Partisi, MHP), led by the charismatic figure of the late Alparslan Türkeş but unable to enter parliament, but above all the Islamic-conservatives (the RP), led by the equally charismatic Necmettin Erbakan. In the countryside especially, these two parties grew immensely, but as a whole the Islamists gained the upper hand. This was the case mainly because of the RP's excellent countrywide organization, and because of its seemingly unlimited funds, which enabled it to gain the support of the rural migrants to the big cities by humanitarian actions, distribution of food, finding jobs for people, etc. It is widely believed that the RP received funding from abroad, mainly from Saudi Arabia, without which its dramatic rise in popularity would probably have been impossible. Whatever the origins of its wealth, the RP managed to replace the social democratic parties as the main hope of the urban poor; indeed, one of the RP's many identities has been characterized as representing the 'new left' in Turkey.

Nevertheless, in the municipal elections of Spring 1994, the Welfare Party managed to gain power in a number of municipalities, among them the capital Ankara as well as Istanbul. This was a surprise for many, but most observers were still caught unprepared when Welfare became the largest party in the parliamentary elections of December 1995.

After several rounds of failed negotiations, among others between the ANAP and Welfare,[10] a coalition between the two democratic right parties was formed, allegedly under military pressure but in fact against the wishes of both party leaders.[11] It was widely believed that the collapse of the coalition talks between Welfare and ANAP was a result of military intervention. The two parties had come so far as to negotiate the distribution of ministries between them, when the talks abruptly crashed only two days before the government was to be officially announced.[12] The given reason was disagreement over the ministries of Defence and the Interior – perhaps a somewhat light reason for the failure of a coalition. The media seriously speculated that Mr Yılmaz' wife might have influenced him by talking him out of coalescing with Islamists.[13] Nevertheless, a formidable coalition of crucial business circles, the secularist media, and – most importantly – the military had exerted pressure on the ANAP and Yılmaz to abandon all coalition plans to coalesce with the Islamists.

The reluctant ANAP-DYP government which followed was short-lived, hardly surviving three months in office. It foresaw that the party leaders would take one-year turns as Prime Minister starting with Mr Yılmaz. The uneasy 'marriage', as it was termed in the Turkish press, between Mr Yılmaz' ANAP and Mrs Çiller's DYP however only accentuated their enmity as both were jealously watching their own party members, fearing that any fraternizing between the parliamentary groups could be dangerous for their respective positions.[14] When Mr Erbakan presented a file charging Mrs Çiller with corruption, Mr Yılmaz had the bad political judgement of supporting this charge, obviously hoping that getting Çiller off her post by legal proceeding would enable him to take control over the entire democratic right. As the DYP deputies saw this happening, they instinctively united around their leader, breaking the coalition.[15] Meanwhile, Mrs Çiller produced a similar file as the one on herself, regarding Mr Erbakan's assets and businesses. It seemed clear, then, that if Çiller was to go down, she would drag Erbakan with her in the fall, given the fact that the allegations against both were serious enough to have potentially grave consequences should they ever be brought to a courtroom.[16] Both the scandal-hungry media and other political parties subsequently showed considerable interest in these mutual corruption charges, and a process that neither Çiller nor Erbakan could control was starting to develop. However, as all other attempts to forge a new government failed, an obvious solution arose: forming a coalition together, something which would have the happy side-effect of a parliamentary majority guaranteeing that neither of the two would be stripped of their parliamentary immunity.[17]

Whatever the role of the intrigues that were a part of the coalition-building, it would be an exaggeration to suggest that a mere fear of corruption charges pushed Erbakan and Çiller into each other's arms. However important a role such considerations may have played, this alternative remained an untouched option, as Mrs Çiller, prior to the DYP–ANAP government, had portrayed herself as the staunchest defender of secularism and refused even to discuss co-operation with Welfare. Now the list of possible coalitions was expiring, since both democratic left parties were keen on staying in opposition.[18] But if one recalls that only roughly six months earlier, a coalition including Welfare had been aborted owing to the military's refusal, what made such a government possible? How was Welfare allowed to come to power and Erbakan allowed to become Prime Minister? And why would Welfare be 'allowed' to coalesce with DYP and allegedly not with ANAP, which after all was founded during military rule? Many observers actually saw the new coalition as a proof of military non-involvement in politics, revising their earlier opinions.

But a closer examination shows that the military policy has been consistent, and from its own precepts, totally logical during this entire time span. One main factor was that the military's influence in ANAP has traditionally been quite low, whereas the DYP was thought to be very close to the military. Compared with Mr Yılmaz, in any case, Mrs Çiller enjoyed far better personal relations with the army. An illustrating fact is that Doğan Güreş, the former military chief of staff, was elected a member of parliament on a DYP ticket, as well as several security officials such as a former head of the emergency rule in the Southeast.[19] Hence, as far as safeguarding secularism was concerned, the DYP was more trusted than the ANAP. Mr Yılmaz himself is known to be a convinced secularist, but a powerful Islamic-conservative wing was present in his party, a legacy of the Özal era and in fact led by the late President Özal's brother; as a matter of fact, the Sufi Nakşibendi order was heavily represented in the party, although the influence of Islamic groups had gradually declined since Özal's death in 1993.[20] These factors may have been crucial in the military's quest to prevent the ANAP from forming a coalition with the Islamists. Although there was no lack of trust for Mr Yılmaz personally, the question was if he would be able to stand up against both Welfare and his own conservative wing. The DYP, on the other hand, was thought easier to control, through its strong links to the military establishment.[21]

But the decision to let Welfare take part in a government was conditioned by other, additional factors. First of all, the most logical government formula not containing the RP had been tried and had failed. More importantly, all discussions in the political debate were centred on excluding RP from any coalition talks. This led to a certain public irritation, even among people who did not support RP. If Welfare was the largest party in parliament, this was after all the people's choice. And to refuse systematically to negotiate with RP would then be to ignore the people's vote. A coalition government containing RP would moreover not necessarily represent a threat to either democracy, secularism, or the status of the military, as a secular party would form part of the coalition and hence be able to walk out on the RP if necessary. To try to exclude Welfare was thus in a sense both illogical and immoral, especially as RP claimed to be an 'Islamic-Democratic' party along the lines of western European Christian Democratic parties.

However, arguably the most important factor was that isolating Welfare while the other established parties kept discrediting themselves only strengthened the popularity of the Islamists. For years now, Welfare had the privilege of staying in opposition – by force – and being able to criticize each government and amassing popular support because of the simple fact that almost all other parties kept losing in popularity; Welfare could continue to promote itself as the untarnished, pure, and non-corrupt alternative, and above all in the name of God. Thus all political parties actually lost in strength in the 1995 elections except Welfare and Ecevit's DSP.

As the leaders of the democratic right and the democratic left did not show any sign of adopting a more responsible policy – personal enmity remained a priority over almost identical party programmes, and the secular politicians went on squabbling with each other instead of seeking to understand the reasons of Welfare's success – the popularity of Welfare could only be expected to rise. In the by-elections held during the summer of 1996, Welfare captured around 35 per cent of the total vote.[22] These by-elections were not representative for the entire country, as they took place mainly in rural areas and in the eastern part of the country, and where the RP had received similar figures in the December 1995 elections. Nevertheless the outcome was still a definite reason to worry for the secular establishment. Many observers acknowledged that Welfare's popularity could decrease only once the party was in power and would prove unable to fulfil its very far-reaching promises to the electorate.

The decision to let Welfare take part in a government can hence be seen as a calculated risk: the RP's long-term aims of transforming the Turkish state were well-known, but it was believed that the situation could still be kept under control through RP's coalition party, the DYP, which importantly kept control over key ministries such as Defence, Interior, and Foreign Affairs. These were some of the factors which opened the way for Erbakan to become Prime Minister; furthermore, as will be seen below, there may have been other and more covert considerations involved.

The fears many secularists had when seeing the Islamists come to power soon proved not to have been exaggerated. Instead of following the established rules, Welfare soon devoted most of its time and attention to the promotion and financing of Islamic revival in Turkey. In sum, three tendencies crystallized during the near-year that the Welfare-Path government (a popular name of the coalition and a contraction of the two parties' names) stayed in office. First, there was a strengthened role for Islam in the state apparatus and in society, as will be discussed shortly. Secondly, a higher degree of authoritarianism, especially among law enforcement organs, was tangible in the context of anti-government demonstrations, for example; human rights organizations such as Human Rights Watch and Amnesty International have noted that the period of the Welfare-Path government coincided with a deterioration in the human rights situation in the country, which had slowly been improving until 1996. Thirdly, there was a gradual loss of the state agencies' cohesion. Cooperation between different organs of the state suffered notably under Erbakan's premiership, with a growing distrust between agencies known for their secularist character, such as the ministry of Foreign Affairs or the National Intelligence Agency (Milli Istihbarat Teşkilatı), and ministries or agencies that came under the increasing influence of the Islamists.

The main problem, which arose already after the municipal elections of 1994, was Welfare's systematic Islamicization of the local government apparatus wherever it was in power. Secular functionaries were methodically replaced with more loyal persons, something which became clear within a year and could be observed directly by the number of beards and headscarves in the local government offices. The same procedure was then implemented in the ministries that were allocated to RP in the coalition; in particular, the attempts to replace secularist judges around the country with more Islamically minded ones. A parallel procedure, although outside the control of the RP, was the dramatic increase of Islamist students at the social sciences faculties of the Turkish universities – which had as a direct corollary an increase in the number of Islamists seeking employment in the public sector. Several universities, including the dignified Marmara University in Istanbul, were affected by Islamic forces in their higher administrative echelons.

As in other countries in the Middle East, the Islamists focus their efforts on the system of education. As mandatory schooling was only five years in Turkey, parents were free to choose their children's form of schooling from grade six onwards. As a result, many children were put in Islamic Quran schools (*Imam-Hatip*) at an early age when they are easier to influence. The increase in the number and appeal of *Imam-Hatip* schools – which often have practical advantages as there are fewer students in each classroom –

has constituted an organized and deliberate effort to increase the Islamic consciousness of the young generation.[23] At the beginning of 1997, furthermore, a debate regarding the introduction of Sharia, Islamic law, arose – although this would be in direct contradiction with the Turkish constitution. Mr Erbakan defended the proponents of Sharia by claiming that secularists only make up three per cent of the country's population – despite the fact that over 75 per cent of the electorate voted for secular-oriented parties. As a response, a storm of protests and women rallies erupted, encouraged by the military and wholeheartedly supported by the democratic left. The unprecedented was the cold response these protests got from the democratic right. Mrs Çiller made some vague statements that every Muslim should follow Sharia, whereas Mr Yılmaz refused to endorse the protests since 'one could not protest against Islam'.[24] The actual reason is that both the DYP and the ANAP are to a significant degree dependent on the vote of traditional and conservative citizens, and were therefore careful not to appear as opponents of religion.[25]

The event that in retrospect can be termed the beginning of the end for Welfare was a larger demonstration in favour of Sharia which occurred in February 1997.[26] The demonstration took place in Sincan, a suburb of the capital Ankara, where the local RP mayor pronounced himself in favour of Sharia with sharp wordings.[27] A disturbing fact was that he was ardently supported in person by the Iranian ambassador, who thus made himself guilty of a flagrant breach of the principle of non-intervention in his host country's internal affairs.[28] Subsequently, the mayor was jailed[29] and the ambassador returned to his home country,[30] but the scandal only got worse when the jailed mayor was visited by Şevket Kazan, the RP minister of Justice, in an obvious show of solidarity.[31]

In the midst of the scandal, the peaceful popular demonstrations increased in number and magnitude,[32] but were met by a surprisingly harsh reaction from the authorities. Through leaks from the Interior ministry it soon became clear that the police had received orders to deal harshly with demonstrations directed at either Islam or the government. This was a clear sign that the government did not hesitate to use violence against its opponents – hence a stronger authoritarian tendency.

This flow of events in the first months of 1997 was followed closely by the military leadership, which saw the situation as disturbing enough to proceed to action carefully but effectively. The first signals of military dissatisfaction actually came relatively early. The forum used was the powerful National Security Council (Milli Güvenlik Kurulu, MGK), which includes the President, the Prime Minister, and the ministers of Defence, the

Interior, and Foreign Affairs, as well as five high-level military officials. The MGK is a consultative body with the authority to make policy recommendations to the government. Already in the autumn of 1996 the military contingent in the MGK began to complain of the level of Islamicization of the state. As this criticism was ignored by the government, the military tone rose. By January, the Commander of the Naval forces publicly stated that Islamic fundamentalism had grown to be a greater threat to the republic than the PKK.[33] During the February Sincan events, a contingent of tanks was sent through the town, in an obvious demonstration of force, and as a sign that the level of military tolerance was reached.[34] As no measures were still taken by the government, the generals saw themselves forced to take concrete measures. A MGK meeting scheduled for 28 February was chosen as the occasion, a meeting which lasted for an unprecedented nine hours.[35] Here the military leadership showed an unexpectedly strong reaction. A list of over 20 points was presented, on which a change in government policy was requested. Among these, the most important were:[36]

(i) Obligatory public schooling was to be extended from five to eight years. This would entail that children could not be put in religious schools until after grade eight, when their minds would presumably be more difficult to indoctrinate;
(ii) The systematic admission of Islamists into public service had to cease;
(iii) Control was to be established over religious sects, and their financial sources investigated;
(iv) The independence of the judiciary needed to be safeguarded (clearly pointing at the systematic appointment of Islamist judges);
(v) The principles of the constitution were to be followed;
(vi) Political parties were to be made legally accountable for members' statements.[37]

The government was given two months to change its policies in these and other fields.[38] During the MGK meeting, Prime Minister Erbakan was the only Islamist present, confronted with five high officers and secular politicians from the DYP. Erbakan claimed after the meeting that all decisions had been unanimous;[39] however it soon became clear that Erbakan had been highly reluctant to accept many of the provisions, and accepted them only in order not to lose face by going against an unanimous MGK.[40] Furthermore Erbakan did not immediately make it clear that he would sign the protocol of the meeting, which was necessary to give it legal force.[41]

The military behaviour has been termed as an ultimatum and has been criticized for being undemocratic as it instructs the popularly elected government to change its policy, on subjective grounds. Mr Erbakan quickly stated that policy 'is made in the parliament, not in the MGK'.[42] Answering this, the military claimed – not without reason – that it merely urged the government to follow the law. Indeed, the judicial provisions that prohibit use of religion in politics have obviously not been followed. In fact a number of laws had been side-stepped, perhaps deemed obsolete or unfitting, but the fact remains that these provisions had not been abrogated and hence remained legally binding. Hence the military could hardly be said to commit any unconstitutional act by urging the government to ensure that certain laws were implemented. Furthermore, taking the events in the perspective of post-war Turkish history, the military seems to have opted for democratic means to influence the politics of the country. In 1960 and 1980 coups were undertaken to restore chaotic situations; in 1971 a clearly unconstitutional military ultimatum was used. This time the military influenced government policy through a constitutionally regulated organ, the National Security Council. In fact, one could argue that the MGK's role was increased in the 1982 constitution precisely to allow the military a channel of constitutional control over civilian politics.

Whatever the legal aspect, the result of the MGK meeting was a sizeable humiliation for the government. It soon became known as a government which had been reprimanded and taught a lesson. This increased the already existing tensions within the coalition and especially within the junior partner, Mrs Çiller's DYP.[43] A rising number of DYP deputies had been pressurizing the leadership to terminate the coalition with the Islamists as the government, in their opinion, was causing harm to the country. Such views, however, found no understanding with Mrs Çiller, who had acquired many enemies through her ambition and recklessness as well as her increasingly authoritarian control over the DYP. Hence the dissatisfaction within the party reached rebellious proportions and the long awaited defections started to occur. The DYP, once the second party in parliament with over 130 deputies, dropped dramatically in size as its deputies in large numbers defected to either Mr Yılmaz' ANAP or to the newly formed DTP (Democratic Turkey Party) under the leadership of Mrs Çiller's rival, former parliament speaker Hüsamettin Cindoruk.[44] Mr Cindoruk's aim to regain control over the DYP was not exactly hampered by Mrs Çiller's recklessness and self-inflicted unpopularity. In retrospect, her struggle to hang on to the government coalition with RP was, seen in the right context, totally understandable. The main reason seems to have been that Mrs Çiller feared that if she fell from power, the corruption charges against her would surface once again. Indeed, for over three years Mrs Çiller has been playing a very high game, in which she undoubtedly has been fairly successful, in staying in power until the summer of 1997 and still remaining leader of the DYP by late 1999. The popular anger at her that is widespread among large sections of Turkey's especially urban and intellectual population is well illustrated by the abundance of sarcastic comments and caricatures of a power-hungry and opportunistic Çiller.[45]

And the government's problems were only beginning. On 21 May, state prosecutor Vural Savaş initiated a lawsuit in the constitutional court to ban the then still incumbent Welfare party on grounds of anti-secularism and anti-republicanism.[46] This lawsuit and its basis (such as a collection of statements of Erbakan and other RP officials) further discredited the coalition in the eyes of many secularist DYP deputies, and was certainly a factor which accelerated the defections from that party. As a result, the DYP's parliamentary group plunged to around 90 deputies. Hence the government rapidly saw its parliamentary majority withering away. As a remedy, Mr Erbakan tried to attract a small religious-nationalist party, the Grand Unity Party (GUP), a splinter-group from the ANAP that had nine seats in the parliament.[47] As the GUP demanded two ministerial posts and a lowering of the threshold barrier in parliamentary elections against small parties from ten to five per cent as condition for supporting the government, and as the rate of defections from the DYP in any case would give the government at best another three weeks even with the support of the GUP, Mr Erbakan threw in the towel and submitted his letter of resignation.[48] This move seems to have been conditioned by two factors: the first was a concern to answer the general belief shared by many secularists that 'the Islamists will never give up power willingly'. Hence Erbakan once again tried to show that RP was not anti-systemic, but similar to any other political party. But more importantly, Erbakan and Çiller seem to have believed that President Demirel would again give Mr Erbakan the duty to form a government, as it was an unofficial rule that the leader of the largest party in parliament should receive this duty first, others being assigned it when and if this first attempt would fail. In any case the two leaders seem to have thought that Mesut Yılmaz would prove unable to form a government if given that duty and that they could hence again form a government within a short time and this time with increased legitimacy.[49]

Thrashing the hopes of Erbakan and Çiller, President Demirel immediately gave Mr Yılmaz the task of form a new government, hence taking a clear stance against the Welfare-Path government.[50] The latter then proceeded to collect the support of all political forces that had been in opposition to the Islamist-led government.[51] In a quick act of lobbying, he further managed to receive the support of a sufficient number of DYP deputies to secure a majority.[52] Thus while the media were discussing the risk of early elections and deadlock, Mr Yılmaz announced the forming of a new government.[53]

This government, the 55th in republican history, became a minority government as the leftist Republican People's Party (CHP) refused to take an active part in it,[54] seeing it as a transitional government whose primary function would be to pave the way for early elections.[55] Nevertheless, the parliamentary majority of the government rested upon four political parties as well as on a number of independent deputies, two of whom reached ministerial rank.[56] Hence the government consisted of a coalition between Yılmaz' ANAP, Ecevit's DSP, and Cindoruk's DTP, with the two smaller parties strongly represented in the cabinet despite their weakness in parliament compared to the ANAP.

Despite Mr Yılmaz' success in forming a government in an unexpectedly short period of time, this should not be taken for an emerging consensus in the Turkish political climate. Even if Mrs Çiller were to depart from politics, her role in contesting Mr Yılmaz for the leadership of the democratic right could presumably have been taken over by Mr Cindoruk, who had repeatedly announced his intention to reunite the democratic right – presumably under his own leadership. However, Mesut Yılmaz had a rare chance to increase his stature in Turkish politics. He was, one could argue, the first leader since Atatürk who received wholehearted support both from the people and the military as well as from the media. The coalition however rested on shaky grounds, based as it was on the support of four parties from two different ideological traditions.

The 1997 events in Turkey were described in a variety of ways both in Turkey and in the West. Depending on one's perspective, one may call the developments either a military near-coup – or the world's first 'post-modern coup', as some observers like to put it – or a general rebellion on the part of the secular establishment against the Islamist-led government. An illustrating fact in this context is that Mrs Çiller was considered by many secularists worse than Mr Erbakan: Erbakan may have been the enemy, but Çiller was the traitor.

What has in fact taken place in Turkey is a clear campaign, inspired from military headquarters, to eradicate the Welfare Party. The lawsuit in the constitutional court to ban the party was only the open, legal aspect of the campaign. Thus the Turkish military defended and increased its role in the politics of the country, although certainly more by perceived necessity than for its own interests.[57] In fact, 1997 marked a new trend for military involvement in Turkish politics. Hitherto, the military had basically left the government of the country to civilian administrations, while reserving the right to intervene massively when things got out of hand, as was done in 1960, 1971 and 1980. But this time, military policy was different. The more subtle form of intervention that was practised in 1997 had as a consequence that, unlike in earlier military interventions, the same political forces and leaders were left to govern the country. This in turn meant that the military could not create a 'clean break' with the mistakes of the past, as was done at least in 1960 and 1980. Consequently, the military was unable to retire from the political scene as it had actually done on the aftermath of the two earlier coups, but continued to play an important role in day-to-day politics. This fact was proven recently when a group of disgruntled deputies, who had been left out of their respective parties' electoral lists,[58] tried to delay the April 1999 elections, when the new chief of staff Hasan Kıvrıkoğlu stated his opinion that delaying the elections would be detrimental to the country.[59] In fact, the military leadership has been drawn into politics to a larger degree than has been tangible earlier. This is by itself a development that causes worry, as this brings a risk of politicization of the military that would be detrimental to its position in society.

Going back to the 1997 events, it is notable that many observers wondered why the military waited so long to take action against Welfare although the coalition government, in the military's eyes, was harming the country by its policies. The reason, when analysed, is simple and has an undeniable logic. If the military wanted once and for all to staunch the progress of political Islam, forcing Welfare out of government and closing down the party would hardly be sufficient, although it would slow down the progress of Islamism. But as the organizational abilities and financial resources of RP and other Islamist organizations were well known, it was necessary to go deeper, so to speak to pull the movement up with its roots.

An analogy here is the military coup of 1980. Since mid-1979, anarchy and civil violence was taking a toll of over 20 deaths daily in the big cities, and large portions of the population were actually demanding a military intervention to put an end to the chaos. But the military waited a whole year, until 12 September 1980, to intervene. When the intervention took place, it proved to be well-planned and bloodless, in comparison with most military coups in history. Within a week, 138,000 persons had been arrested, and the widespread violence that plagued the country disappeared literally overnight. The military had thus used a year to map the extremist groups responsible for the anarchic condition in order to crack down on them quickly and effectively. In a sense, it can be argued that a similar strategy has been adopted this time. When RP members insulted the army publicly, no measures were taken either politically or judicially although the possibilities were present. Instead, military intelligence tracked down the various Islamist movements – especially the more extreme ones – as well as their organizational network and financial sources. In this endeavour, they were assisted by the fact that Islamic movements, which had previously been operating underground, exposed themselves more openly during RP's time in government, obviously in the belief that they could now voice their claims with impunity. Hence, within 48 hours of the formation of Mr Yılmaz's government, two hundred officials were expelled from their positions, a yet unknown number of arrests were made, and the financial sources of a number of radical Islamist movements were frozen. Files intended for legal action have been prepared on several RP deputies and municipal politicians; the trial of the above-mentioned mayor of Sincan has already been concluded with prison terms for the mayor and several of the involved persons. In another case, Istanbul mayor Reccep Tayıp Erdoğan was sentenced to a year's imprisonment for reciting a poem deemed to incite hatred and create divisions on religious grounds; the sentence was upheld in October 1998, effectively putting an end to Erdoğan's future political career. Mrs Çiller herself as well as her former associate and minister of the Interior, Mrs Akşener, were threatened by various legal proceedings for embezzlement and other charges.[60] Mrs Çiller has, among other charges, been targeted with the relatively absurd accusation of having been a spy for the CIA for a quarter of a century, something which shows the tone that the campaign against the Welfare-Path government took.[61]

The closure case against the RP received mixed but predominantly negative reactions abroad. First of all, there was doubt regarding the judicial process in the Constitutional Court and regarding the fairness of the Turkish judicial system in general, criticism that has recurred in the context of the trial of PKK leader Abdullah Öcalan, who was apprehended in Kenya in February 1999.[62] Western observers seemed to interpret the process as a show with a predetermined outcome. Secondly, there has been a reaction in Turkey as well as abroad on the very principle of banning political parties. The issue at stake, then, is whether banning a political party – notably as it is the largest party in parliament and hence not a marginal, extremist formation – is compatible with democracy.[63] In Turkey both Islamists as well as many secularists have reacted against the idea, seeing such a development as unfit for the democratic society they want Turkey to be.[64] As an answer, those in favour of the ban have argued that although political parties are a cornerstone of democracy, this does not mean that there are no limitations on them – they must be required to operate within the spirit of the constitution.[65] In late 1997, the US State Department declared that the US was against the closure of the RP,[66] and responded negatively when the decision became public.[67] Nevertheless, in conjunction with many Turkish observers, the respected *Wall Street Journal* showed understanding for the outlawing of a party whose leader claimed that Islamic values will prevail, whether the transition period will be smooth or bloody.[68]

On 16 January 1998, the constitutional court announced the banning of the Welfare Party with nine votes against two. As expected, Erbakan, former Justice Minister Şevket Kazan and six other RP officials were banned from participation in politics for five years. The RP took the decision with a mixture of shock and resignation. Until the end, supporters had hoped for a favourable decision. But the work to start a new party had already begun, under the leadership of long-time Erbakan ally Recai Kutan. However, younger forces within the new-born party, the Virtue Party or Fazilet Partisi (FP) initially seemed to take on a higher profile than they had in the RP. These included among others the new vice chairman Abdullah Gül, widely seen as a moderate Islamist,[69] and then Istanbul mayor Reccep Tayyıp Erdoğan. In the first days after the decision, the general belief seemed to be that the FP, would move increasingly toward the centre. Under the leadership of the young cadres of the RP, the Islamic political movement would develop into an Islamic-democratic party. However, it remained clear that despite the political ban imposed on him, Necmettin Erbakan retained the reins of the party through his loyal ally Kutan who remained the head of the new party. This situation was analogous to the years after the 1980 coup, when most political leaders, including Ecevit and Demirel, were remote-controlling their respective parties from their seclusion on an island in the Marmara sea.

At the eve of the April 1999 elections, there was an impression that Turkey had regained some of its lost political stability. The ANAP-led government that stayed in power for little over a year arguably seemed to be more serious than previous ones, and comparatively more interested in the country's future than in personal enmities and intrigues. Political and religious extremism were successfully subdued, and the economy was flourishing despite the political crises of recent times. By late 1998, the government had succeeded in achieving its aim of halving inflation to 50 per cent on a yearly basis, a notable improvement from the close to 150 per cent that was seen during Çiller's premiership a few years earlier. A much-needed tax reform was pushed through the legislature, and most important, the different state agencies that had drifted apart were brought back on the same track. Also, in the domain of human rights and democratization, the struggle was taken up where it was left in mid-1996, and several improvements in this field have been noted by respected agencies such as Human Rights Watch.

The path of integration with Europe nevertheless suffered tremendously from the episode. A severe setback was the December 1997 Luxembourg summit of the EU, where Turkey was once again sidelined, this time in a more undiplomatic and tactless way than ever, from the list of membership candidates. As far as relations with the EU is concerned, it is certain that the Islamist government played an important role in dissuading Europe even further from embracing Turkey. However, an equal amount of damage was done by the military role in politics, which brought back memories of the 1980 coup for the Europeans and further hampered Turkey's reputation in the EU. The Turks nevertheless felt offended by misplaced statements from EU officials, including Luxembourg Prime Minister Jean-Claude Juncker's opinion that 'it cannot be that a country in which torture is still going on can sit at table of the EU'.[70] Yılmaz's government responded by freezing political relations with the EU, and openly hinted at Germany's role in opposing Turkish membership, arguing instead that Germany's advocacy of the membership of the Central European countries reflected its need for '*Lebensraum*'. While such statements may have increased the gap with the EU, in the eyes of the Turkish public they restored some of the lost national honour. In the long run, however, the rejection by the EU may serve Turkey, in that it now knows that it needs to rely on itself and build connections to other trade partners elsewhere. Indeed, Turkey soon embarked on a renewed diplomatic offensive in the Caucasus and Central Asia, while intensifying its contacts with Israel in every field.[71] Through the new successes that ensued, Turkey gained back some of its self-confidence in the international arena. This was boosted even further by the gradual decimation of the rebellious Kurdish separatist PKK, a process that culminated in 1998–99 in first a standoff with Syria that resulted in Syria expelling the PKK and its leader Öcalan under the threat of Turkish military action, and finally in February 1999 in the capture of the PKK leader in Kenya.

However, the closure of the Welfare Party did not necessarily imply that the Islamist movement was defeated. Initially, there were some fears that part of the Islamist movement, feeling excluded from politics, would opt for non-democratic forms of pursuing their struggle. Nevertheless, the new Virtue party was able to keep the Party discipline of the RP – in fact all former RP parliamentarians with no exception joined the FP – and the party continued to develop in the opposite direction, that is, towards a reconciliation with the secular state. This said, cracks have appeared within the party with different forces pulling the party in different directions; nevertheless the FP has succeeded in keeping a united profile to the outside.

The secular–Islamic divide also remains in society. In the young generation, especially, a clear dichotomy can be seen between a larger, mainly urban secular stratum, and a smaller, Islamic-oriented stratum which predominantly has rural roots. This circumstance is clearly in concordance with Samuel Huntington's well-founded description of Turkey as 'a torn country'. On the other hand, the distinguished observer and historian, Professor İlber Ortaylı, puts forward the view that the secularist–Islamist tension is actually an appearance, only on the surface. A reconciliation process is under way in the civil society despite the polarization in the political sphere. Rather, in this view, the problem is one of westernization:

> It looks [like a democratization problem] but it is directly a westernization problem. In fact all of them [secularists as well as islamists] are individuals of a society which is modernizing, industrializing rapidly, which is opening to the outside world rapidly, and neither of the sides know either the East or the West, neither Islam nor Christianity nor secularism–none correctly know these ... Reconciliation will be achieved when society ... starts to know itself. We are already seeing the positive developments of this process. There is a growing interest in these subjects ... as well as moderation toward the other.[72]

Similarly, many politically active Turks agree that Islamism is not a major threat to the republic and its stability. The old conflict between the extreme left and the extreme right is considered by many to have accentuated in later years. Naturally, the extreme right includes the Islamists and extreme leftists are secularists. But the controversy over Islam's role in the society is not the overshadowing concern for many Turks.

According to sources close to the military, it was thought in 1997 that the RP could have received a quarter of the votes in a national election if it kept its leadership, its financial resources, its organizational structure, and less tangible factors such as the very aura the party had created for itself. But with a new name, new faces and a financial capacity comparable to other parties, the figure would fall to only 12–15 per cent. This is believed by many observers to be the range of the actual support that Islamism commands in Turkish society, even given the recent Islamic revival. The RP, besides diehard Islamists, also attracted protest voters disillusioned with the infighting in the democratic right as well as what could be termed gratitude voters from the urban slums. Hence the argument goes that people who voted for RP for these reasons would not necessarily go on voting for Islamists under a different shape, but return to their former parties such as the DYP or ANAP. This thesis is supported by a diversity of sociological investigations, which asked Welfare voters (among others) to define their political identity. The result of the poll is seen in Table 1. As the table clearly shows, only half of the RP voters classify themselves politically as 'Muslims'. Hence it seems safe to assume that a distinctively lower proportion could be termed religious extremists. The core group of Islamic voters does seem to consist of somewhere between 10 to 15 per cent of the electorate.

TABLE 1

POLITICAL SELF-IDENTIFICATION OF WELFARE PARTY VOTERS, 1997[73]

Political Self-identification	Percentage
Muslim	51.5
Muslim Democrat	28.2
Democrat	7.8
Nationalist	4.9
Liberal Democrat	1

The interim period between the fall of the RP–DYP coalition and the next general elections, which were subsequently determined to be held on 18 April 1999, was as noted earlier characterized by a return to stability. However, the government rested on the parliamentary support of two conservative parties and of two social-democrat parties. The only common denominator among the four parties was their aversion for Islamism and in particular the former government. Their co-operation was conditioned by a crisis mentality, in other words a perception of being a kind of national unity government. The economic and social policies of the parties differed according to their place in the political spectrum; and *within* the centre-left as well as the centre-right were dormant personal enmities and competition between antagonistic party leaders. The main 'spoiler' was CHP leader Deniz Baykal, who has earned notoriety as a career-minded politician whose main ambition has been to be the sole leader of the democratic left. However, the party had continuously lost votes since 1991 and Baykal attempted to exploit being in opposition. When allegations of corruption on the part of Mesut Yılmaz emerged in the fall of 1998, Baykal withdrew his party's parliamentary support for the government, with the assertion that a prime minister facing corruption charges should immediately resign – something which would limit the life span of almost all Turkish governments drastically. In retrospect, Baykal's move was immensely counterproductive. It opened the way for the formation of a minority caretaker government composed solely of Mr Ecevit's DSP, resting on the support of ANAP and DYP.

Although this government followed policies little different from the previous one in which it had also taken part, the five months it stayed in power boosted the popularity of the DSP considerably. First and foremost, Ecevit's government was lucky in being in power at the time of the apprehension of the country's most wanted man, PKK leader Abdullah Öcalan. Credit for Öcalan's capture was given to the DSP government's judicious handling of the matter, in particular the diplomatic campaign that had dissuaded several European governments that had been vocal on the

Kurdish issue from granting the terrorist leader refuge. In particular, the diplomatic efforts that resulted in a blatant exposure of Greece as a state sponsoring terrorism showed the competence of the DSP administration, especially Foreign Minister Ismail Cem. A new assertiveness in Turkish foreign policy could be detected, propelled as mentioned earlier by the feeling of strength as compared to the two arch-rivals Syria and Greece. The Turkish military strength even allowed some observers to claim that the Turkish military is about to become the 'second most effective military force in the world', after the United States[74] – perhaps an unlikely statement at first sight, but the Turkish military's modernization programme of $150 billion in the next 25 years nevertheless gives corroboration to the view of Turkey as an emerging regional great power.[75] In fact a few days before the 1999 elections, Ecevit declared that 'Europe may isolate Turkey as much as it desires to; Turkey is nevertheless a leader in its region.'[76] Besides these factors, the party's popularity also benefited immensely from the charisma and spotless reputation of its leader. Ecevit is among the few leading politicians who has never been accused of dishonesty despite his more than 30 years in politics.

The electoral campaign for the April 1999 elections differed little from its 1995 precursor. Again, the established parties' leaderships were totally unable to learn from the blatant mistakes of the past. The DYP's Çiller and ANAP's Yılmaz concentrated their respective campaigns on castigating each other's personalities, both tendering their resignation should their party fall behind the other. Their electoral campaign was hence more of an internal competition for the command of the democratic right than a campaign on the level of the whole country. An interesting development can nevertheless be noted in the profiles of the two parties, very much as a result of the political events surrounding the DYP–RP coalition. Tansu Çiller, whose campaign in 1995 had been based on fierce secularist rhetoric and on preventing the RP from coming to power, now competed with the FP for the religious votes of the Anatolian countryside. Çiller herself on some electoral posters even appears covering her hair, though far from wearing the Islamist type of headscarf. ANAP, on the other hand, developed a stronger secularist rhetoric than before and rid of its old Islamic wing turned into a neo-liberal party whereas the DYP became an openly stated conservative (*Mühafazakar*) party. In sum, the electorate of the two parties had diverged increasingly. But no party was judged to be in a position to compete for a first or second place in the polls shortly before the vote.

The FP, meanwhile, was predicted to be a front-runner in the elections, competing for the first place with the DSP.[77] However, Recai Kutan was unable to match the charisma of Necmettin Erbakan, and the tarnished record of its one-year rule meant that it was aiming at sustaining its share of a fifth of the votes rather than increasing it. In March the FP, much like the CHP had done a few months earlier, made a move which turned out to be counter-productive. When the above-mentioned disgruntled deputies announced their intention to overthrow the DSP minority government, the FP approached them to clinch a deal. Accordingly, the FP would support their motion to overthrow the DSP government and subsequently vote to postpone the elections and give the disgruntled a new chance to be registered for the elections. In return, the disgruntled would support a FP motion to lift the article in the penal code on which Erbakan and his associates had been banned from politics. This Machiavellian scheme nevertheless failed to materialize and by the time the FP realized that the public reaction was vehemently negative to this political game, it had already lost a great deal of its credibility. The episode nevertheless gave another proof of the duplicity that all too often surrounds Turkish politics. In fact, it probably gave yet another push to Ecevit's popularity.

On the left, positions were changing as well. CHP leader Baykal displayed his usual attitude, lashing out at all parties but especially, of course, his rival Ecevit. The CHP continued to attract most leftist intellectuals and a good portion of the Alevi voters; however it was far from the mass-appeal party that it had been in the 1970s or even in 1991, when it mustered the support of over 20 per cent of the population, coming in third after the DYP. Many former supporters, including active politicians, had moreover abandoned the party in opposition to the leadership style of Mr Baykal and the lack of intra-party democracy. Meanwhile, the DSP was increasingly appearing to take a position as a centrist party, now very marginally on the left of centre. Ecevit on several different occasions publicly declared that the time of ideological rivalry is relegated to the past both globally and in Turkey; moreover he explained his surprisingly good relations with Turkish industrialists with the simple words that 'without industrialists there would be no jobs'.[78]

Finally, the nationalist MHP was also thought to pass the 10 per cent threshold and enter parliament. Under the leadership of the academic Devlet Bahçeli, the MHP had dissociated itself from some of its more extremist, quasi-criminal youth wings and waged an election campaign on the stated aim to clean up the dirty politics of the country and eradicate corruption. Undoubtedly, the MHP also rode on the same nationalist tendency that helped the DSP.

The results of the elections nevertheless served several surprises, and were instructive as to the mood of the people. The deep fragmentation was still present, and a government would this time necessitate the support of at least three parties The winner of the election was the DSP, which received little over 22 per cent of the votes. The FP unexpectedly lost over a million votes and came in third with 15 per cent; ANAP and DYP were once again fighting an even race, but in a lower division this time. In the end, ANAP gathered an uneasy 13.2 per cent and DYP a disastrous 12.1 per cent. The CHP, not unexpectedly, fell below the threshold gathering 8.7 per cent. The most remarkable development was that the MHP more than doubled its vote, finishing as the second largest party with over 18 per cent of the vote.

TABLE 2

1999 ELECTION RESULTS

Party	Percentage	Seats
Democratic Left (Ecevit)	22.1	136
Nationalist Movement (Bahçeli)	18.1	129
Virtue (Kutan)	15.2	110
Motherland (Yılmaz)	13.2	86
True Path (Çiller)	12.2	85
Republican People's (Baykal)	8.7	0
People's Democracy (Bozlak)	4.7	0
Independent Deputies	0.9	3

Western analysts immediately after the elections ascribed the success of the DSP and the MHP to a nationalist wave emanating after an 'euphoria' following the arrest of PKK leader Öcalan.[79] This analysis nevertheless presents only part of the truth, in the sense that a nationalist wind was blowing in Turkey, the MHP profiting from its demand actually to implement the death penalty passed on Abdullah Öcalan. But in fact, the main reason for the success of these two parties was related to public dissatisfaction with the four other main parties, their leaders, and very importantly, the corruption of the state. As mentioned earlier, the DSP benefited from the honest and statesmanlike aura of its leader, attracting especially former ANAP and CHP voters.[80] Meanwhile, the MHP benefited especially from former RP voters, that is potential FP voters, and secondly from former DYP voters.[81] In its campaign, the MHP was successful in projecting itself as a reformed nationalist party, instead of the band of extremist brigands many Turks recalled from the late 1970s. Moreover, its nationalist-conservative image with an allegiance both to the secularism of the republic and 'Turkish Islam' appealed to both Islamic- and secularist-minded voters. But the election, and especially the Nationalist performance, sheds light on the 1995 elections and the RP victory as well. In retrospect, it is now possible to conclude that the WP victory was the result less of a genuine Islamic revival in large tracts of the population than a popular display of disappointment with the traditional political parties.

The RP was unable to sustain on the national level the popularity it had received by virtue of being an untried alternative. It managed to hold on to the municipalities of Ankara and Istanbul that it had captured in 1994, being rewarded for its accomplishments on the local level. But its short term in government had not impressed the electorate, which seemed to conclude that the RP, or now the FP, was no better than the established parties. In 1999 there remained only one untried alternative, one channel for the disappointed voters who desired neither to vote for the 'old' parties or for the FP. The MHP, astutely sensing the trend, had adjusted its profile and campaign – with an emphasis on anti-corruption measures – to attract these voters. Moreover, close to three million young people voted for the first time; the MHP was according to surveys able to capture over 30 per cent of the first-time voters. The result was beyond the wildest expectations of the party leadership.[82]

If a single conclusion is to be drawn from the 1999 elections, it is that voters sent signals that could no longer be misunderstood. In 1995, public disappointment had reduced the centre-right from 52 per cent in 1991 to 38 per cent. In 1999, the DYP and ANAP gathered no more than 26 per cent of the vote – half of what it had mustered eight years earlier. The message from the electorate to the DYP and ANAP was then obvious: the public was weary of the infighting in the centre-right, and the only way for the two parties to regain their lost credibility was to effect what they have been talking about for years – unity.

TABLE 3

MAJOR SHIFTS IN TURKISH ELECTIONS 1991–99 (PER CENT)

Political Orientation	1991	1995	1999
Centre-Right	52	38	26
Centre-Left	34[83]	26	31
Extreme Right	17	29	33

As far as the FP and, to a lesser extent, the DYP, is concerned, the elections proved that the climax of the utilization of religion in Turkish politics belongs to the past. The Islamic upsurge in politics may very well have turned out to be a wind that blew in with great force but exhausted itself, with the not so negligible 'help' of the military. In its place, a nationalist breeze is sweeping through the Turkish political landscape, a breeze that shows no signs of being significantly more enduring, being based just like the RP's popularity on dissatisfaction.

The underlying reason for both winds blowing into Turkish politics with such ease remains the division of the democratic right which left a suitable opening for them. And despite the clarity of the public message, most defeated party leaders pledged to stay in their posts. As the daily *Sabah* noted on 19 April, the leaders of the CHP, ANAP and DYP never won an election. All three lost every consecutive election that they have taken part in, only Deniz Baykal taking the consequences and resigning on 23 April.[84]

In a sense, the character of Turkish politics remains unchanged. The deep rifts within the democratic left and the democratic right that enabled first Welfare and later the Nationalists to reach their respective popularity show few signs of healing. Quite to the contrary, the underlying determinant of politics with some notable exceptions seems to remain personal ambition.

On the whole, there seems to be both reasons for optimism and pessimism as concerns Turkish politics and society. On the negative side, the great variations in political parties' electoral support have ultimately led to the extreme right being the largest political faction in 1999, surpassing both the democratic right and the democratic left. This is undoubtedly a cause for worry. But at the same time, the Turkish voters are showing their refusal to accept the workings of the current political system. It is no coincidence that the two parties least tainted by corruption, and who moreover waged campaigns against corruption, came out victorious in the elections. This shows to a growing political culture among the Turkish electorate and will unequivocally, sooner or later, have to lead to the reform of the political system.

Turkey is therefore at a crossroads. Will the country be able to clear up its various problems or will the Turkish politicians remain unable to refrain from operating in a complicated political environment of intrigues and personal differences? The near future will doubtlessly show the path Turkey will embark upon. Turkey is muddling through internally and increasing its regional stature externally, but the question whether any comprehensive reforms of the political system can be expected remains unanswered.

NOTES

1. 'Islamists Come First', *Middle East International*, No.516, 5 Jan. 1996.
2. Ibid.
3. For a detailed overview of the 1995 parliamentary elections, see Harald Schüler, 'Parlamentswahlen in der Türkei', *Orient*, Vol.37, No.2 (1996).
4. See also 'Unedifying Race for Power', in *Middle East International*, No.517, 19 Jan. 1996.
5. *NTV* Private Television Channel, 7 April 1999.
6. On the issue of fragmentation, see also M. Hakan Yavuz, 'Turkey's Imagined Enemies: Kurds and Islamists', *The World Today* (April 1996).

7. For an account of the episode, see 'The Özal Era', in Erik Cornell, *Turkey in the Twenty-First Century: Challenges, Opportunities, Threats* (Richmond, 1999); or 'The Özal Revolution', in Nicole and Hugh Pope, *Turkey Unveiled* (New York, 1998).
8. See Ersin Kalaycioğlu, 'The Logic of Contemporary Turkish Politics', *Middle East Review of International Affairs*, Vol.1, No.3 (Sept. 1997).
9. Pope and Pope, *Turkey Unveiled*, p.331.
10. 'Islamists Close In', *Middle East International*, No.518, 2 Feb. 1996.
11. 'New Government at Last', in *Middle East International*, No.521, 15 March 1996.
12. *Milliyet* and *Turkish Daily News*, 26–28 Feb. 1996.
13. Private Television Channel *ATV*, 27 Feb. 1996.
14. 'Tensions Rise with Damascus', *Middle East International*, No.528, 21 June 1996.
15. 'Islamists Consolidate', *Middle East International*, No.527, 7 June 1996.
16. See also the biography of Çiller: Faruk Bildirici, *Maskeli Leydi: Tekmili Birden Tansu Çiller* (Istanbul, 1997).
17. The leader of the Democratic Left Party, Bülent Ecevit, hence reduced the formation of the WP-TPP government to a 'Money-Laundering Operation'. See 'Erbakan at the Helm', *Middle East International*, No.529, 5 July 1996; also Pope and Pope, *Turkey Unveiled*, p.335.
18. See 'The Erbakan Whirlwind Sweep through Turkey', in *Middle East International*, No.530, 19 July 1996.
19. See e.g., Pope and Pope, *Turkey Unveiled*, p.313.
20. See Sencer Ayata, 'Patronage, Party, and State: The Politicization of Islam in Turkey', *The Middle East Journal*, Vol.50, No.1, 1996, p.44. See also Şerif Mardin, 'The Nakshibendi Order in Turkish History', in Richard Tapper (ed.), *Islam in Modern Turkey: Religion, Politics and Literature in a Secular State* (London, 1991).
21. For the Motherland Party, see Üstün Ergüder, 'The Motherland Party, 1983–89', and for the TPP, Feride Acar, 'The True Path Party, 1983–89', in Metin Heper and Jacob Landau (eds.), *Political Parties and Democracy in Turkey* (London, 1991).
22. See 'Islamists Consolidate', *Middle East International*, No.527, 7 June 1996. In Nov. of the same year another set of by-elections was held, where the WP still polled over 30 per cent. See, e.g., 'A Troubled System, in *Middle East International*, No.537, 8 Nov. 1996.
23. See Sencer Ayata, 'Patronage, Party, and State', pp.47–8.
24. See Doğu Ergil, 'Shariah and Darkness', *Turkish Probe*, 21 Feb. 1997.
25. For a detailed analysis of Islam in Turkey, see Svante E. Cornell and Ingvar Svanberg, 'Turkey', in David Westerlund and Ingvar Svanberg (eds.), *Islam Outside the Arab World* (Richmond, 1999).
26. See *Hürriyet*, 3 Feb. 1997; *Milliyet*, 3 and 4 Feb. 1997.
27. See M. Akif Beki, 'The Coup Conflict', *Turkish Probe*, 7 Feb. 1997. See also 'Uncomfortable Questions', *Middle East International*, No.543, 7 Feb. 1997.
28. See *Hürriyet,* 4 and 6 Feb. 1997.
29. See *Hürriyet,* 5 Feb. 1997.
30. See *Hürriyet,* 5 Feb. 1997.
31. *Hürriyet*, 16 and 17 Feb. 1997. See Raşit Gürdilek, 'Not the Best of Images', *Turkish Probe*, 21 Feb. 1997. See also See *Hürriyet,* 16 and 17 Feb. 1997.
32. See 'Secular Forces Rally', in *Middle East International*, No.544, 21 Feb. 1997.
33. *Milliyet*, 25 Feb. 1997.
34. See *Hürriyet,* 5 and 6 Feb. 1997.
35. See 'Turbulent Times', *Middle East International*, No.545, 7 March 1997. See also accounts in *Cumhuriyet, Yeni Yüzyil, Hürriyet, Milliyet*, 1 and 2 March 1997.
36. See newspaper reports, for example *Cumhuriyet* (Istanbul), 2 March 1997; *Radikal* (Istanbul), 1 and 2 March 1997.
37. See *Hürriyet*, 2 March 1997.
38. For the implementation of these decisions, in particular the education bill, see 'Education at Issue', *Middle East International*, No.557, 8 Aug. 1997.
39. See *Milliyet*, 3 March 1997. See also Fikret Bila, 'Genelkurmay: Erbakanla Uyum Yok', [Chiefs of Staff: No Unanimity with Erbakan], *Milliyet*, 3 March 1997.
40. See, e.g., *Yeni Yüzyil*, 3 March 1997.

41. See *Milliyet*, 6 March 1997; *Hürriyet*, 6 March 1997.
42. See *Hürriyet*, 4 March 1997. Also television new broadcast in private channels *InterStar* and *Kanal D*, 3 March 1997.
43. See 'Temporary Relief', in *Middle East International*, No.547, 4 April 1997.
44. 'The Crisis Drags On', in *Middle East International*, No.552, 13 June 1997.
45. See e.g., Üstün Reinart, 'Ambition for All Seasons', *Middle East Review of International Affairs*, Vol.3, No.1 (March 1999).
46. See *Hürriyet* and *Milliyet*, May 1997; and *Turkish Daily News*, 8 Oct. 1997, 11 Nov. 1997, and 29 Dec. 1997.
47. See *Hürriyet*, 12 June 1997. See also 'The Crisis Drags On', *Middle East International*, No.552, 13 June 1997.
48. See 'Erbakan Forced Out', in *Middle East International*, No.553, 27 June 1997, *Hürriyet*, 18 March 1997.
49. Ibid.
50. See *Hürriyet* and *Milliyet*, 20 and 21 June 1997.
51. See *Hürriyet*, 24 and 25 June 1997
52. For defections from the TPP, see e.g., *Hürriyet*, 21, 23, 26, 27, 28, and 29 June 1997.
53. See *Milliyet* and *Hürriyet*, 30 June and 1 July 1997; 'An Unlikely alliance', *Middle East International*, No.554, 11 July 1997.
54. *Hürriyet*, 26 June 1997.
55. See *Hürriyet*, 3 July 1997; *Turkish Daily News*, 10 Oct. 1997.
56. See *Hürriyet*, 30 June 1997.
57. See the chapter on the military in Erik Cornell, *Turkey in the Twenty-First Century* (Lund, 1997) (forthcoming in English).
58. The so-called *Küskünler* or 'the disgruntled'.
59. See *Cumhuriyet*, 19 March 1999.
60. Regarding the accusations against Aksener, see *Hürriyet*, 2 July 1997; 'Turkey's Watergate', *Middle East International*, No.555, 25 July 1997.
61. See Robert Olson, 'The Rose of Istanbul', *Middle East International*, No.556, 8 Aug. 1997.
62. See Svante E. Cornell, 'Beyond Öcalan: A Window of Opportunity?', *Turkistan Newsletter*, Vol.3, No.31, 21 Feb. 1999.
63. See also the discussion in Sami Kohen, 'Possible Ban on Party Divides Turkey', *Christian Science Monitor*, 26 Nov. 1997.
64. See for example the editorials of the editor-in-chief of *Turkish Daily News*, 12 Nov. 1997, 13 and 19 Jan. 1998, among others.
65. A statement which was repeated in the very words of the chairman of the Constitutional Court while making the decision public. See *Hürriyet*, 17 Jan. 1998.
66. See *Milliyet*, 14 Dec. 1997.
67. See *Turkish Daily News*, 19 Jan. 1998; *New York Times*, 17 Jan. 1998.
68. See *The Wall Street Journal*, 20 Jan. 1998.
69. See interview with Gül in Scott Peterson, 'Can Miniskirts and Veils Walk amid Mosques?', *Christian Science Monitor*, 20 Jan. 1998.
70. Originally stated in an interview with *Luxemburger Wort*. See *Xinhua*, 13 Dec. 1997, *Turkistan Newsletter*, Vol.97–1, No.112, 15 Dec. 1997.
71. On the Caucasus, see chapter 7, 'Turkey: Priority to Azerbaijan', in Svante E. Cornell, *Small Nations and Great Powers: A Study of Ethnopolitical Conflict in the Caucasus* (Richmond, 1999); on ties to Israel, see Amikam Nachmani, 'The Remarkable Turkish-Israeli Tie', *Middle East Quarterly* (June 1998), pp.19–29, and Joseph Leitmann-Santa Cruz and Çağrı Erdem, 'Turkey: Benefiting from David's Army: Turkish-Israeli Defense Cooperation', *The International Relations Journal*, Winter 1997.
72. Interview with Professor Ortayli in *Turkish Daily News*, 5 Jan. 1998.
73. The table is taken from an opinion poll published in *Cumhuriyet*, 24 Oct. 1997.
74. Private Communication by sources close to the military, Ankara, April 1998.
75. Of the $150 billion, $65 billion will be allocated to the air force, $60 million to the ground forces, and $25 billion to the navy. See e.g. Nachmani, 'The Remarkable Turkish-Israeli Tie', *Middle East Quarterly* (June 1998), p.25.

76. *NTV* private television interview with Ecevit, 11 April 1999.
77. *Turkish Daily News*, 16 April 1999.
78. *NTV* private television interview with Ecevit, 11 April 1999.
79. See e.g. Andrew Finkle, 'Ecevit Quits as Turkey Veers to the Right', *The Times*, 20 April 1999; Evangelos Antonaros, 'Die Wahren Sieger sind die Rechtsextremisten', *Die Welt*, 20 April 1999; 'Fascister Går Framåt i Turkiskt Val', *Svenska Dagbladet*, 19 April 1999; Howard Schneider, 'Rightist Party's Gain Could Stir Ethnic Tension in Turkey', *The Washington Post*, 20 April 1999.
80. The 2 per cent drop in CHP votes and the 6 per cent drop of ANAP votes accurately make up for the 7.5 per cent upsurge of the DSP.
81. As shown by the sociological research conducted in the months before the election by Tarhan Erdem. Erdem's projections on election day proved very close to the final result (displayed continuously on private *NTV* television), and his account of the voters' movements also shed light on the developments. See also Taner Altunay, '18 Nisan'ın Sırrı', *Milliyet*, 22 April 1999.
82. 'Bu Kadar Oy Beklemyorduk' ['We Didn't Expect This Many Votes'], *Cumhuriyet*, 20 April 1999.
83. The SHP which was the largest party of the left in 1991 had an electoral alliance with the pro-Kurdish DEP party, which was subsequently closed down. Its successor HADEP appeared on its own in 1995 and 1999, at both occasions gathering around 4.5 per cent of the vote. Hence the centre-left's figures for 1991 are in fact slightly exaggerated.
84. *Hurriyet*, 24 April 1999; *Turkish Daily News*, 24 April 1999.

Index

For Product Safety Concerns and Information please contact our EU representative GPSR@taylorandfrancis.com Taylor & Francis Verlag GmbH, Kaufingerstraße 24, 80331 München, Germany

T - #0119 - 270225 - C0 - 216/138/13 - PB - 9780714680996 - Gloss Lamination